Purging the Odious Scourge of Atrocities

Purging the Odious Scourge of Atrocities

The Limits of Consent in International Law

BRUCE CRONIN

Oxford University Press is a department of the University of Oxford. It furthers the University's objective of excellence in research, scholarship, and education by publishing worldwide. Oxford is a registered trade mark of Oxford University Press in the UK and certain other countries.

Published in the United States of America by Oxford University Press
198 Madison Avenue, New York, NY 10016, United States of America.

© Oxford University Press 2023

All rights reserved. No part of this publication may be reproduced, stored in a retrieval system, or transmitted, in any form or by any means, without the prior permission in writing of Oxford University Press, or as expressly permitted by law, by license, or under terms agreed with the appropriate reproduction rights organization. Inquiries concerning reproduction outside the scope of the above should be sent to the Rights Department, Oxford University Press, at the address above.

You must not circulate this work in any other form
and you must impose this same condition on any acquirer.

Library of Congress Cataloging-in-Publication Data
Names: Cronin, Bruce, 1957– author.
Title: Purging the odious scourge of atrocities : the limits of consent in international law / Bruce Cronin.
Description: New York : Oxford University Press, [2023] | Includes index.
Identifiers: LCCN 2023014255 (print) | LCCN 2023014256 (ebook) |
ISBN 9780197693308 (hardback) | ISBN 9780197693315 (epub)
Subjects: LCSH: Consent (Law) | Torture (International law) |
Responsibility to protect (International law) | Minorities—Crimes against. |
Political atrocities. | Political violence. | International law and human rights.
Classification: LCC K579 .I6 C76 2023 (print) | LCC K579 .I6 (ebook) |
DDC 342.08/5—dc23/eng/20230714
LC record available at https://lccn.loc.gov/2023014255
LC ebook record available at https://lccn.loc.gov/2023014256

DOI: 10.1093/oso/9780197693308.001.0001

Printed by Integrated Books International, United States of America

Contents

1. Introduction: The Limits of Consent in International Law   1
2. A Theory of Consensus-Based International Law   37
3. The Universal Ban on Extreme Internal State Violence   73
4. The Violent Persecution of Minorities   96
5. Torture   131
6. Civilian Immunity in Domestic Armed Conflicts   157
7. International Consensus and the Future of International Law   182

Index   201

1
Introduction: The Limits of Consent in International Law

In 2018, the UN High Commissioner for Human Rights accused the government of Myanmar of committing "grave offenses" under international law by engaging in crimes against humanity and ethnic cleansing against its Rohingya Muslim population.[1] Yet the only legally binding document that specifically cites crimes against humanity as a violation of international law is the Statute of the International Criminal Court (ICC), and Myanmar was not a party to the treaty. It was also not a party to the 1977 Second Protocol to the 1949 Geneva Conventions—which provides extensive protections to civilians during internal conflicts and civil wars—and is therefore not technically bound by its provisions. Indeed, although the term "ethnic cleansing" has become a regular part of human rights discourse, it is not mentioned in any treaty, nor is it even considered a core crime in the ICC Statute. In fact, the term has never even been legally defined.

This raises a number of questions regarding the doctrine of consent in international law, particularly as it pertains to internal state violence: Can states legally commit genocide if they explicitly refuse to ratify the 1948 Genocide Convention?[2] Are governments free to launch indiscriminate attacks against their own citizens during civil wars or insurrections if they are not parties to the Second Protocol to the Geneva Conventions?[3] Can they legally inflict severe pain and suffering on political opponents at home or abroad if they have not signed the UN Convention against Torture?[4]

---

[1] United Nations Human Rights Council, "Report of the Special Rapporteur on the Situation of Human Rights in Myanmar," 37th session, 26 February–23 March 2018.

[2] As of 2021, 42 countries have refused to ratify the Convention. See United Nations Treaty Collection, Status of Treaties, Chapter IV, Human Rights, (1), Convention on the Prevention and Punishment of the Crime of Genocide.

[3] The Second Protocol extends civilian protection to non-international armed conflicts. Currently, 26 countries, including the United States, Syria, and Iraq, have declined to ratify the Protocol.

[4] Twenty-three countries have refused to ratify the Convention against Torture and Other Cruel, Inhuman or Degrading Treatment. See United Nations Treaty Collection, Status of Treaties, Chapter IV, Human Rights, (9), Convention Against Torture and Other Cruel, Inhuman or Degrading Treatment or Punishment.

Moreover, can states who have signed the above treaties release themselves from their obligations by withdrawing from these agreements, as guaranteed by the Vienna Convention on the Law of Treaties?[5] Does a state's explicit refusal to ratify the above-mentioned conventions constitute a clear, persistent objection that would exempt it from the prohibition even if it were considered part of customary international law? Does the lack of widespread, consistent practice in these areas negate the presumption that such bans are even part of customary law?

According to contemporary theories of international law and international relations, the answers to these questions would generally be yes. Under the principle of sovereignty, states have considerable autonomy to engage in a wide range of nefarious practices within their own borders, and with few exceptions these actions are shielded from international legal scrutiny. This autonomy can be constrained by international law and diplomatic agreement; however, the legal doctrine of *state consent* stipulates that governments are obligated to follow only those rules that they have agreed to accept, either explicitly by ratifying a specific treaty or implicitly by the existence of a long-term general practice that the international community recognizes as a legal norm.[6]

At the same time, many public officials and legal scholars have taken the position that governments are indeed legally prohibited from engaging in such actions even when perpetrated within their own borders and even in the absence of their consent to abide by them. As a number of legal scholars argue, despite a steady increase in the number of state parties to international human rights treaties in recent years, reliance upon legal agreements alone provides an unsatisfactory patchwork quilt of obligations, while continuing to leave many states largely untouched.[7] Rather, in a gradual shift from 19th- and 20th-century practice, states are increasingly recognizing a limited body

---

[5] The fundamental right to renounce one's legal commitment by withdrawing from a treaty is discussed in Laurence R. Helfer, "Terminating Treaties," in Duncan Hollis (ed.), *The Oxford Guide to Treaties* (Oxford University Press, 2012), pp. 634–649. This right is cited in Article XIV of the Convention on the Prevention and Punishment of the Crime of Genocide.

[6] There is a large literature on the doctrine of consent as the foundation for modern international law. Contemporary works include Louis Henkin, *International Law: Politics and Values* (Springer, 1995); James Brierly, *The Law of Nations: An Introduction to the Modern Law of Peace* (Oxford University Press, 1978), pp. 51–54; Ian Brownlie, *Principles of Public International Law* (Oxford University Press, 2003), chapter 1; and Michael J. Glennon, "How International Rules Die," *Georgetown Law Journal*, vol. 93, no. 3, March 2005.

[7] See, for example, Bruno Simma and Philip Alston, "The Sources of Human Rights Law: Custom, Jus Cogens, and General Principles," *Austrian Yearbook of International Law*, vol. 12, 1988.

of international law as having *general* applicability that is binding on all states regardless of whether they are parties to specific agreements or whether the laws are based on a long-term general customary practice.

This suggests that states are pursuing new ways of addressing the uneasy balance between sovereignty and responsibility in world politics, and that there are limits to the doctrine of consent. However, at the moment current theories regarding the sources of international law lack a foundation for explaining how states can be required to assume legal obligations that transcend state consent.

This book will attempt to provide such a foundation by proposing a theory of sources that is based on collective international consensus rather than individual state consent, and suggesting a method for determining which legal norms fall into this category. It does so by offering a model that merges the legal with the political. In the following pages, I argue that qualitative changes in the form of global governance are leading to an expansion in the theoretical underpinnings of international law and its role in contemporary world politics. Specifically, in limited and well-defined areas of international law, states have begun to recognize the authority of collective international consensus over individual state consent as the source of some legal rules. I do not argue that these norms are *replacing* consent-based rules, nor do I claim that they even provide the bulk of them within the body of international law. Rather, I simply maintain that they are becoming increasingly significant in influencing the way international law is practiced in the 21st century, particularly in regulating internal state violence.

In developing a theory of consensus-based international law, I try to explain the existence and growth of a limited body of human rights law that is based, not on individual state consent or consistent state practice, but rather on collective agreement within the international community that is developed through an established multilateral process within a complex array of international institutions.[8] The body of law I examine in this book involves atrocities committed by states against their own people, a practice that the Genocide Convention refers to an "odious scourge."[9]

---

[8] The international community can be defined as an identifiable group of recognized political actors who maintain ongoing, formal relations based on a set of constitutional elements that define basic criteria for rights and obligations under international law and diplomatic practice. See Bardo Fassbender, *The United Nations Charter as the Constitution of the International Community* (Martinus Nijhof, 2009).

[9] UN General Assembly, *Convention on the Prevention and Punishment of the Crime of Genocide*, 9 December 1948, United Nations, Treaty Series, vol. 78, preamble.

The transformation of some human rights norms into general legal obligations provides a unique opportunity to study the evolution of international consensus as a foundation for law. Unlike much of contemporary international law, the protection of human rights is not rooted in long-term state practice (like freedom of navigation on the high seas), principles of reciprocity (such as the laws of armed conflict or diplomatic immunity), or classical notions of natural or Roman law (such as the principle of proportionality). Rather, they are *erga omnes* (obligations that all states owe to the international community as a whole). Their recent vintage and expansion beyond the traditional scope of international law is directly tied to changes in the structure of the global political environment to which I allude below.

Building from this premise, the project will attempt to explain how the regulation of certain acts of state violence committed within its own borders can be legally binding on governments in the absence of either explicit consent or a common customary practice. As such, these regulations are part of general international law.[10] Since human rights violations exist on a continuum—from government censorship to massacring an entire race of people—the project will also establish which sets of rights are considered to be universal rather than normative or relative, and how we can determine this.[11]

In this vein, I argue that while the violation of many international human rights protections, such as freedom of expression and due process, are tolerated—and governed by the doctrine of consent in international law—the international community has developed a consensus around the legal control of what I call "excessive internal state violence." I define this as a level of coercive force that the international community considers to be disproportionate and illegitimate for pursuing state interests within its own borders.

---

[10] The term "general international law" (GIL) is a broad concept that refers to the entire corpus of international law that is binding on all states. The International Law Commission refers to GIL as "rules of international law of general application, whether treaty law or customary international law or general principles of law." See United Nations, "Draft Conclusions on Identification of Customary International Law, with Commentaries, Adopted by the International Law Commission at its Seventieth Session, in 2018" (A/73/10). Christian Tomuschat defines GIL as "rules without a precise classification, but which are legal propositions expressing genuine consensus of the international community." See his "General International Law: A New Source of International Law?," in Riccardo Pisillo Mazzeschi and Pasquale De Sena (eds.), *Global Justice, Human Rights and the Modernization of International Law* (Springer, 2018). Traditionally, this was limited primarily to customary law; however, this has changed As far back as 1955, Lassa Oppenheim and Hersch Lauterpacht posited that universal international law "is created when all or practically all the members of the Family of Nations are parties to multilateral treaties. . . . Many law-making treaties have been concluded which contain general international law because the majority of states, including the leading Powers, are parties to them." See Lassa Oppenheim and Hersch Lauterpacht (eds.), *International Law* (Longmans, Green and Co., 1955), p. 28.

[11] Universal legal norms apply to all states and are not subject to consent.

This includes violent persecution (including genocide, ethnic cleansing, and apartheid); large-scale, systematic violence against domestic populations; torture; and attacks on civilians during internal armed conflicts. In these cases, state action is subject to general international law that overrides their consent.

The types of legal obligations assumed by states have important consequences for the conduct of international relations, particularly in regard to human rights. Governments treat legal obligations more seriously than diplomatic agreements and normative commitments. The degree to which internal state violence violates international law influences how states and international and regional organizations decide to employ economic and political sanctions, engage in humanitarian intervention, issue diplomatic condemnation, and prosecute individual perpetrators in international criminal tribunals. It also determines the degree to which domestic courts will exercise universal jurisdiction, that is, the authority to investigate and prosecute certain international crimes, even if they were not committed on its territory or against one of its nationals. Like most political actors, jurists are influenced by the general beliefs held by the societies in which they operate.

In addition, international legal norms enable domestic legal systems to prosecute their own leaders in cases where the state has failed to ratify specific treaties. In fact, transnational prosecutions can catalyze domestic prosecutions by legitimizing what might otherwise be controversial actions taken against national leaders by prosecutors.[12] Finally, violations of international law help nongovernmental organizations mobilize populations and create public pressure on governments and prosecutors.

The Political Foundation of International Legal Obligation

The inherent tension between national autonomy and international coexistence is the most challenging feature in a global system of sovereign states. On the one hand, the principle of sovereignty holds that states are neither subject to the authority of any higher institution nor part of any larger

---

[12] See Naomi Roht-Arriaza, "The Pinochet Precedent and Universal Jurisdiction," *New England Law Review*, vol. 35, no. 2, Winter 2001, pp. 315–316.

constitutional arrangement, except that which they explicitly accept.[13] Foreign policy officials tend to be highly jealous of this autonomy and resist accepting regulations that significantly limit their freedom of action. On the other hand, while sovereignty provides a wide latitude for governments to pursue their own interests, states also participate in a complex pattern of relationships that impose limitations on their will to be independent. Most political leaders recognize that a stable, predictable, and functional international order requires formal rules that define acceptable behavior, regulate political interaction, provide for the realization of common interests, and facilitate the resolution of disputes. In practice, even powerful states accept constraints on their autonomy as necessary for maintaining political and economic relations with other states and for pursuing common goals that they cannot achieve independently.[14]

For most of the 19th and 20th centuries, political leaders attempted to resolve this tension by creating international institutions that were based on the principle of voluntary state consent. In a consent-based political order, states freely choose which organizations they wish to join and which rules they wish to adopt as legal commitments. Since there is no legal hierarchy of organizations in international law or diplomatic practice, no international institution has greater authority than any other. As a result, a state's membership—or lack thereof—in one association does not affect its status in others, and the rules of an organization cannot be extended beyond its membership. This protects state sovereignty while still providing for general rules that would facilitate cooperation and coexistence. States can therefore follow global rules without ceding their independence because they have to comply only with those rules that they have accepted.

Consent-based international law consists of an assortment of empirically verifiable customary practices and voluntarily accepted legal agreements that commit the signatories as long as they remain parties to the specific legal arrangements. Treaty commitments are made on a purely voluntary basis, and each state chooses which rules it wishes to adopt as legal obligations and which ones it does not. Although these commitments are binding so long as

---

[13] See Allen James, *Sovereign Statehood: The Basis of International Society* (Allen and Unwin, 1986), p. 25.

[14] See, for example, Harold Hongju Koh, "Why Do Nations Obey International Law," *Yale Law Journal*, vol. 106, no. 8, June 1997 and Kenneth W. Abbott and Duncan Snidal, "Why States Act through Formal International Organizations," *The Journal of Conflict Resolution*, vol. 42, no. 1, February 1998.

a state remains a signatory to the treaty, each party can ultimately opt out so long as it follows the proper procedures for treaty withdrawal. This is because consent theories hold that treaties are not like legislation and therefore do not constitute a source of universal or general law. They bind only those who specifically sign and ratify them.[15] Moreover, since states are not beholden to any higher principle, their treaty obligations do not go beyond written text or verifiable acts of state practice, a concept known as "positive law."[16] Thus, states resolve any ambiguities in the law through self-interpretation, negotiation, or military force, although they may sometimes consent to impartial arbitration by an international court.

From this perspective, customary law reflects implied consent inasmuch as it is derived from verifiable state practice that has not only continued consistently over time but has been publicly accepted by a wide range of states within the international community as a legal obligation.[17] This concept of *opinio juris* (an unambiguous belief by state officials that a particular practice is in fact a legal obligation) makes law based on practice a consensual act. Thus, under a legal positivist approach, political leaders and legal scholars can infer some legal obligations from state behavior by discovering exactly what states have consented to. The consensual nature of this form of the law is underlined by the fact that states can exclude themselves from customary law by voicing a persistent objection to its principles while the practice is in its early stage of development.

Thus, while states may hold each other accountable politically and diplomatically for violating broadly held norms and principles, political realists, liberal institutionalists, and legal positivists all agree that states are required to adhere only to those international legal commitments that they either specifically adopt or accept as consistent with long-term practice that is widespread, representative, consistent, and broadly acknowledged as a legal obligation. Under contemporary theories of international law, state

---

[15] The principle of *pacta tertiis nec nocent nec prosunt* is enshrined in the Vienna Convention on the Law of Treaties, which maintains that "a treaty does not create either obligations or rights for a third State without its consent." See Vienna Convention, concluded at Vienna on 23 May 1969, United Nations, Treaty Series, vol. 1155, Article 24.

[16] See, for example, Lassa Oppenheim, "The Science of International Law: Its Task and Method," *American Journal of International Law*, vol. 2, 1908 and John Austin, *The Province of Jurisprudence Determined* (1832), edited by Wilfrid E. Rumble (Cambridge University Press, 1995).

[17] There is a vast literature on customary law, and its examination has been experiencing a revival over the past two decades (*see below*). For a good discussion on the political role of contemporary law, see Michael Byers, *Custom, Power and the Power of Rules: International Relations and Customary International Law* (Cambridge University Press, 1999).

consent legitimizes legal obligation.[18] For political realists, this preserves a state's right to reject any principle or obligation that it does not deem to be in its interest to assume, and for liberal institutionalists and positivists it strengthens the international legal system by committing states to adhere to those rules that they themselves have agreed to follow. For these reasons, consent-based legal norms have dominated international law for more than a century.

For hundreds of years international law has provided a mechanism for political leaders to define and evaluate acceptable state behavior in international relations. Like most forms of cooperation, international law is an institution designed to achieve common goals and provide for stable and predictable relationships among international political actors. Unlike other cooperative institutions, however, it is based on generalized principles of conduct that are both authoritatively binding on governments and applicable in a wide variety of circumstances. Following these rules is not simply a policy choice for political leaders, but an obligation that is fundamental for international coexistence and domestic legitimacy.[19] States may sometimes violate the rules—and when they do there may be few coercive mechanisms to sanction them—however, all members are expected to observe them and there are often political and diplomatic consequences when they do not. In fact, in most cases, political leaders regard those who flagrantly violate these rules to be committing a hostile act not only against a particular state or group of states but against the international community as a whole.[20] Such violators often become pariahs and lose the political, economic, and security benefits that multilateral institutions and diplomacy provide.[21]

---

[18] See Matthew Lister, "The Legitimizing Role of Consent in International Law," *Chicago Journal of International Law*, vol. 11, no. 2, 2011.

[19] The authority of international law goes well beyond obligations owed to other states. In most cases, states incorporate international law into their domestic legal systems, thereby creating legal liabilities for governments through their own judicial institutions. See Antonio Cassesse, *International Law* (Oxford University Press, 2005), chapter 12.

[20] See J. L. Brierly, *The Outlook for International Law* (Oxford University Press, 1946).

[21] The concept of a "pariah state" has a long history in diplomatic relations, despite the imprecision and controversial definition of the term. Robert Harkavy defines a pariah state as one whose refusal to conform to prevailing international norms places it in a condition of diplomatic isolation and thus sparks a challenge to its legitimacy by the international community. Harkavy argues that one can measure such as state by the number and identity of nations with which they maintain formal diplomatic relations, by the outcomes of critical votes involving said states within international and regional organizations, by the overall trade and cultural relations it has with other states, and by its membership in international and regional organizations. See his "Pariah States and Nuclear Proliferation," *International Organization*, vol. 35, no. 1, Winter 1981, particularly p. 140. See also Olawale Lawal, "Pariah State System and Enforcement Mechanism of International Law," *Journal of Alternative Perspectives in the Social Sciences*, vol. 4, no. 1, 2012.

All of this distinguishes international law from diplomatic practice, a distinction that is particularly important when addressing human rights regulations. Governments routinely judge and condemn each other over their policies and actions—including a state's behavior toward its own population—but this does not necessarily involve an accusation that the target state has violated international law. The practice of "naming and shaming" is a regular part of international diplomacy, particularly regarding human rights. However, political leaders generally accept that governments may pursue a variety of nefarious policies without violating their legal obligations, even though they may levy political and economic sanctions against those who act contrary to certain values. Thus, condemnation or praise of a state's behavior alone, even if widespread, does not necessarily indicate a belief that a particular act violates a legal norm.

Over the past century, international law has played a greater role in world politics than during any other period of the nation-state system. The dramatic increase in economic, political, and cultural interdependence among states and societies has led to a rising demand for more precise and binding commitments by governments.[22] This in turn has led to a corresponding increase in the depth and complexity of the international legal system.

For example, while the scope of international law was traditionally limited to issues related primarily to bilateral relations (such as diplomatic interactions, behavior in wartime, and division of territory) and the use of common pool resources (such as the high seas), since the end of World War II it has expanded to address such previously untouched areas as the protection of refugees, human rights, international trade, the natural environment, and international criminal activity. Moreover, political leaders are increasingly framing their political actions in legal terms, and the rise in international criminal tribunals and international legal institutions have made questions of legality central to political action.[23]

At the same time, since international law operates within an environment that lacks a constitutional foundation, there is no single body of legal principles or institutions from which states and international

---

[22] See "Legalization and World Politics," special issue of *International Organization,* vol. 54, no. 3, Summer 2000.

[23] See, for example, Ian Hurd, "The Strategic Use of Liberal Internationalism: Libya and the UN Sanctions, 1992–2003," *International Organization,* vol. 59, no. 3, Summer 2005.

organizations can develop a comprehensive set of rules and obligations. Instead, international law is derived from a highly diverse collection of multilateral treaties and customary practices that are often confirmed by judicial opinions and supported by legal principles that are common to all domestic systems.[24] Moreover, unlike most domestic legal systems, the international community lacks a central power with the authority to enact legislation, interpret rules, and punish transgressors. This has several implications.

First, the international legal system has traditionally been highly decentralized. Its main functions (codification, interpretation, adjudication, and enforcement) are not primarily provided by global legal institutions but rather by individual states, who must often interpret and execute the rules themselves. It is therefore heavily dependent upon national governments and domestic courts for implementation. Second, the range of issues over which international law has jurisdiction is still limited compared to those within domestic societies. While legal norms do cover a wide range of state practices, beyond these limits states have considerable legal autonomy to design their foreign and domestic policies as they choose. Third, governments continue to jealously guard their sovereignty and are wary of making commitments to follow general principles that would apply in unforeseen future circumstances. This makes it difficult to create new legal rules that would extend the reach of international law into new areas of politics. Often the most innovative attempts to do so are hindered by the limited number of signatories who voluntarily agree to adopt them. International law is thus difficult to develop and hard to implement.

Finally, traditionally, the lack of a "social contract" among states in the international system—as well as differences in cultural norms and practices—often hampered their ability to establish a more cohesive legal system. This has encouraged a minimalist approach to the development of international law.

For these reasons, it has been very difficult to develop general or universal rules that apply to all states under all circumstances, even if all states agree to abide by them, and therefore it is difficult to reconcile universal human rights norms with a voluntarist legal system.

---

[24] This is commonly known in legal circles as the "Doctrine of Sources," as articulated in Article 38 of the Statute of the International Court of Justice.

Expanding Customary Law to Accommodate Universal Legal Norms

So how do we reconcile universal legal norms with an international legal system based on state consent? A growing number of international law scholars and jurists have sought to expand the concept of customary international law (CIL) to include certain types of legal norms that form over a short period of time without necessarily reflecting widespread, consistent state practice. The advantage of applying customary law in this context is that it is binding on all states, including newly created sovereign entities, regardless of whether they participated in its formation.

Traditionally, for a legal norm to gain acceptance in customary law, two elements are required in sequence: a practice that is general, widespread, representative, consistent, and virtually uniform, followed by a general acknowledgment that such practice constitutes a legal obligation (*opinio juris*).[25] While *opinio juris* is the key element in transforming a common practice into a legal obligation, the emphasis on state practice means that custom develops over time, whereby conduct that was initially voluntary becomes habitual and then obligatory.[26] For a practice to become part of customary law, then, it must be uniform and sustained by constant repetition, which gives rise to a legitimate expectation of similar conduct in the future.[27] Legal scholars and political leaders therefore traditionally determined the existence of custom by examining years of state practice before exploring the degree to which the practice is in fact an obligation.

This has made it difficult to frame human rights obligations, or any newly minted legal norm, as reflecting customary law inasmuch as most are of relatively recent vintage, have not evolved over time, have not been either consistent or uniform, and are often not reflected in widespread or general practice.

Some recent approaches to customary law, however, suggest that modern versions of customary law allow us to replace the strictly additive (two-element) model of custom formation with a single-element theory, mostly by

---

[25] This principle is best articulated in a famous ruling by the International Court of Justice, North Sea Continental Shelf (FRG/Den.; FRG/Neth.), 1969 ICJ REP. 3, 44 (Feb. 20). See also United Nations, "Draft Conclusions on Identification of Customary International Law, with Commentaries, Adopted by the International Law Commission at its Seventieth Session, in 2018" (A/73/10), pp. 135–136.

[26] H. L. A. Hart, *The Concept of Law* (Clarendon Press, 1961), pp. 121–132.

[27] International Law Association, London Conference, Committee on Formation of Customary (General) International Law, Final Report of the Committee, 2000, pp. 8 and 20.

de-emphasizing one of the two standard requirements or by displacing them altogether.[28] Thus, its proponents argue, international custom can be derived by narrowing the requirements by either focusing on *opinio juris* without an accompanying practice or by redefining *opinio juris* itself as a form of practice. This method was first suggested decades ago by Bin Cheng, who proposed that customary law can be based exclusively on *opinio juris* (articulated, for example, through United Nations General Assembly resolutions) so long as it is not rejected by member states of the international community.[29] Indeed, in a comprehensive study of contemporary customary law, the International Law Commission (ILC) posits that it is now generally accepted that verbal conduct (whether written or oral) may also count as practice and that practice may even at times consist entirely of verbal acts, for example, diplomatic protests.[30]

Since customary law places the emphasis on the wills of individual states, proponents argue that we can examine diplomatic correspondence, advice of legal advisors, official government declarations, domestic court decisions, and government manuals for evidence of *opinio juris* even if practice is absent or sparse.[31] Thus, Anthea Elizabeth Roberts argues that modern (as opposed to traditional) customary law is derived through a *deductive* process that begins with general statements of rules rather than first waiting for a long-standing practice to emerge.[32] Such evidence of *opinio juris*, she argues, can be derived from multilateral treaties and declarations by international organizations leading to what legal scholars such as Christopher Joyner have called "instant custom."[33]

Consistent with this formulation, the ILC recently held that "conduct in connection with resolutions adopted by an international organization or at an intergovernmental conference likewise includes acts by States related to

---

[28] International Law Commission, "Formation and Evidence of Customary International Law," Document A/CN.4/663, First report on formation and evidence of customary international law, by Sir Michael Wood, 2013, p. 148.

[29] Bing Cheng, *Studies in International Space Law* (Oxford University Press, 1997), chapter 7.

[30] United Nations, "Draft Conclusions on Identification of Customary International Law, with Commentaries, Adopted by the International Law Commission at its Seventieth Session, in 2018" (A/73/10), p. 133.

[31] Michael Scharf, "Accelerated Formation of Customary International Law," *Case Western Reserve University School of Law Commons*, Faculty Publications, 2014, p. 312.

[32] Anthea Elizabeth Roberts, "Traditional and Modern Approaches to Customary International Law: A Reconciliation," *The American Journal of International Law*, vol. 95, no. 4, October 2001.

[33] Christopher Joyner, "United Nations General Assembly Resolutions and International Law: Rethinking the Contemporary Dynamics of Norm-Creation," *California Western Law Review*, vol. 11, 1981, p. 445.

the negotiation, adoption and implementation of resolutions, decisions and other acts adopted within international organizations or at intergovernmental conferences."[34] Moreover, the practice of international organizations when concluding treaties, serving as treaty depositaries, in deploying military forces (for example, for peacekeeping), in administering territories, or in taking positions on the scope of the privileges and immunities of the organization and its officials may contribute to the formation, or expression, of rules of CIL in those areas.

These approaches have been particularly popular among those seeking to explain how recent norms, such as the protection of human rights and the promotion of humanitarian intervention, can become general legal obligations for all states in the international community, even though they do not reflect the actual practice of states.[35] In doing so, they try to reconcile the international normative commitment to human rights with inconsistent state practice. Thus, Frederic Kirgis argues that custom exists on a sliding scale, requiring different standards for evaluation based on the legal norm: "The more destabilising or morally distasteful the activity—for example, the offensive use of force or the deprivation of fundamental human rights—the more readily international decision makers will substitute one element (*opinio juris*) for the other (state practice) provided that the asserted restrictive rule seems reasonable."[36]

If this is the case, it suggests that political and legal stakeholders are becoming less demanding about the consistency and duration of practice required to signify consent; this would account for their willingness to change the formula for designating a practice to be part of CIL. Thus, for example, Meron suggests that we adopt a "more relaxed approach to customary international law" compared with the "traditional approach" of a detailed discussion of the evidence.[37]

---

[34] United Nations, International Law Commission, "Draft Conclusions on Identification of Customary International Law, with Commentaries," adopted by the International Law Commission at its 70th session (A/73/10), 2018, p. 131.

[35] See, for example, Olivier De Schutter, *International Human Rights Law: Cases, Materials, Commentary* (Cambridge University Press, 2014); Brian Lepard, *Customary International Law: A New Theory with Practical Applications* (Cambridge University Press, 2010); John Merriam, "Kosovo and the Law of Humanitarian Intervention," *Case Western Reserve Journal of International Law*, vol 33, no. 1, Winter 2001; and Jean-Pierre Fonteyne, "The Customary International Law Doctrine of Humanitarian Intervention: Its Current Validity under the U.N. Charter," in Tarcisio Gazzini (ed.), *The Use of Force in International Law* (Routledge, 2017).

[36] Frederic Kirgis, "Custom on a Sliding Scale," *American Journal of International Law*, vol. 81, no. 1, January 1987, p. 149.

[37] Theodor Meron, *The Making of International Criminal Justice: The View from the Bench: Selected Speeches* (Oxford University Press, 2011), p. 31.

In this vein, several legal scholars argue that many, most, or even all of the articles in the Universal Declaration of Human Rights and the Covenant on Civil and Political Rights have become firmly embedded in customary law.[38] They cite as evidence the widespread reference to these documents by a large number of states, citation by national and international courts, its incorporation into the national law of many countries, and widespread condemnation by governments when others violate its provisions. As one of the primary authors of the Universal Declaration, John Humphrey, observed, "[T]he Declaration has been invoked so many times both within and without the United Nations that lawyers are now saying that, whatever the intention of its authors may have been, the Declaration is now part of the customary law of nations and therefore binding on all states."[39]

Under this formulation, the widespread violation of much of the Declaration by many states around the world would not necessarily invalidate it as a rule of customary law. As the International Court of Justice opined, "[I]nstances of State conduct inconsistent with a given rule should generally have been treated as breaches of that rule, not as indications of the recognition of a new rule. If a State acts in a way *prima facie* incompatible with a recognized rule, but defends its conduct by appealing to exceptions or justifications contained within the rule itself, then whether or not the State's conduct is in fact justifiable on that basis, the significance of that attitude is to confirm rather than to weaken the rule."[40]

Clearly, then, some legal scholars, international jurists, and courts are looking for a way to expand customary law to meet contemporary needs, particularly in the area of extreme human rights violations. Since customary law has long been widely accepted as the primary source of general international law binding on all states, this seems to be a reasonable approach. Why

---

[38] See, for example, Louis Henkin, *The Age of Rights* (Columbia University Press, 1990); Thomas Meron, *Human Rights and Humanitarian Norms as Customary Law* (Oxford University Press, 1991); Hurst Hannum, "The Status of the Universal Declaration of Human Rights in National and International Law," *Georgia Journal of International and Comparative Law*, vol. 25, 1995–1996; Richard Lillich, "The Growing Importance of Customary International Human Rights Law," *Georgia Journal of International and Comparative Law*, vol. 25, 1995–1996; and Philip Alston, "The Universal Declaration at 35: Western and Passe or Alive and Universal?," *The Review of the International Commission of Jurists*, no. 31, December 1983.

[39] Quoted in Mary Ann Glendon, "John P. Humphrey and the Drafting of the Universal Declaration of Human Rights," *Journal of the History of International Law*, vol. 2, 2000.

[40] Quoted in United Nations, International Law Commission, "Draft Conclusions on Identification of Customary International Law, with Commentaries," adopted by the International Law Commission at its 70th session (A/73/10), 2018, p. 138.

invent a new source of law when we can reformulate an existing one to meet contemporary challenges?

Although this scholarship offers an innovative way to provide flexibility in adapting international law to changing human rights norms, it also stretches the concept of international custom well beyond its meaning. As the International Court of Justice held in the most widely cited case regarding customary law (*North Continental Shelf*), while the passage of a long period of time is not required for CIL, it is an "indispensible requirement" that state practice, including those whose interests are specially affected, be "both extensive and virtually uniform."[41] This is necessary to eliminate the ambiguity that is inherent in any source of law that is based on interpreting behavior. This serves to ensure that the exercise of identifying rules of CIL results in determining only such rules as actually exist.[42] More important, as an empirical matter, there is little evidence that new interpretations emphasizing one constituent element over the other or even excluding one element altogether have been adopted either by states or in the case law.[43]

I have to agree with Robert Jennings that this "modern" concept of custom is "not only *not* customary law: it does not even faintly resemble customary law."[44] This is because the foundation of international custom has long been state practice, with *opinio juris* being the secondary component for transforming the practice into a legal obligation. To remove action from the concept is to make the very concept a caricature of itself.[45] Practice is the only way dissenting states can be obligated to follow a customary rule while remaining consistent with the doctrine of consent.[46] Redefining or eliminating practice from the formula not only removes the element of implied consent; it also changes the fundamental concept of customary law that the international community has accepted for hundreds of years.

As A. Mark Weisburd observes, the only real evidence for determining practice is behavior, in particular behavior that creates expectations for

---

[41] International Court of Justice, *Analysis of North Sea Continental Shelf Cases (Federal Republic of Germany v. Denmark; Federal Republic of Germany v. Netherlands)*, 20 February 1969, available at: https://www.refworld.org/docid/4023a4c04.html (accessed 14 November 2020).

[42] United Nations, International Law Commission, "Draft Conclusions on Identification of Customary International Law, with Commentaries," 2018, p. 4.

[43] United Nations, "Draft Conclusions on Identification of Customary International Law," p. 126.

[44] Robert Jennings, "The Identification of International Law," in Bin Cheng (ed.), *International Law: Teaching and Practice* (Stevens and Son, 1982), p. 3.

[45] See Anthony D'Amato, "Trashing Customary International Law," *The American Journal of International Law*, vol. 81, no. 1, January 1987.

[46] Niels Petersen, "Customary Law without Custom? Rules, Principles, and the Role of State Practice in International Norm Creation," *American University Law Review*, vol. 23, no. 2, 1988.

future behavior.[47] However, there is an inherent problem basing a source of law on interpreting state practice in a world of 195 states with a wide diversity in history, tradition, regime type, and level of development. This is particularly the case when there is a dramatic increase in the formation of new states over a short period of time, as has been the case after decolonization and the end of the Cold War.[48] As the ILC noted, CIL must be "distinguished from conduct by international actors that neither generates a legal right or obligation nor carries such a legal implication. Not all international acts bear legal significance: acts of comity and courtesy, or mere usage, even if carried out as a matter of tradition, thus lie outside the scope of customary international law and the present topic."[49]

Certainly one can be sympathetic to the efforts of legal scholars to elevate the concept of *opinio juris* to a higher explanatory level in determining the extent to which political leaders accept a legal norm as binding. I do so myself in this book. However, once one embarks on this line of thinking, one is no longer talking about custom, at least not as it has developed over the past several hundred years. For these reasons J. Patrick Kelly (among others) argues that customary law is rapidly becoming both outdated and a barrier to the progressive development of international law, inasmuch as it lacks the four standards of legitimacy for a legal rule developed by Thomas Franck (determinacy, symbolic validation, coherence, and adherence).[50]

These problems are particularly acute when trying to determine *which* norms restricting internal state violence have passed into customary law. As mentioned above, the concept of human rights exists on a sliding scale, encompassing a very wide range of protections. The most egregious aspects of internal violence are loosely regulated through a series of multilateral treaties; however, a number of states have refused to sign or ratify them. According to contemporary theories of international law, even if one could establish that particular human rights treaty norms have become embedded

---

[47] A. Mark Weisburd, "Customary International Law and Torture: The Case of India," *Chicago Journal of International Law*, vol. 2, no. 1, Spring 2001.

[48] Between 1945 and 1990, 96 new states were created as a result of decolonization. See A. J. Christopher, *The Atlas of States: Global Change, 1900-2000* (Wiley, 1999). Following the end of the Cold War (1990-1995), 22 new states formed. A. J. Christopher, "New States in a New Millennium," *Area*, vol. 31, no. 4, 1999, p. 327.

[49] International Law Commission, "Formation and Evidence of Customary International Law," Document A/CN.4/663, First report on formation and evidence of customary international law, by Sir Michael Wood, 2013, p. 125.

[50] J. Patrick Kelly, "The Twilight of Customary International Law," *Virginia Journal of International Law*, vol. 40, 2000.

into CIL, nonparty states would theoretically be exempt from the obligations stipulated in the agreements, since the one element that frees a state from a customary norm is a persistent objection made at the time the rule began to transition into a customary law. The persistent objector exception has traditionally been viewed by legal analysts and political leaders as necessary for customary law to remain consistent with the traditional doctrine of consent, which is still the foundation of contemporary international law.[51] Clearly, an explicit refusal of a state to sign and ratify a treaty as it is being drafted is clear evidence of a persistent objection made at the time of the rule's inception.

For these reasons, CIL has traditionally been reserved for those practices that have a long lineage, or at least those that have developed through repeated practice by a wide range of states and by many different governments. For example, it is generally recognized within political and legal circles that the basic principles underlying the laws of international armed conflict have become firmly rooted in customary law applicable to newly formed states even if they have not signed the four Geneva Conventions.[52] However, the regulation of warfare (both *jus ad bellum* and *jus in bello*) has long been one of the primary goals of international law, dating back to the publication of Hugo Grotius's *De Jure Belli ac Pacis* in 1625. Over the past 400 years, its basic principles have been repeatedly evoked in diplomatic correspondence, treaties, conventions, and government military manuals and has been acknowledged throughout scores of conflicts in all parts of the world. The four Geneva Conventions of 1949 were only a modern articulation of these principles.

Similarly, much of international law governing the use of the high seas was deeply embedded in customary law long before the Law of the Seas Convention entered into force in 1994. Freedom of navigation was at the origins of modern international law and one of the oldest and most recognized principles in the legal regime governing the high seas ever since it was enshrined in Grotius's *De Mare Liberum* in 1609.[53]

---

[51] Jonathan I. Charney, "The Persistent Objector Rule and the Development of Customary International Law," *British Yearbook of International Law*, vol. 56, no. 1, 1985.

[52] This principle was the basis for prosecuting grave breaches of the laws of armed conflict during the trials conducted by the UN-sponsored International Tribunal for the Former Yugoslavia. See *Prosecutor v. Delalić, Mucić also known as "Pavo," Delić, Landzo also known as "Zenga"* (Judgement) IT-96-21-A (20 February 2001) para. 113.

[53] See Rüdiger Wolfrum, "Freedom of Navigation: New Challenges," International Tribunal for the Law of The Sea, in *Freedom of Seas, Passage Rights and the 1982 Law of the Seas Convention*, Center for Oceans Law and Policy, vol. 13, 2009.

So too is diplomatic law, long considered to be one of the pillars of international relations dating back to French king Louis XIV in the mid-17th century. Long before the conclusion of the 1961 Vienna Convention on Diplomatic Relations, governments conducted diplomacy according to a set of informal rules that came to be part of CIL.[54]

For this reason, renowned legal scholar Louis Henkin holds that given the modern origins of human rights law, and the fact that unlike customary law it has been consciously created, it could not be regarded as customary-based.[55]

Most important, as I demonstrate below, CIL reflects a very particular period of European history, and the structural conditions in the international system that gave rise to this form have changed dramatically. CIL emerged during a period when there was a small number of European states whose shared culture and traditions enabled them to recognize a common set of practices as constituting voluntarily accepted legal norms. Indeed, the concept of sovereign equality as a constitutive principle of the international system did not emerge in practice until after World War II, when most of the world was either under colonial rule or excluded from the European state system. Moreover, in the absence of international institutions or multilateral treaties, and with a low density of interaction among governments, common practice was the most effective standard. In fact, according to several legal scholars, most contemporary customs are founded on the basis of practice by fewer than a dozen states.[56] Thus, reconceptualizing contemporary human rights norms that are based on collective agreement without a corresponding practice as customary law takes us backward rather than forward.

If this is correct, we need to posit a new source of international law to explain some types of contemporary practice that are not based on individual state consent, particularly in the area of human rights. It is apparent from the above discussion that many legal scholars are searching for a method to explain how some legal norms can apply to all states in the absence of consistent, widespread state practice. While many still refer to this as a new form of customary law, for the reasons stated above I don't believe that this is the best approach toward explaining what I hope to show is a new way of practicing international law. At the same time, the extensive literature among international law scholars drawing from customary law to explain emerging

---

[54] See Harold Nicolson, *Diplomacy* (Institute for the Study of Diplomacy, 1988).
[55] Louis Henkin, "Human Rights and State Sovereignty," *Georgia Journal of International and Comparative Law*, vol. 25, no. 1, 1996, p. 35.
[56] See Scharf, "Accelerated Formation of Customary International Law," p. 317.

human rights norms reveals keen insights and innovative ideas that we can incorporate into a theory of consensus-based law.

The Evolution of International Law

Rather than rewrite the concept of customary law to reconcile universal legal norms with the doctrine of consent, I suggest that we posit a new source of international law that is rooted in the structure of the contemporary international system. I start by examining how and why different types of international legal systems evolve in the first place and how the sources of international law are derivative of the structure of the international order. Michael Scharf argues that fundamental changes in the international system can alter the legal paradigm, producing new principles of international law with exceptional speed, a process that he calls a "Grotian moment."[57] Although he advances this notion to explain what he calls "rapid custom," the idea of a "tipping point" can be useful to explain how fundamental changes in the principles underlying international relations can produce parallel changes in international law, without involving custom.

The evolution of international law has been historically linked to four variables that characterize the structure of the international system: (1) the nature of the constitutive units (kingdoms, empires, states); (2) the organizing principles of the system (international hierarchy, anarchy, sovereignty, globalization); (3) the density of interaction among the units (which John Ruggie defines as the volume, velocity, and diversity of interactions among political actors within international society);[58] and (4) the scope and depth of institutionalization within the system (defined largely by the number and scope of authority of international organizations and the level of global governance).

During the early years of the European state system, monarchs recognized a small but influential body of natural law as providing a standard from which they could evaluate and regulate each another's behavior. Natural law theory holds that there are certain principles of right and wrong inherent in

---

[57] Michael Scharf, "Seizing the 'Grotian Moment': Accelerated Formation of Customary International Law in Times of Fundamental Change," *Cornell International Law Journal*, vol. 43, April 2010.

[58] Drawing from sociologist Emil Durkheim, John Ruggie first introduced this concept of "dynamic density" into the study of international relations in 1983. See John Ruggie, "Continuity and Transformation in the World Polity: Toward a Neorealist Synthesis," *World Politics*, vol. 35, no. 2, 1983.

all human societies that are necessary for the maintenance of social order. These principles are binding on both the individual members of the community and the authorities that govern them. Its precepts date back to classical Roman philosophy, particularly that of the Stoics, and the concept was further developed by Christian theologians in the 13th century.[59]

This form of universal law was the primary form of legal obligation accepted by rulers during the late Middle Ages and early modern period in Europe (16th–18th centuries) and remained dominant until the early 19th century.[60] During this period, there was no strict line between the domestic and the international or between the public and the private sectors. There was only *jus naturae et gentium* (natural law binding on all humankind), and therefore the legal principles of the realm were also applicable in the king's relations with other monarchs.

For example, sovereigns acknowledged limits on the conditions under which a monarch could initiate hostilities that drew from just war doctrine (*jus ad bellum*).[61] The code of chivalry regulated the combatants' behavior in battle, and the king's armies accepted rules governing the choice of targets and the treatment of neutrals and noncombatants.[62] As the European system continued to evolve, the king's army became the state's army, and many of these values became embedded within the military organizations. While these limits were not always followed, they did force monarchs to provide justifications for their behavior, and when they failed to live up to them, it often led to diplomatic and military consequences within the community of recognized European royal families.

This form of international law reflected the political structure of the early modern European system: a loose cosmopolitan association of kingdoms, principalities, duchies, counties, and Free Imperial Cities, all of which were part of the universal Kingdom of God and beholden to its transnational representatives on earth, the Holy See and Holy Roman Emperor.[63]

---

[59] See Marcus Tullius Cicero, *On the Commonwealth* and *On the Laws*, edited by James E. G. Zetzel (Cambridge University Press, 1999) and Thomas Aquinas, *The Treatise on Law* [being *Summa theologiae*, I–II; QQ. 90 through 97] (University of Notre Dame Press, 1993).

[60] See, for example, Adam Roberts and Richard Guelff, *Documents on the Laws of War* (Oxford University Press, 2002), pp. 3–4.

[61] See Hugo Grotius, *The Rights of War and Peace: Including the Law of Nature and Nations* (Hard Press Publishing, 1913 [1625]).

[62] See Maurice Keen, *The Laws of War in the Late Middle Ages* (Routledge, 1965).

[63] Although the rulers within the Holy Roman Empire had a fair degree of independence, they were legally vassals of the emperor. Similarly, Catholic kings accepted limits on their authority imposed by Canon Law, a transnational legal code imposed by the Holy See. Anders Winroth and John C. Wei (eds.), *The Cambridge History of Medieval Canon Law* (Cambridge University Press, 2022).

The idea of a *res publica Christiana* (a European Christian republic that transcended the authority of the monarchs) provided the foundation for a higher authority above the individual rulers. The obligation to follow natural law was closely connected to the legitimation of the king's divine right to rule and to his responsibilities as a European monarch. Just as the king's authority was derived from the "natural order of things" as dictated by a supreme being, his responsibility to adhere to the restrictions imposed by natural law was the flipside of this authority.[64] As such, universal natural law provided the foundation for a hierarchical system of legal obligation among sovereigns.

Religious justifications for natural law steadily diminished during the 18th-century Enlightenment, and with the rise of secularism in Western Europe modern natural law theories shifted toward the rational. By the mid-18th century, human reason had largely replaced divine inspiration as the source of natural law. This was accepted by political actors as forming the foundation for an unwritten body of universal moral principles and ethical and legal norms by which their conduct could be evaluated and governed.[65]

Although the Peace of Westphalia in 1648 symbolically ushered in a new political order in Europe based on a rudimentary form of state sovereignty, the idea of a positivist Law of Nations rooted in custom—as conceived by such 17th-century jurists as Hugo Grotius and Emer de Vattel—was not actually reflected in state practice until after the conclusion of the Napoleonic wars in the early 19th century.[66] This is because the territorial nation-state as the principal, if not exclusive, legitimate political form did not dominate until that time. Personal relationships and royal charters, rather than fixed territory, remained the major factor in creating and governing political communities.

During the period between the Peace of Westphalia and the 1815 Congress of Vienna, dynastic ties among European rulers had created political and social bonds that cut across territorial boundaries.[67] Both governments and

---

[64] During the late Middle Ages and early years of the European state system, social order was maintained largely by the commonly held belief that the structure of society was determined by an unchanging hierarchy that stipulated each person's role. The "natural order" was thus the moral source from which natural law derived its authority. It encompassed the natural relations of beings to one another that existed in the absence of human law. See Norman F. Cantor, *The Civilization of the Middle Ages* (Perennial, 1994).

[65] See Stephen Pope, "Reason and Natural Law," in Gilbert Meilaender and William Werpehowski (eds.), *The Oxford Handbook of Theological Ethics* (Oxford University Press, 2007).

[66] See Simone Zurbuchen, *The Law of Nations and Natural Law, 1625–1800* (Brill, 2019).

[67] See Jeremy Black, *The Rise of the European Powers* (Routledge, Chapman and Hall, 1990), p. 150.

their populations (who were considered to be subjects rather than citizens) were built upon loyalty to the king, emperor, and Church. The recognition of natural law as a guide for the relationships among sovereigns flowed largely from the nature of their regimes and the dynastic system that dominated the continent.

The French Revolution of 1789 and its expansion through Napoleon's continental empire destroyed this system by undermining absolute monarchy and dynastic succession as legitimate foundations for the state.[68] As Napoleon's armies moved across Europe, they formally abolished feudalism and eliminated dozens of petty principalities and duchies by consolidating their territories into large administrative units. The ultimate defeat of Napoleon left half of the continent without government, but it was not possible to simply restore the old order.[69] Napoleon had abolished the Holy Roman Empire in 1806, and the power of the Catholic Church, which had been steadily losing ground to secular rulers, was dramatically reduced. This formally ended the last vestiges of political hierarchy in Europe. International anarchy, based on the absence of a central authority, was now firmly entrenched.

The 1815 Congress of Vienna (the largest meeting of European political leaders and diplomats ever assembled to date) reorganized the system of states by recognizing territory rather than dynastic lineage as the legitimate foundation of statehood, a principle that had already been slowly evolving over the past century. The Congress was the first collective effort to base the Law of Nations on sovereign will.[70] To facilitate relations among themselves, the major powers created two informal institutional structures that would formalize their relations and the rules to guide them, the Congress system and the Concert of Europe.

As a result, the transition from transnational hierarchy to international anarchy in Europe led to the parallel development of an international legal order founded not on the universality of natural law but on individual state consent. The emerging volunteerist school of law rejected universal sources

---

[68] Albert Sorel, *Europe and the French Revolution: The Political Tradition of the Old Regime* (Fontana Library, 1969 [1885]); Alexis de Tocqueville, *The Old Regime and the French Revolution* (Anchor, 1955); and E. J. Hobsbawm, *The Age of Revolution: 1789-1848* (New American Library, 1962).

[69] Guglielmo Ferrero, *The Reconstruction of Europe: Talleyrand and the Congress of Vienna, 1814-1815* (Putnam, 1941), p. 141.

[70] "Part 1: The Progressive Development of International Law," *The American Journal of International Law*, vol. 41, no. 4, 1947, pp. 32-49.

of international law, such as God, reason, or transnational authority, and replaced it with one grounded in state autonomy. As Vattel had defined it a half-century earlier, sovereignty provides a "freedom that is limited only by voluntarily-accepted restraints" because the natural state of nations is an independence that does not acknowledge a social bond among them. "Nations or sovereign states must be regarded as so many free persons living together in a state of nature. States are independent not only from each other but also from any higher principle except that to which they specifically agree."[71]

This new decentralized legal order rooted in consent thus grew out of an international system based on international anarchy and state sovereignty. The principle of anarchy holds that no central authority exists that can create laws, enforce agreements, or adjudicate disputes. The principle of sovereignty stipulates that even if such an authority were to exist, states would be under no obligation to obey it. Following from this, the doctrine of consent maintains that since states are not beholden to any universal principle or supranational authority, they are only obligated to follow those rules that they have specifically agreed to accept. Modern consent theories therefore reject both natural law and global hierarchy as a foundation of international obligation, and as a result, the foundation of legal obligation emanates solely from the explicit and voluntary will of each member of the international community.[72]

During the 19th century, customary practice was the primary source of positive international law accepted by governments. The increasing density of interaction among the European states during this period, as well as their shared culture and traditions, enabled them to recognize certain common practices as constituting voluntarily accepted legal norms. At that time, customary law was highly Eurocentric, facilitated by the cultural and social cohesiveness of the European community of states, its common history and religion, and its common legal tradition based on Roman law (*ius gentium*).[73]

---

[71] Emeric Vattel, *The Law of Nations or Principles of the Law of Nature, Applied to the Conduct and Affairs of Nations and Sovereigns* (Abraham Small, 1817), p. 13.

[72] See, for example, Louis Henkin, *International Law: Politics and Values* (Martinus Nijhoff, 1995) and Anthony Arend, *Legal Rules and International Society* (Oxford University Press, 1999), chapter 2.

[73] See, for example, Milos Vec, "From the Congress of Vienna to the Peace Treaties of 1919," in Bardo Fassbender and Anne Peters (eds.), *Oxford Handbook of the History of International Law* (Oxford University Press, 2012), p. 658 and Arthur Nussbaum, "Significance of Roman Law in the History of International Law," *University of Pennsylvania Law Review*, vol. 100, 1951–1952.

This cohesiveness was maintained, at least in part, by the exclusion of other regional legal systems, such as the Qānūn and Sharia codes of the Ottoman Empire, the Chinese tributary system, and the customary practices and legal traditions in precolonial Africa. During this period, non-Western societies and less powerful Western nations played little role in the formation of international legal norms. Some non-European polities (such as the Ottoman Empire) were permitted to participate in European politics, but only on the basis of European institutions.[74] Custom as practice was therefore accepted as a legitimate source of interstate law so long as European governments publicly acknowledged its legal authority.

As a result, state officials accepted a set of legal obligations based on reciprocity regarding the means and methods of warfare, the use of the high seas, and diplomatic rules that reflected long-standing state behavior and traditions passed down through royal families, sovereign rulers, and government bureaucracies.

This changed in the 20th century. The increased formalization and institutionalization of international relations encouraged states to develop more defined and better-articulated legal mechanisms for facilitating cooperation. Thus, customary practice, while still an important part of international law, largely gave way to written agreements as the primary foundation of legal obligation. This was largely an outgrowth of a modest increase in the dynamic density of interaction and the proliferation of intergovernmental institutions, such as the League of Nations, the International Labor Organization, the United Nations, regional security associations (such as the Organization of American States), and dozens of other formal bodies.

In pursuing this approach, political leaders sought to remove the ambiguity that is inherent in CIL by codifying, clarifying, and expanding its most important principles into multilateral conventions and treaties. For example, the Hague Conventions of 1899 and 1907 and the Four Geneva Conventions of 1949 on the laws of armed conflict; the Vienna Convention on Diplomatic Relations (1961); the Law of the Seas Conventions (1994); and the Montevideo Convention on the Rights and Duties of States (1933), all codified into positive law rules that had previously been based on long-standing practice and normative principle.

---

[74] See J. Patrick Kelly, "Customary International Law in Historical Context: The Exercise of Power with General Acceptance," Widener University Delaware Law School Legal Studies Research Paper Series no. 17-06, April 2018.

International Consensus as a Source of Legal Obligation

Yet even as consent-based international law continues to dominate diplomatic and legal circles, political leaders have begun to consider legal norms that have a more universal effect on states. Much as the political and structural conditions in the 19th century provided a framework for the development of positive international law based on state consent, there is some evidence that changes in the structure of authority within the international system are producing another transformation in the nature of international legal obligation. These changes have been slowly advancing over the past 75 years. Specifically, in attempting to deal with discrete problems in international relations, political leaders have contemplated ways of creating *opinio juris* through collective deliberation through formal institutions among the active members of the international community rather than simply relying on state practice and public pronouncements by individual states.

This movement has been reflected in some recent scholarship questioning the degree to which consent should remain the foundation of international legal obligation. Nico Krisch and Andrew Guzman, for example, argue that an international legal system based primarily on individual state consent is inadequate to solve many global problems, as national goals become increasingly dependent on, and vulnerable to, forces and dynamics outside their own boundaries.[75] Requiring consent from all decision-making states frustrates many potential arrangements that would improve the lot of states as a whole, which in turn greatly restricts the ability of states to generate collective gains. This prevents many forms of cooperation that are necessary to achieve essential outcomes, such as the provision of vital collective goods like combating climate change, preventing the spread of terrorism, nuclear nonproliferation, stable global trade, and economic development.[76] It also frustrates the ability of international law to provide a greater degree of protection for certain types of fundamental human rights that reflect broad support within the international community.

Thus, Laurence Helfer holds that there is an increasing erosion of the consent requirement, producing a change of paradigm that is manifesting itself in the weakening of the persistent-objector rule, third-party effects of

---

[75] Nico Krisch, "The Decay of Consent: International Law in an Age of Global Public Goods," *American Journal of International Law*, vol. 108, no. 1, January 2014 and Andrew Guzman, "Against Consent," *Virginia Journal of International Law*, vol. 52, no. 4, 2012.

[76] Guzman, "Against Consent," p. 758.

treaties, and majority voting within treaty bodies and international organizations.[77] He posits the rise of what he terms "nonconsensual international lawmaking," which he defines as a legal obligation that binds a member state of a treaty or an international organization even where that country has not ratified, acceded to, or otherwise affirmatively accepted that obligation.

This approach is also represented by the efforts of the United Nations, with the strong support of its member states, to define the conditions under which individual states can exercise universal jurisdiction to prosecute specific, defined offenses committed outside of their sovereign territory. According to the principle of universal jurisdiction, certain crimes violate the fundamental principles of the international community as a whole, and as a result any national court may assert jurisdiction over their perpetrators without relying on the traditional bases of jurisdiction, territory, extradition, or nationality.[78] A claim to universal jurisdiction is not made against those within the domestic legal community but, rather, is a claim to authority in relation to states and individuals external to it.[79]

In 2017, the General Assembly tasked its Sixth Committee (which addresses questions of international law) with initiating a process that would institutionalize this practice.[80] They began at its 70th session, bringing together hundreds of representatives from member states to discuss, debate, and develop a set of principles that would integrate the universal enforcement of certain offenses into international law.[81]

So what is going on? Just as the transition from international hierarchy to international anarchy brought forth a parallel change from natural law to state consent as the foundation for international law, the increased globalization of world politics through the growth and expansion of multilateral institutions has been leading to a larger role for international consensus as the foundation for legal rules.

The evolution of international law to include factors in which international consensus plays an increasingly important role has been facilitated

---

[77] Laurence R. Helfer, "Nonconsensual International Lawmaking," *University of Illinois Law Review*, vol. 2008, no. 1, 2008.

[78] See Kenneth C. Randall, "Universal Jurisdiction under International Law," *Texas Law Review*, vol. 66, 1987–1988.

[79] Devika Hovell, "The Authority of Universal Jurisdiction," *The European Journal of International Law*, vol. 29, no. 2, 2018.

[80] UN General Assembly, "The Scope and Application of the Principle of Universal Jurisdiction," resolution adopted on 14 December 2015, A/70/119.

[81] United Nations Sixth Committee, 71st session, "The Scope and Application of the Principle of Universal Jurisdiction" (Agenda item 85), 3 October to 11 November 2016.

by four relatively recent developments in what many scholars have termed "global governance":[82] (1) the proliferation of universal membership organizations with broad mandates to address a wide range of issues in global politics, (2) the domination of multilateralism as the legitimate institutional form of international cooperation, (3) the increased use of collective deliberation among a wide range of states as the legitimate process for making decisions in international affairs, and (4) the development of independent institutions that reflect the principles of transnationalism.

Since the end of World War II, there has been a dramatic growth in the number and scope of multilateral organizations with broad mandates to address a wide range of issues within the international system. Such organizations provide increased governance functions because many of them are open to all states and are characterized both by a centralization of authority and at least some degree of autonomy from the individual states that characterized them.[83] This provides an institutional mechanism for states to collectively develop principles that reflect the consensus of the international community.

Most of these organizations require their members to sign legally binding charters committing them to a process of consultation and collective decision-making on a wide range of issues.[84] This in turn has (1) reduced the range of actions that states can pursue purely on the basis of self-help, (2) increased the number of forums for negotiating multilateral treaties and other agreements, and (3) expanded the diversity and number of states involved in such negotiations.[85] This has produced what a reviewer of this manuscript termed "attenuated consent," a second-order form in which states agree to accept the authority of specific institutions they had agreed to join,

---

[82] Global governance is a process through which political actors define, develop, legitimize and implement collective rules and procedures for the international community of states. This is a large literature on the effect of global governance on the structure of the international system. See, inter alia, Martin Hewson and Timothy J. Sinclair (eds.), *Approaches to Global Governance Theory* (State University of New York Press, 1999); Joseph Nye and John Donanu (eds.), *Governance in a Globalizing World* (Brookings Institution, 2000); Paul F. Diehl (ed.), *The Politics of Global Governance: International Organizations in an Interdependent World* (Lynne Reinner, 2001); and Lloyd Gruber, *Ruling the World: Power Politics and the Rise of Supranational Institutions* (Princeton University Press, 2000).

[83] Kenneth Abbott and Duncan Snidal, "Why States Act through Formal International Organizations," *Journal of Conflict Resolution*, vol. 42, no. 1, February 1998.

[84] See, for example, the United Nations Charter; Agreement Establishing the World Trade Organization; Charter of the Organization of American States; Constitutive Act of the African Union; the Bangkok Declaration (establishing ASEAN); and the Maastricht Treaty on European Union.

[85] Jose Alvarez, *International Organizations as Law-Makers* (Oxford University Press, 2006), pp. 283–291.

based on a defined process and decision rules. It has also led to what Daniel Deudney calls "institutional binding," a process through which states agree to accept mutual constraints by adopting a variety of multilateral treaties, interlocking organizations, and joint management responsibilities. This web of commitments makes it difficult and costly to defect in the future.[86]

Most of these organizations rely heavily on formal deliberative processes for collective decision-making based on the principle of multilateralism. Multilateralism is a form of institutionalism that commits political leaders to follow generalized principles of conduct that apply without regard to the particularistic interests of the parties or the strategic exigencies that may exist in a particular occurrence—the very essence of a legal commitment.[87] As Ruggie argues, multilateralism has come to embody a procedural norm in its own right, changing the expectations for how new rules could be developed and implemented.[88] Since World War II foreign policy officials have accepted multilateralism as the primary legitimate form of collective decision-making within the international community.[89] Multilateralism legitimizes such decision-making by creating a process through which all interested and affected states can participate according to well-established and generally accepted procedures.

The historical record over the past half-century clearly suggests that this has been extended to the area of legal obligation. Even a cursory examination of the most important treaties and conventions signed over the past generation demonstrates that multilateral forums have become the preferred method for conceptualizing and creating general international law. If this is correct, it provides the international community with the means to develop a type of virtual legislative process for establishing new legal obligations without creating either a world government or a supranational authority. In this sense, the products of multilateral forums substantially advance and formalize the international lawmaking process. When such a process is conducted within international organizations encompassing a

---

[86] See Daniel Deudney, "Binding Sovereigns: Authorities, Structures, and Geopolitics in Philadelphian Systems," in Thomas Biersteker and Cynthia Weber (eds.), *State Sovereignty as Social Construct* (Cambridge University Press, 1996).

[87] See John Ruggie, "Multilateralism: The Anatomy of an Institution," *International Organization*, vol. 46, 1992, p. 571.

[88] John Ruggie, "Multilateralism: The Anatomy of an Institution," in John Ruggie (ed.), *Multilateralism Matters: The Theory and Praxis of an Institutional Form* (Columbia University Press, 1993), p. 23.

[89] See G. John Ikenberry, *After Victory: Institutions, Strategic Restraint and the Rebuilding of Order after Major Wars* (Princeton University Press, 2000) and Ruggie, "Multilateralism."

broad membership, the outcome is legitimized by the fact that the members of these organizations have already legally committed themselves to this process by signing the organizational charters.

If, as Jonathan Charney argues, multilateral forums such as international organizations or negotiating conferences represent a different way of creating international law, they can provide more relevance to broad, multilateral consensus than can state practice.[90] In particular, as I discuss in Chapter 2, multilateral conferences sponsored by the universal-membership United Nations for the purpose of developing lawmaking treaties can create a new type of general international law that can bind all states. Thus, although states continue to retain broad autonomy in establishing their own foreign policies, over the past several decades they have accepted a growing number of legal obligations collectively developed through multilateral institutions such as the United Nations, regional security bodies, and the World Trade Organization.[91]

The deliberative process upon which multilateralism is based provides a mechanism for states to collectively develop certain legal and political principles that they can then argue apply more broadly within the international community. Roy Lee argues, for example, that the very process of creating new legal norms through international organizations—from deliberation to decision-making—provides the necessary source materials for assessing the degree of support and commitment to particular legal norms.[92] Similarly, international law scholar Ian Johnstone holds that collective decisions that are the product of extensive deliberation achieve a high level of legitimacy among states, particularly when they are justified through appeals to impartial and mutually acceptable principles.[93]

As such, a deliberative process requires argumentation and appeals to abstract principles and collective interest that reach beyond narrow self-help. Even if such arguments are motivated by particular interests, the

---

[90] Jonathan Charney, "Universal International Law," *The American Journal of International Law*, vol. 87, no. 4 (October 1993), pp. 529–551.

[91] See Judith O. Goldstein, Miles Kahler, Robert Keohane, and Anne-Marie Slaughter (eds.), "Legalization and World Politics," *International Organization* special issue, vol. 54, no. 3, August 2000.

[92] Roy Lee, "Rule-Making in the United Nations: Opinio Communitatis," *NYU Journal of International Law and Politics*, vol. 27, 1994–1995.

[93] Johnstone argues that the purpose of deliberation is both to get better outcomes and to give people the sense that their concerns have been taken into account, regardless of the outcome. See his "Deliberation and Legal Argumentation in International Decision-Making," in Hillary Charlesworth and Jean-Marc Coicaud (eds.), *The Faultlines of Legitimacy* (United Nations University Press, 2007) and Ian Johnstone, "Discursive Power in the UN Security Council," *Journal of International Law and International Relations*, vol. 2, no. 1, 2005.

generalization of these arguments on the basis of abstract principles ensures that the decisions themselves will be applicable in a wide range of (often unforeseen) circumstances even when they may not favor such interests in the future. In this sense, the authority of the decisions is derived internally from within the community (in this case, the community of states) based on commonly held principles rather from an external actor such as a supranational legislative body. This applies equally to what has been termed "soft law," an avenue that political leaders have been increasingly pursuing over the past decade. I discuss this in greater detail in the next chapter.

At the same time, even as the international system based on the principle of state sovereignty consolidated and expanded to dominate all parts of the world, there has been a parallel growth in nongovernmental organizations (NGOs), most of which act independently of states. Since they do not represent states, they are not bound by the limitations imposed by the principle of sovereignty and can therefore represent a wider range of global opinion than many governments. While NGOs have neither legal authority nor direct political power over territory and populations, they play an important role in international norm and policy setting, mass mobilization, and monitoring state behavior. Many of them are active in helping to develop policies within the UN and other international organizations.[94] As a result, they are also playing an increasing role in the progressive development of international law.[95]

Increasingly both states and international and regional organizations such as the UN, NATO, The Economic Community of West African States, and the Organization of American States subcontract to NGOs many tasks such as peacekeeping, internal security, caring for refugees, monitoring elections, and engaging in sustainable development. This in turn gives them influence in decision-making.[96] Their influence is particularly felt at international

---

[94] Currently 138 NGOs have general consultative status with the UN Economic and Social Council, the highest level that guarantees significant participation in the organization. Approximately 4,000 others have special status, which limits their participation to specific issue areas. See Economic and Social Council, "List of Non-Governmental Organizations in Consultative Status with the Economic and Social Council as of 1 September 2018," E/2018/INF/5.

[95] See, for example, Karsten Nowrot, "Legal Consequences of Globalization: The Status of Non-Governmental Organizations under International Law," *Indiana Journal of Global Legal Studies*, vol. 6, no. 2, 1999; Isabelle Gunning, "Modernizing Customary International Law: The Challenge of Human Rights," *Virginia Journal of International Law*, vol. 31, 1991; Kenneth Anderson, "The Ottawa Convention Banning Landmines, the Role of International Non-Governmental Organizations, and the Idea of International Civil Society," *European Journal of International Law*, vol. 11, 2000.

[96] See Thomas Weiss (ed.), *Beyond UN Subcontracting: Task-Sharing with Regional Security Arrangements and Service Providing NGOs* (Palgrave, 1998).

conferences where treaties are drafted, and their specialized knowledge and professional leadership help to shape the outcomes. Indeed, NGOs have influenced the content of a number of international agreements, including the UN Convention Against Torture, the Rome Statute of the International Criminal Court, the Ottawa Convention banning landmines, and the Convention on the Rights of the Child.[97] This expands the global base of support for international legal norms beyond governments.

One of the most important contributions to the development of universal international law by NGOs might be their ability or potential to mobilize domestic populations in support of legal norms and empower domestic political actors to convince their governments to accept the norm. Thus, even if governments do not accept a particular principle as legally binding, pressure from civil society could encourage or force them to act as if they did.

In addition to the political role played by nonstate actors through NGOs, the literature on epistemic communities explains how transnational networks of knowledge-based experts develop, transmit, and legitimize sets of ideas and beliefs across national borders. These ideas help state officials to identify their interests, frame the issues for collective debate, and clarify salient points for negotiation. Ernst Haas, for example, demonstrates how communities of knowledge among independent professionals can lead to policy consensus among state elites. This sometimes leads to general understandings about cause-and-effect relationships in a given issue area, a phenomenon known as "consensual knowledge."[98] The generation of consensual knowledge—and its adoption by political leaders and opinion leaders—significantly influences the development, evolution, and outcome of international negotiations.

In this sense, the legitimation of certain ideas—such as decolonization, environmentalism, self-determination, and human rights—influences how political leaders frame and understand their political and legal obligations. The revolution in communications—from television to the internet to social media—dramatically accelerated this process, giving nongovernmental actors increased visibility and influence.

One of the most important epistemic communities in terms of international law is legal advisors who work for foreign ministries, national security

---

[97] See Zoe Pearson, "Non-Governmental Organizations and the International Criminal Court: Changing Landscapes of International Law," *Cornell International Law Journal*, vol. 39, no. 2, 2006, p. 251, fn. 12; and Nicola Short, "The Role of NGOs in the Ottawa Process to Ban Landmines," *International Negotiation*, vol. 4, no. 3, 1999.

[98] Ernst Haas, *When Knowledge Is Power: Three Models of Change in International Organizations* (University of California Press, 1990).

departments, military organizations, and other executive branch agencies. These counselors, in their official capacity, apply, interpret, and make policy recommendations to government officials on a wide range of issues related to the implementation of international law in a given situation.[99] In addition to advising policymakers to conform with international law, legal advisors often play leading roles in promoting the evolution of such law, particularly in areas that they consider best suited to national interests. Their common training, experience, and interaction among them create a transnational community of legal professionals who influence how international law is perceived within their own countries.

Thus, judicial decisions by domestic and international courts and the teachings of highly qualified publicists of the various nations are listed by the Statute of the International Court of Justice as subsidiary sources of international law. This is generally accepted by legal scholars and analysts, as evidenced by the frequent citation of court rulings and legal opinions in law journals and government documents. However from a strict positivist perspective, such rulings and opinions should not be binding on states inasmuch as they are not created through consent. Rather, the authority of such opinions actually stems from a general consensus among legal scholars and political leaders that they reflect the collective beliefs and will of the international community.

This does not mean that policymakers will always adhere to legal requirements at the expense of national interest. However, legal advisors do significantly influence said policymakers' perception of interest and their beliefs regarding their obligations under international law.[100]

Consensus and Customary Law

Through their participation in global forums, both states and NGOs engage in extensive consultations, deliberation, and negotiation. This enables

---

[99] See Andraz Zidar and Jean-Pierre Gauci (eds.), *The Role of Legal Advisors in International Law* (British Institute of International and Comparative Law, 2017) and Antonio Cassese, "The Role of Legal Advisors in Ensuring That Foreign Policy Conforms to International Legal Standards," *Michigan Journal of International Law*, vol. 14, no. 1, Fall 1992.

[100] During the 2003 U.S. invasion of Iraq, for example, military lawyers were intricately involved in approving individual targets for attack, ensuring that they complied with the laws of armed conflict. This frustrated many military leaders, who saw this as impinging on military necessity and their ability to prosecute the war. See Stephen Komarow, "US Attorneys Dispatched to Advise Military," *USA Today*, 11 March 2003, p. 9A.

political leaders to articulate in unambiguous terms their intention to accept collective norms.[101] Unlike customary law, we do not derive this type of *opinio juris* by aggregating the beliefs, intentions, and practices of individual states. This is the key difference between customary and consensus-based legal norms. Customary law does not require discussion or deliberation; it evolves over time. Consensus, however, can be traced as it develops within a global or regional collective through deliberation and interaction and is then appropriated individually by each state. We therefore shift the focus from examining statements and documents from individual states to exploring the quality of discourse within international institutions. In this way, the development of global governance structures that require formal deliberation among the membership provides a permissive condition for the evolution of a new form of international law, one that is rooted not in individual will, but in a convergence of international opinion among sovereign states. I refer to this as "consensus-based" international law.

The advantage of focusing on deliberation through multilateral institutions as the foundation of consensus-based law is that the standards are determined by the decision rules of the institutions. This is enhanced by the requirement that consensus must be developed and documented through multiple institutions. There must be a clear pattern, something which I test in the four empirical chapters.

A theory of consensus-based law—which I detail in Chapter 2—holds that under certain conditions, international legal obligations can be derived from a widespread agreement among the members of the international community concerning the authority of basic principles underlying specific legal rules. Once developed by states through a series of legitimately accepted political processes, such legal norms can become part of general international law applicable to all states, much in the same way that customary law is considered to be universally binding after it has been accepted as such by the international community. Unlike customary law, however, consensus-based norms are not rooted in a long-standing *practice*, nor can states separate themselves from a legal obligation by maintaining a persistent objection. In fact consensus-based international law turns customary law on its head; the norm *precedes* the practice rather than the other way around. Thus consensus international law does not *reflect* state practice as much as it *creates* it. This is an important distinction because some of the most important

---

[101] Lee, "Rule-Making in the United Nations," pp. 575–576.

consensus-based human rights norms (such as the prohibition against torture or widespread attacks on civilian populations) are created by political leaders precisely because the practice of states does not conform to the principle.

Consensus-based legal norms differ from those drawn from both natural and consent law in that they introduce a political dimension to state obligation. The obligation to follow natural law is imposed on states by forces that are external to the will of the actors (such as divine revelation, ethical principle, or human reason), while the responsibility to follow legal principles based on consent is derived *internally* by each state individually. A consensus-based legal norm, on the other hand, is neither external nor internal, but rather intersubjective, that is, one based on shared understandings among the members of the international community developed through their interaction.[102] In this way, it subjects universal legal obligations to deliberation and negotiation—thereby merging law with politics—an important connection in a decentralized system of sovereign states.

Thus, international legal norms produced through consensus are not either externally imposed on all states or adopted internally by each state, but rather binding political principles developed collectively by the members of the international community through deliberation and interaction. States are required to comply with these obligations as the price of membership in the international community of states. For consensus-based legal norms, then, the power of consent is held collectively by the international community—rather than individually by each state—at least in those areas in which there is widespread agreement.[103] In these cases, collective agreement can override an individual objection. In this vein, noted international law scholar Lassa Oppenheim speaks of "common consent" within the international community, a concept that is similar to the idea of general consensus.[104]

An examination of customary law suggests that an element of consensus has long been at least part of the international legal system. Although

---

[102] See, for example, Alexander Wendt, "Anarchy Is What States Make of It: The Social Construction of Power Politics," *International Organization*, vol. 46, no. 2, Spring 1992.

[103] Gerhard von Glahn refers to this as "common consent," while Bernard Oxman calls it "diffuse consent." See Gerhard von Glahn, *Law among Nations* (Allyn and Bacon, 1996), p. 39 and Bernard Oxman, "The Duty to Respect Generally Accepted Standards," *NYU Journal of International Law and Politics*, vol. 24, 1991, pp. 143–144.

[104] Lassa Oppenheim, *International Law: A Treatise* (Franklin Classics, 2018–1920). For an interesting interpretation of this, see Hirofumi Oguri, "Pacta Sunt Servanda as the Intersubjective but Universal Principle: Oppenheim's Common Consent within the Family of Nations," *European Society of International Law Conference Paper Series*, Conference Paper No. 14, 2018.

international law scholars consider customary law to be based on implied state consent as reflected in general practice, the second necessary element, *opinio juris,* reflects a form of universal consensus. That is, over time some practices have become so widespread and widely accepted that they come to reflect an international consensus that cannot be overridden by individual choice. Thus, it is a fine line between "implied consent" (which is implied only because it is accepted widely over time) and international consensus.

Moreover, if practices must be accompanied by a broad acknowledgment that they are legal obligations, the concept of *opinio juris* reflects a shared belief (consensus) held by the members of a particular international community.[105] As Michael Byers argues, the creation of customary law involves "collective knowledge," in which states hold shared understandings regarding the distinction between legally binding and nonbinding state practice. *Opinio juris* therefore represents a diffuse consensus among states as to the legal relevance of different kinds of behavior in different situations.[106] Thus, whether a particular practice has achieved the status of *opinio juris* is not determined individually by each state through their own practice or acknowledgment (a characteristic of a consent-based CIL) or by abstract moral principles (reflecting natural law), but by agreement within the international community as a whole.

This has important practical implications for current debates among international law scholars and political leaders over whether specific principles, such as human rights, have achieved the status of customary law. These debates are difficult to resolve because there has never been a standard for determining how much, for how long, and among how many states practice has to continue in order for it to become part of the body of customary law. Thus, for example, scholars and practitioners continue to debate whether human rights or humanitarian intervention are legal obligations that go beyond the text of specific treaties. A theory of consensus-based legal obligation can contribute to this debate because it can deal with practices that are of recent vintage that lack consistent state practice and with norms that have been developed in the course of addressing contemporary problems.

---

[105] Although the concept of *opinio juris* is broadly accepted by most legal scholars, it is not without its critics. For a brief overview of the contrary arguments, see Christian Dahlman, "The Function of Opinio Juris in Customary International Law," *Nordic Journal of International Law*, vol. 81, no. 3, 2012, pp. 332–335. I should note that while Dahlman discusses the critiques in detail, he personally accepts *opinio juris* in both theory and practice.

[106] Byers, *Custom, Power and the Power of Rules*, p. 19.

Organization of the Book

The next chapter will develop a theory of consensus-based international law and discuss the processes and institutions that facilitate its development. Subsequent chapters will apply this to what I call "excessive state violence" (atrocities) that states employ within their borders. I hope to demonstrate that political leaders have generally agreed that at least four specific practices exceed the limit of internal state violence that governments can employ in the pursuit of national interest: widespread, systematic attacks on a civilian population; violent persecution of defined human groups (including genocide, ethnic cleansing, and apartheid); torture; and the violation of civilian immunity in internal armed conflicts. I am not including slavery in this list because it is not only legally prohibited in every country on earth; its ban is one of the few legal norms that have achieved the status of *jus cogens* and is unambiguously part of CIL. It is therefore unnecessary to add it to the list of consensus-based legal norms.

I argue that the universal opposition to this level of extreme internal state violence constitutes a general convergence in political values that provides a permissive condition for the emergence of consensus-based legal norms. I will examine how a universal ban on each of these practices evolved into a consensus-based legal obligation.

2
A Theory of Consensus-Based International Law

Are there conditions under which the international community will recognize some emerging legal norms as universally binding, even if some states do not agree to accept them and the norms do not reflect general practice? Under the prevailing philosophies of international law—legal positivism and state consent—the answer is clearly no. These philosophies hold that all law emanates from human will, as expressed in written rules or customary practices that have been explicitly adopted or contracted. As such, it is independent from any external source, higher principle, or universal notions of right and wrong. From this perspective, a state's legal obligations can be determined only through a set of verifiable conditions that provide an objective standard of legal validation; such obligations do not go beyond the letter of a treaty's text or specific and verifiable acts of state practice.

At the same time, as I argued in the previous chapter, qualitative changes in global governance are prompting political leaders to recognize a limited body of international law that is based, not on explicit state consent or customary practice, but rather on collective consensus among states within the international community. To account for this, this chapter will advance a theory of consensus-based international law that holds that under certain well-defined conditions, some international legal obligations can be derived from a widespread agreement among the members of the international community, even in the absence of state practice. In doing so, I will examine the conditions under which such legal norms can emerge, the sources of such norms, and the processes and institutions that enable states to develop them. I will then apply this theory to the regulation of internal state violence and the universal ban on atrocities.

The Sources of Consensus-Based International Legal Norms

International law scholar Louis Henkin argues that there is an emerging category of "non-conventional" (nontreaty) law of human rights that differs significantly from customary law. "Traditional customary law was not made," he maintains, "it resulted. Most of it was always there in the constitutional law implicit in the conception of a system of states.... [S]tate practice recognized the law as having happened.... Now, non-conventional law is being made, purposely, knowingly," and human rights is a principal instance.[1] While his long experience in both academia and international legal practice informed this view, he did not offer a theory to explain how this type of law emerged and why it arose when it did. This is one of the tasks I hope to accomplish in this chapter.

Consensus-based international law differs from both treaty and customary international law in that it is both universally binding and consciously created by states through multilateral processes and forums. This emerging form of law can be explained by changes in the density of interaction among states and the expanded scope and depth of institutionalization within the system. The growth and proliferation of these institutions of global governance and the adoption of multilateralism as the legitimate process for creating new rules have made this new form of international law possible.

The sources of consensus laws are neither random nor arbitrary, nor are they imposed by a small number of powerful states on the international system, although the major powers may exercise significant influence on their development. Rather, they are derived from a variety of definable sources that in total offer evidence of international consensus. I emphasize "in total" because none of the sources cited below is in and of itself sufficient to demonstrate consensus. Instead, political leaders, diplomats, and legal analysts derive consensus-based legal norms from a combination of the following: (1) a body of multilateral lawmaking treaties and conventions, (2) a corpus of soft law supported by a consistent pattern of unanimous or near-unanimous resolutions passed by decision-making bodies within various intergovernmental organizations, (3) principles of international law that have achieved the status of *jus cogens*, and (4) legal interpretations made by

---

[1] Louis Henkin, "Human Rights and State Sovereignty," *Georgia Journal of International and Comparative Law*, vol. 25, nos. 1–2, 1995–1996, p. 37.

international courts and institutions (such as the ILC) that are broadly cited by legal analysts and political leaders.

Lawmaking Treaties

A primary source of consensus-based legal norms is multilateral conventions that are designed to further the progressive development of international law. The term "progressive development" refers to the preparation of multilateral conventions on subjects that either have not been regulated by international law or have not been sufficiently developed in the practice of states.[2] Many legal analysts distinguish progressive development from the traditional notion of "codification"; the latter attempts to enshrine existing customary law into a multilateral agreement rather than create new legal norms.[3] Others, however, argue that this distinction is a false one, pointing out that there is a dynamic relationship between the two, and that even a new legal norm often includes elements of a customary rule already in existence.[4] Either way, any effort to create new binding rules in areas where it had not previously existed can be considered a form of lawmaking.

The concept of progressive development emerged after World War II, when it was discussed extensively during the San Francisco conference that drafted the United Nations charter in 1945. While there was broad agreement by the assembled states not to endow the General Assembly with legislative authority, they agreed to task the body with promoting the progressive development of international law by initiating processes that would result in the creation of new legal norms.[5]

As a result, since the mid-20th century there has been a growing trend to develop emerging legal norms into a form of general law through the

---

[2] Statute of the International Law Commission, adopted by the General Assembly in resolution 174 (II) of 21 November 1947, as amended by resolutions 485 (V) of 12 December 1950, 984 (X) of 3 December 1955, 985 (X) of 3 December 1955, and 36/39 of 18 November 1981, Article 15.

[3] See, for example, Paul Szasz, "International Norm-Making," in Edith Brown Weiss, ed., *Environmental Change and International Law: New Challenges and Dimensions* (United Nations University Press, 1992) and Arnold Pronto, "Codification and Progressive Development of International Law: A Legislative Article 13(1)(a) of the Charter of the United Nations," *Florida International University Law Review*, vol. 13, no. 6, 2019.

[4] See, for example, Pavel Sturma, "The International Law Commission between Codification, Progressive Development, or a Search for a New Role," *FIU Law Review*, vol. 13, no. 6, 2019, pp. 1133–1134.

[5] See Pronto, "Codification and Progressive Development of International Law," p. 1104. Also see Article 13 (1) of the United Nations Charter.

advancement of "lawmaking treaties." Lawmaking treaties are multilateral agreements that articulate principles of international law designed to be binding on an overwhelming majority of states, with the intention of becoming part of general international law. Unlike traditional agreements based on the principle of reciprocity (that have been generally viewed as akin to contracts), lawmaking treaties are designed to establish general principles of conduct that would apply widely across the international community. Malcolm Shaw argues that by virtue of their widespread support and acceptance, such treaties have an effect *generally* rather than *restrictively*. That is, lawmaking treaties elaborate a common perception of international law in a given topic and establish new rules to guide states in their international conduct.[6] As Grigory Tunki, a former member of the ILC, argues, as a result of the codification and progressive development of international law, a number of general multilateral treaties have become or are becoming part of general international law.[7]

These treaties therefore articulate a general consensus around the emergence of new legal norms rather than simply codifying existing practices.

According to Oscar Schachter, in order to be considered a lawmaking treaty, a specific agreement must be designed to regulate a particular kind of behavior that applies in a wide variety of circumstances without regard to specific claims to the contrary. For Schachter, it must also articulate a rule formally adopted by an authorized body of an international organization.[8] Frederic Kirgis concurs, but argues that such agreements should also fulfill at least one of the following conditions: (1) codifying preexisting customary law, (2) reflecting general principles of law recognized by a wide range of states, (3) crystallizing "emerging rules of law" (as opposed to simply codifying existing practices), or (4) generating new custom by encouraging new practice.[9] While the first two conditions are consistent with consent-based legal norms, the latter two suggest a broader application that moves beyond individual state consent. I consider those that fulfill the latter two conditions as constituting one piece of evidence for the emergence of a universal legal norm based on international consensus.

---

[6] Malcolm Shaw, *International Law* (Cambridge University Press, 1997), p. 75.
[7] Grigory Tunki, "Is General International Law Customary Law Only?," *EJIL*, vol. 4, 1993, p. 538.
[8] See Oscar Schachter, *International Law in Theory and Practice* (Kluwer Academic Publishers, 1999), p. 5.
[9] Frederic Kirgis, "Specialized Law-making Processes," in Christopher Joyner (ed.), *The United Nations and International Law* (Cambridge University Press, 1999), p. 66.

As I argue below, it is not the specific text of the treaties themselves that bind nonsignatories, but rather the legal principles represented within them and the process through which the agreements were drafted. For example, the definitions of genocide and torture accepted by virtually all states are drawn directly from the respective conventions. These concepts are used in a wide variety of forums and documents that are independent of the treaties themselves. So too is the principle that both practices are illegal under any and all circumstances. Both were early examples of treaties developed through a multilateral process within international organizations, involving considerable deliberation and widespread participation by most states in the world.

The impact of a particular multilateral treaty can be determined by several factors. A number of legal analysts argue that a major indication of whether a human rights norm has become part of general international law is the density of acceptance, that is, the degree to which a particular norm has been repeated in multiple treaties, agreements, and conventions.[10] In this sense, a succession of treaties articulating the same legal principle can lead to recognition by the international community as a whole that a rule is one of general, and not just particular, law.[11] This includes both international and regional accords.[12] Moreover, multilateral treaties can spark new rules by creating state practice, once again turning customary law on its head.[13]

The increase in academic and legal research on the role of multilateral lawmaking treaties in international law suggests a growing interest in mechanisms that create legal norms that apply generally (throughout the entire international community) rather than restrictively (only among selected states). This research has not progressed as far as it could, however, because the concept of lawmaking treaties as a legislative instrument is inconsistent with the principles of state consent and state sovereignty and therefore cannot be reconciled with current theories of international law. While international legal scholars and political scientists might agree that such treaties

---

[10] See, for example, Thomas Meron, *Human Rights and Humanitarian Norms as Customary Law* (London: Clarendon Press, 1989), p. 94; Andrea Bianchi, "Human Rights and the Magic of Jus Cogens, *European Journal of International Law*, vol. 19, no. 3, 2008. Although Meron applies this to customary law, it is even more applicable to a consensus-based legal norm.

[11] International Law Association, London Conference, Committee on Formation of Customary (General) International Law, Final Report of the Committee, 2000, p. 48.

[12] See American Law Institute, *Third Restatement of the Law, The Foreign Relations Law of the United States*, 1987, §701, note 2.

[13] International Law Association, London Conference, Committee on Formation of Customary (General) International Law, Final Report of the Committee, 2000, pp. 46–47. I should note again that this argument was made in regard to customary law.

can generate new principles of law that are broadly applied, few consider them to be akin to legislation.

Thus, despite references to "international lawmaking" by scholars such as Paul Szasz, Vera Gowlland-Debbas, and Theodor Meron, few legal theorists have addressed the conundrum of how the international community can create the equivalent of international legislation without creating a global legislature. However, within a more general theory of consensus-based legal norms, one can view the development of lawmaking treaties as one component in the process of creating general international law.

The general legal effect of such treaties is multiplied when accompanied by regional agreements that articulate the same principles. For example, we can find common principles regarding specific human rights protections addressing extreme state violence in the European Convention on Human Rights, the European Convention for the Prevention of Torture, the American Declaration on the Rights and Duties of Man, the American Convention on Human Rights, and the African Charter on Human and Peoples' Rights. The key is to examine the agreements for common principles and determine the degree to which this represents a global consensus.

Soft Law and Resolutions from International Organizations

A second instrument that contributes to consensus-based legal norms is a body of rules and principles that have some indicia of international law but lack the explicit legal-bindingness of a treaty.[14] Such rules lack the sense of absolute obligation, precision, and delegation that characterizes treaties, but they entail a much stronger commitment than purely political arrangements in which legalization is largely absent.[15] These instruments are known as soft law. They include a corpus of standards, commitments, joint statements, and declarations of policy or intention by broad-based international organizations.[16] On another level, they also encompass those rules that interpret or inform our understanding of binding legal rules that create expectations

---

[14] Kal Raustiala and Anne-Marie Slaughter, "International Law, International Relations, and Compliance," in Thomas Risse, Beth A. Simmons, and Walter Carlsnaes (eds.), *Handbook of International Relations* (Sage Publications, 2002), p. 540.
[15] Kenneth W. Abbott and Duncan Snidal, "Hard and Soft Law in International Governance," *International Organization,* vol. 54, no. 3, Summer 2000, p. 422.
[16] Antonio Cassese, *International Law* (Oxford University Press, 2005), p. 196.

about future conduct.[17] The law is "soft" because it lacks the standard criteria for an obligatory legal norm; however, since international law is often as much about politics as it is about law, it can exhibit the same compliance pull as a formal treaty.

Soft law can assume the character of an obligation because in international politics the primary consumers of the law are not courts, judges, or litigants—members of a legal community that rely heavily on precise, verifiable text—but political leaders and their legal advisors, who are not limited to formal documents that form the basis of positive law. For many of them, resolutions adopted by international organizations are taken into account when determining a particular legal obligation.[18] Courts issue judgments and judges articulate doctrine, but ultimately the implementation of international law rarely relies on pronouncements by courts or as a result of legal proceedings; it is usually performed by political leaders acting within the political community of diplomats, foreign secretaries, chief executives, and legal analysts.

In this context, obligations are as much about collective perceptions as they are about objective validation. Indeed, the very concept of *opinio juris*, a widely accepted notion that is central to customary international law, is based primarily on the collective perceptions of political leaders concerning the legality of a particular legal norm. This is particularly important in international relations, where political leaders and diplomats rely far more heavily on understandings and expectations than one might see in domestic politics.[19] These perceptions are not subjective but rather intersubjective, that is, based on collective understandings and beliefs acquired through interaction among the principal participants in the international community.

Soft law is particularly useful for articulating principles and commitments that address behavior that is internal to states. One of the problems states face with using soft law to create obligations is uncertainty

---

[17] Andrew T. Guzman and Timothy L. Meyer, "International Soft Law," *Journal of Legal Analysis*, vol. 2, no. 1, Spring 2010, p. 173.

[18] In a series of interviews conducted by legal scholar Antonio Cassese, many legal advisors reported a direct correlation between conformity with international legal standards and the need to take into account the pronouncements of regional and global organizations. See his "The Role of Legal Advisers in Ensuring That Foreign Policy Conforms to International Legal Standards," *Michigan Journal of International Law*, vol. 14, no. 1, 1992, p. 162.

[19] This, of course, gets to the heart of the difference between political science and jurisprudence as academic disciplines. International law scholars and practitioners are trained in law schools, which heavily privilege legal text, precedent, and interpretation and give greater credence to court rulings and judgments than do political scientists, who focus more on political institutions, diplomacy, and relationships within the international community of states.

over the degree to which other states will honor these commitments. When political leaders conclude agreements that rest on the principle of reciprocity, such as arms control and trade, trust that other states will comply is paramount. On the other hand, commitments to protect certain types of human rights within a state are not dependent upon reciprocal compliance by other states, and therefore the costs of defection by others can be relatively low.

Part of the problem in the debate over soft law is that the term itself is imprecise and includes a wide range of instruments, including resolutions, declarations, and joint statements by states and international organizations. Thus it is not accurate to consider a particular instrument of soft law itself as a source of legal obligation; rather one must examine the particular forms that it takes. While soft law instruments may not be legally binding in and of themselves, I consider them to be one piece of evidence for the existence of a consensus-based legal norm.

Some analysts have argued that the recent interest in soft law reflects a general global trend moving from hard law norms enshrined in treaties toward principles that are more amenable to gradual development, interpretation, and evolution.[20] In this way, soft law helps to shape state practice and direct decision-makers', scholars', and advocates' attention in such a way as to encourage constructive development of new law. As a result, many political actors in the global community have treated soft law norms as a "persuasive authority."[21]

Probably the most important source of soft law is a consistent pattern of broadly supported resolutions passed by decision-making bodies within various intergovernmental organizations. There has been a lot of research and debate concerning the legal effects of such resolutions, particularly those approved by the UN General Assembly.[22] Although such resolutions are almost always advisory rather than obligatory, they can represent an international consensus that goes beyond the jurisdiction of the specific organization. For this reason, the American Law Institute has held that the

---

[20] See, for example, Elena Baylis, "The International Law Commission's Soft Law Influence." *FIU Law Review*, vol. 13, no. 6, 2019, p. 1010.

[21] Baylis, "The International Law Commission's Soft Law Influence," p. 1010.

[22] For a good overview of the literature in this area, see Marco Divak Oberg, "The Legal Effects of Resolutions of the Security Council and General Assembly in the Jurisprudence of the ICJ," *European Journal of International Law*, vol. 16, no. 5, 2005. See also Jorge Castaneda, *The Legal Effects of UN Resolutions* (Columbia University Press, 1969).

evidentiary value of a resolution passed by an international organization is high if it is passed by consensus or "virtual unanimity."[23]

For Ian Johnstone, the resolutions themselves could have legal validity because they—and the discussions surrounding their approval—reflect the prevailing beliefs and values of states concerning international law. He argues that the international legal order operates primarily through this process of "justificatory discourse" that determines what does and does not count as legitimate legal argument. Such discourse occurs within interpretive communities, which are composed of the participants in a field of practice who set the parameters of what constitutes reasoned argumentation for that practice.[24]

Thus it is not the resolutions themselves that are binding; they are not. Rather, the principles represented in the text as well as the content of the discourse surrounding the deliberations leading to the resolutions provide evidence of *opinio juris* around the principles that the resolution articulates, even in the absence of corresponding state practice. Once a principle is broadly accepted at an international forum involving all or most states (usually through consensus), it can constitute a type of *opinio juris* confirming that these principles apply generally across the international community. To determine this, we must examine not only the content of the resolution but also the intent of the state representatives (garnered through the official transcript/record of discussion, debate, and negotiations, known as the *travaux préparatoires*); the level of support (unanimous or near unanimous); the level of dissent and abstentions; and the identity of the dissenters. This will, among other things, help distinguish a resolution that expresses a purely political view from one that seeks to enshrine a more general legal principle.[25]

Michael Bothe argues that declarations and resolutions intended to create new principles of international law can express a general consensus of the

---

[23] American Law Institute, *Third Restatement of the Law, The Foreign Relations Law of the United States*, §103, Reporter's Notes 2, 1987, p. 38

[24] See Ian Johnstone, "Treaty Interpretation: The Authority of Interpretive Communities," *Michigan Journal of International Law*, vol. 12, no. 2, 1991 and Ian Johnstone, "Security Council Deliberations: The Power of the Better Argument," *European Journal of International Law*, vol. 14, no. 3, 2003.

[25] A number of legal scholars and political scientists argue that not all General Assembly resolutions are alike, and that the type of resolution helps to determine the degree to which its sponsors and supporters consider it to be binding. See, for example, Rainer Lagoni, "Resolution, Declaration, Decision," in Rudiger Wolfrum and Christiane Philippet (eds.), *United Nations: Law, Policies, and Practice* (Springer, 1995) and Marko Divac Öberg, "The Legal Effects of Resolutions of the UN Security Council and General Assembly in the Jurisprudence of the ICJ," *The European Journal of International Law*, vol. 16, no. 5, 2005.

international community and should therefore be regarded as a source of law beyond Article 38 of the International Court of Justice (ICJ) Statue.[26] Of particular importance are those resolutions that seek to interpret or clarify fundamental principles found in the UN Charter. Because the Charter is a legally binding document, and because every recognized state in the world is a member of the UN, such interpretations could assume a general legal character. Again, while a particular resolution itself may not be the sole source of a legal norm, it could contribute to a general consensus-based norm if the intent of the resolution was in fact designed to do so. One could consider this a form of attenuated consent inasmuch as the member states delegated some authority over the maintenance of peace and security to the Charter in general, the Security Council in particular, and the General Assembly secondarily.

For example, the principle that colonialism is illegal did not emerge either from a treaty or from customary practice. Rather, it can be largely traced to a process that culminated in a unanimous resolution passed by the United Nations General Assembly, which declared that the subjection of peoples to alien rule, domination, and exploitation constitutes a denial of fundamental human rights.[27] The Assembly's 1960 Declaration on the Granting of Independence to Colonial Countries and Peoples has been cited many times by a wide range of political leaders and legal analysts as the legal basis of decolonization, most of whom view the resolution as a key step in the progressive development of the principle of self-determination.[28] It could not be considered to be reflective of customary law because at the time of its passage it did not reflect common practice. Many of the colonial powers continued to hold colonies until the late 1960s and mid-1970s, thereby meeting the criteria of a persistent objection. For that reason, at the time the resolution was viewed as purely normative.

The resolution, however, can be credited with providing pressure on colonial states to relinquish their colonies; in these cases, the norm preceded the practice. Since that time, virtually all states have considered the prohibition of colonial rule to be legally binding, even though there is no treaty specifically outlawing the practice. This is because this resolution articulated what

---

[26] Michael Bothe, "Legal and Non-Legal Norms—A Meaningful Distinction in International Relations," *Netherland Yearbook of International Law*, vol. 11, 1980, p. 76.

[27] United Nations Resolution 1514 (XV), "Declaration on the Granting of Independence to Colonial Countries and Peoples," General Assembly, 14 December 1960, Article 1.

[28] See Helen Quane, "The United Nations and the Evolving Right to Self-Determination." *The International and Comparative Law Quarterly*, vol. 47, no. 3, 1998, p. 563.

has become a fundamental principle in international law, the right of self-determination for all peoples, which one could argue has achieved the status of *jus cogens* (see below). This concept is articulated in vague form in Article 1(2) of the Charter. It was this resolution that provided the justification for the Security Council—whose resolutions are legally binding—to declare in 1975 that East Timor is an independent state and calling on Indonesia to immediately vacate the territory.[29] It also provided the foundation for the Council's actions against South Africa's possession of Namibia.[30]

Similarly, the Security Council and other decision-making bodies consistently evoke other General Assembly resolutions—such as the Declaration on Principles of International Law Concerning Friendly Relations—when providing a legal justification for their actions. Thus, for example, there is broad agreement that General Assembly Resolution 95 (which affirmed the principles adopted by the Nuremberg Tribunal) has become part of general international law, not because states have ceased committing atrocities (they clearly have not) but because those who do so are violating generally accepted principles of conduct.[31]

Jus Cogens Norms

Most legal scholars recognize a very limited number of legal principles to have achieved the status of *jus cogens* (literally, "compelling law"). Such principles are considered to be peremptory, that is, so fundamental to the international community that no state may either derogate from or override them either by individual acts or collective will, including treaty. Peremptory norms reflect and protect fundamental values of the international community, are hierarchically superior to other rules of international law, and are universally applicable.[32] As such, they are binding on all legal subjects regardless of whether the subjects have specifically consented to them on an individual basis.

---

[29] Security Council Resolution 384, S/RES/384 (1975).
[30] Security Council Resolution 264, S/RES/264 (1969).
[31] See, for example, Mary Metlay Kaufman, "Judgement at Nuremberg—An Appraisal of Its Significance on Its Twentieth Anniversary," *The Guild Practitioner*, vol. 25, 1966.
[32] International Law Commission, "Report on the Work of the Seventy-first Session," Chapter V (2019), p. 140, Document A/74/10; Dire Tladi, "Codification, Progressive Development, New Law, Doctrine, and the Work of the International Law Commission on Peremptory Norms of General International Law (Jus Cogens): Personal Reflections of the Special Rapporteur." *Florida International University Law Review*, vol. 13, no. 6, 2019, p. 1143.

Political leaders consider violations of peremptory norms shocking to the sensibilities of the international community and therefore bind the members of that community, irrespective of protest, recognition, or acquiescence.[33] Moreover, such violations would be seriously detrimental to the international legal system itself, inasmuch as they are so important to the international society of states—and to how that society defines itself—that legal analysts cannot conceive of an exception.[34]

These norms are not derived from natural law—which exists apart from the members of the international community—but rather are recognized through broad agreement among the subjects of international law. They can be modified only by a subsequent norm of general international law having the same character.[35]

The concept of *jus cogens* is a challenge to—and in many ways is in conflict with—our conventional notions of positivism and state consent. It departs from the essential characteristics of contemporary international law because its principles cannot be nullified even through contract and agreement (thus, they are nonderogable), and its norms are hierarchically superior to other rules of international law. They cannot be objectively verified in the same way as a treaty, although rulings and judgments by domestic and international courts and legal analysts provide evidence that they represent a consensus among political actors within the international community.

For this reason, some legal scholars are uncomfortable with the entire concept, arguing that only black-letter law (treaties) and long-term customary practices can serve as a basis of legal obligation.[36] It is for this same reason that some states, such as France, refused to sign the Vienna Convention on the Law of Treaties, which attempted to codify *jus cogens* into general international law.[37] As international law scholar Anthony D'Amato rhetorically

---

[33] See International Law Commission, "Draft Articles on State Responsibility," Art. 19, *Yearbook of the ILC*, vol. 2, 1976, p. 73.

[34] Michael Byers, "Conceptualising the Relationship between *Jus Cogens* and *Erga Omnes* Rules," *Nordic Journal of International Law*, vol. 66, nos. 2–3, 1997, p. 221.

[35] International Law Commission, *Yearbook of the International Law Commission: Summary Records of the Third Session, 16 May–27 July 1951*, vol. 1 (1963), pp. 291–292.

[36] See, for example, Ulf Linderfalk, "The Effect of Jus Cogens Norms: Whoever Opened Pandora's Box, Did You Ever Think about the Consequences?," *The European Journal of International Law*, vol. 18 no. 5, 2008; Prosper Weil, "Toward Relative Normativity in International Law," *American Journal of International Law*, vol. 77, 1983; and Gennady Danilenko, "International *Jus Cogens*: Issues of Law-Making," *European Journal of International Law*, vol. 2, no. 1, 1991.

[37] Olivier Deleau, "Les Positions Françaises à la Conférence de Vienne sur le Droit des Traités," *Annuaire Francais de Droit International*, vol. 15, 1969.

asks, how does a norm of *jus cogens* arise, and once it does, how can the international community change or get rid of it?[38] Without objective criteria for identifying which norms reflect the fundamental collective values of states, different groups of states or even individual political leaders can make conflicting claims about which norms fall within the category of *jus cogens* and which do not.

Beyond this, scholars disagree over the means to identify the elements of a peremptory norm, how to determine its priority over competing or conflicting norms, how to assess the significance and outcomes of prior application, and how to gauge its future applicability in light of the value-oriented goals sought to be achieved.[39]

Despite these concerns, however, most legal scholars accept both the existence and authority of at least some peremptory norms.[40] Determining which principles fall into this category requires a widespread and general consensus among states. According to the Vienna Convention on the Law of Treaties, principles of *jus cogens* must be "accepted and recognized by the international community of States as a whole."[41] As the ILC stated in its commentary on the draft articles for the international law of the treaties, there is no simple criterion that would allow one to determine whether a rule belongs to *jus cogens*. Only widespread agreement by a wide range of states can give legitimacy to a claim that a peremptory norm exists.[42] This of course raises questions as to precisely how widespread the support must be to be considered a peremptory norm.

There is an obvious difficulty in enumerating precisely which principles achieve the status of *jus cogens*; therefore this determination cannot be arbitrary. Gordon Christenson argues that a norm achieves the status of

---

[38] Anthony D'Amato, "It's a Bird, It's a Plane, It's Jus Cogens!," *Connecticut Journal of International Law*, vol. 6, Fall 1990, p. 6.

[39] M. Cherif Bassiouni, "International Crimes: 'Jus Cogens' and 'Obligatio Erga Omnes,'" in "Accountability for International Crimes and Serious Violations of Fundamental Human Rights," special issue of *Law and Contemporary Problems*, vol. 59, no. 4, Autumn 1996.

[40] See, for example, Dire Tladi (ed.), *Peremptory Norms of General International Law (Jus Cogens): Disquisitions and Disputations*, Developments in International Law series, vol. 75 (Brill/Nijhoff, 2021). See also Thomas Weatherall, *Jus Cogens: International Law and Social Contract* (Cambridge University Press, 2015); Mary Ellen O'Connell, "*Jus Cogens*: International Law's Higher Ethical Norms," in Donald Earl Childress (ed.), *The Role of Ethics in International Law* (Cambridge University Press, 2012); and Robert Kolb, *Peremptory International Law—Jus Cogens: A General Inventory* (Hart Publishing, 2015).

[41] Vienna Convention on the Law of Treaties, concluded at Vienna on 23 May 1969, United Nations, Treaty Series, vol. 1155, article 53.

[42] United Nations International Law Commission, *Yearbook of the International Law Commission* (United Nations, 1966), p. 247.

jus cogens when (1) states view it as indispensable to the existence of the system of public international law and (2) the obligation is indeed peremptory; that is, the international community accepts that the norm possesses an overriding quality, rather than simply having a subjective moral belief in its preeminence.[43] Similarly, Evan Criddle and Evan Fox-Decent hold that peremptory norms must embody general and universalizable principles that are public, clear, feasible, consistent with other like norms, relatively stable over time, and prospective rather than retroactive.[44]

Like other consensus-based legal norms, only a general agreement by states collectively can determine that these conditions exist.

Although it is difficult to articulate a definitive list of all norms that fall within this category, the legal literature appears to agree that the following practices constitute violations of peremptory norms: genocide, piracy, slavery, and terrorism.[45] To this I might add territorial conquest (the nonconsensual annexation of the territory of a recognized sovereign state by another) and colonialism, both of which would constitute a blatant assault on the constitutive principle of state sovereignty, the fundamental building block of the international system. For this reason, these practices are universally condemned as illegal on their face, and can therefore be considered a norm of *jus cogens*. Similarly, national self-determination, despite difficulty in agreeing to a single definition of the concept, provides the legitimate foundation for the existence of the nation-state and can therefore be considered to be peremptory.[46]

Some legal analysts, such as Mahmoud Cherif Bassiouni, have sought to expand this list to include certain fundamental human rights norms, including the prohibitions on crimes against humanity and torture.[47] Others go even further and suggest a wider range of human rights protections, including most of those found in the Universal Declaration.[48]

---

[43] Gordon A. Christenson, "Jus Cogens: Guarding Interests Fundamental to International Society," *Virginia Journal of International Law*, vol. 28, Spring 1988, pp. 592–593.
[44] Evan J. Criddle and Evan Fox-Decent, "Deriving Peremptory Norms from Sovereignty," *American Society of International Law Proceedings*, vol. 103, 2009.
[45] Weatherall discusses this consensus in *Jus Cogens*.
[46] For a set of legal criteria that features self-determination as a necessary condition in the formation of a new state, see Lea Brilmayer, "Secession and Self-Determination: A Territorial Interpretation," *Yale Journal of International Law*, vol. 16, no. 1, 1991.
[47] Bassiouni, "International Crimes."
[48] See, for example, Myres S. McDougal, Harold Lasswell, and Lung-Chu Chen, *Human Rights and World Public Order* (Yale University Press, 1980), p. 345 and Justice M. Haleem, "The Domestic Application of International Human Rights Norms," in *Developing Human Rights Jurisprudence* (Commonwealth Secretariat, 1998), p. 97.

I find this to be overly ambitious. For a legal norm to be truly peremptory it must be so central to the values underlying the international community that no state would recognize an agreement to override it, even if voluntarily contracted and even if it were permitted in domestic law. There is a danger that expanding the list to include anything less would render the concept essentially meaningless.

Some universally accepted norms, such as the prohibition against slavery and the slave trade, are *jus cogens* because they have become so deeply ingrained in the identity of the international community that no government on earth would defend the practice under any circumstances. Nor is it likely that any state would recognize even voluntary servitude as legal. However, while practices such as torture and crimes against humanity may be nefarious and unconscionable, their prevention is not fundamental to the operation of the international community. Both have been practiced widely for centuries (and continue to be practiced) without undermining the fundamental principles embedded in the state system or in the conduct of diplomacy and international relations. While most legal analysts would agree that these practices are in fact illegal under general international law, this does not make their prohibition *jus cogens*.

For this reason, attempts by some legal scholars to pile on a list of human rights protections as constituting peremptory legal norms threatens to undermine the very concept. Rather, I would suggest that we more modestly limit our understanding of *jus cogens* norms to a prohibition of those practices that have indeed been viewed within the international community as constituting an irrefutable assault on its fundamental values. Moreover, the peremptory nature of a particular human rights norm must be based on more than just an assertion or even a particular ruling from a judicial body; it must be supported by other evidence, as discussed in this chapter.

Thus, while each of these elements (lawmaking treaties, soft law, *jus cogens,* and resolutions by international courts and institutions) individually may not offer sufficient evidence of consensus, in their totality they can demonstrate a consistent pattern of agreement on principles that are generally accepted by members of the international community. The demonstration of this proposition will be my central task in the following empirical chapters.

Method for Determining a Consensus-Based Legal Norm

This still leaves us with the tough question of how one can determine whether a specific consensus-based legal norm actually exists outside of the minds of legal scholars, idealists, and theorists, and the degree to which such norms are in fact accepted by the international community of states. Most positivists in the social sciences and legal community would likely object to a theory based on international consensus in part because consensus is itself difficult to measure. For example, international law scholar Richard Falk's definition of consensus as "a convergence of international opinion, an overwhelming majority, a predominance to something more than a simple majority but less than unanimity"[49] lacks the precision that many academics have come to expect in the study of social science and law. Moreover, on a practical level, political leaders would undoubtedly require a more definitive method for determining exactly which rules they are obligated to follow. Certainly legal advisors and political leaders would demand some concrete evidence of a legal obligation, particularly since consensus is difficult to document. Unlike other forms of decision-making, consensus is based on neither a numerical majority (which can be measured) nor a specific command issued by a superior authority (which can be identified).

This problem is particularly acute because a consensus-based legal norm requires a markedly different method for determining obligation than that found in a system based on either natural or traditional positive law. To understand natural law we study philosophy, theology, and history. Since natural law is discovered, either through human reason or divine revelation, its theorists seek the universal principles that underlie legal norms by examining the progression of ideas and ethics over time and in various cultures. On the other hand, traditionally legal positivists have sought evidence of a legal norm by studying texts—such as treaties, court rulings, diplomatic correspondence, or legal opinions of government lawyers—since this represents the most conclusive confirmation of that to which states have agreed. Consensus-based legal norms, however, are not based on eternal principles that can be discovered, nor are they contained either in a particular document or by practices of individual states. Rather, they are founded on principles that are consciously developed collectively over time by defined groups of political actors. It therefore requires a method that examines

---

[49] Richard Falk, *The Status of Law in International Society* (Princeton Press, 1970), p. 142.

the intersubjective (shared) beliefs of an international community at a particular time.

If the authority to create new international law—or amend existing legal obligations—were vested in a specific institution, consensus could be defined in the charter of the proscribed organization. Some international organizations, such as the United Nations Security Council, define consensus as the absence of an official objection by a permanent member of the body (symbolized by what has come to be unofficially called the veto). However, since there is no hierarchy of organizations in international law, neither the United Nations nor any other international body has the authority to create new law. For this reason, consensus-based legal norms cannot emanate from a single source but must be supported by a variety of legitimately constituted institutions that members of the international community consider to be authoritative.

The question of method is a problem not only for academics studying consensus-based international law but also for political leaders and legal advisors practicing it. How do we know when a consensus exists, and how many political actors need to accept it for it to be considered legitimate? In addressing this question, I begin by defining consensus as a broad, general agreement on the fundamental principles related to a specific legal issue that is deep-rooted enough within the international community to hold for an extended period of time and in a wide variety of circumstances. This agreement incorporates a wide range of views among legal subjects but does not imply unanimous assent on all details. The method for determining when a consensus exists then becomes the main issue.

Martha Finnemore and Kathryn Sikkink's efforts to address a similar problem of identifying norms can be helpful in determining the degree to which a consensus may exist around a particular set of principles. Like consensus, norms (generally agreed-upon standards of behavior) lack the type of objective documentation that can provide hard evidence of their existence, particularly for the positivist. Finnemore and Sikkink, however, argue that we can identify a norm by tracing its particular "life-cycle," that is, the process through which a norm moves from an idea held by a small group of actors (whom they call "norm entrepreneurs") to a critical mass of actors converging around a particular standard. By tracing the process, one can determine the "tipping point" after which agreement becomes widespread.[50]

---

[50] Martha Finnemore and Kathryn Sikkink, "International Norm Dynamics and Political Change." *International Organization*, vol. 52, no. 4, 1998, pp. 892–893.

In terms of identifying the norm itself, Finnemore and Sikkink argue that norms usually leave an extensive trail of communication among actors that we can study.[51] We recognize norm-conforming behavior because it produces general praise by members of a community and norm violations when it generates broad disapproval.[52] Once this is done, we look for patterns in behavior or discourse and ask if there are any significant persistent objections. A strong negative reaction, or more specifically a sanction, by a broad swath of states to a perceived breach is evidence of its existence.

Anthony Arend proposes a similar approach for the study of international law by examining how to uncover the authority of a legal rule. Although Arend bases his method on the assumption that all authoritative legal rules are grounded in state consent, his approach can be useful in understanding consensus-based norms as well. Arend suggests that we not only examine the content of a particular legal rule but also note the number of manifestations (or sources) in which the rule or principle appears (for example, multilateral treaties, organizational charters, and General Assembly resolutions). He further suggests investigating its degree of universality by determining how many states accept the rule, how many publicly challenge it, and how frequently and significantly they comply with or violate its mandates.[53]

Similarly, we can identify the evolution of consensus in international law by studying, among other things, (1) the substance of discussions at international conferences where multilateral conventions and lawmaking treaties are developed;[54] (2) the type of discourse that is conducted within the deliberative bodies of formal international organizations such as the UN Security Council, the ILC, and the executive councils of regional organizations; (3) the degree to which states and international organizations make reference to these emerging legal norms when making decisions, articulating policies, and conducting diplomatic interaction; and (4) the development of legal arguments that ultimately lead to the articulation of the particular

---

[51] Finnemore and Sikkink, "International Norm Dynamics and Political Change," pp. 892–893.

[52] See Finnemore and Sikkink, "International Norm Dynamics and Political Change," p. 892 and Fredrich Kratochwil and John Ruggie, "A State of the Art on an Art of the State," *International Organization*, vol. 40, no. 4, 1986, pp. 753–775.

[53] Anthony Arend, *Legal Rules and International Society* (Oxford University Press, 1999), chapter 4.

[54] Many of these organizations and agencies—in particular UN-sponsored lawmaking conferences—maintain very precise records detailing the substance of the discussions, negotiations, and debates, including verbatim statements made by the delegates. These records, known as the *travaux préparatoires*, are available from the Dag Hammarskjöld Library and its depositories. Article 32 of the Vienna Convention on the Law of Treaties specifically refers to these records as sources for helping to interpret a treaty when a particular meaning is ambiguous or contested.

rule within multilateral bodies.[55] In doing so we would note how often the identified legal norm appears and whether there have been significant challenges to it.

Once we trace the principle underlying a particular legal norm, we can further investigate how it is put into practice by multilateral bodies such as the UN Security Council or the World Trade Organization as they attempt to address specific issues and conflicts that are brought before them. The most direct way of doing so is to study the resolutions and directives issued by these organizations as they attempt to address specific issues and conflicts that are brought before them. Unlike customary law, the focus is not on views expressed by individual states but rather on the entirety of discourse conducted within the collective community of states.

In general, the task is to determine whether there is a consistent pattern of agreement over specific obligations within a wide variety of forums. The job of identifying the process and substance of consensus is greatly eased by the nature of the contemporary international community itself. Unlike domestic societies, the international community consists of a very limited, identifiable group of actors, all of whom have the capabilities and legal authority to participate in the creation of new law. At present the number is roughly 195 states, plus a relatively small number of global and regional multilateral organizations.[56] Communication and deliberation among these actors is usually well documented and available to interested parties.

In order to pursue this method, we must determine which international organizations and agencies are considered by political leaders to be legitimate forums for developing obligations. I address this in more detail below. Since there is no official hierarchy of organizations, we cannot rely on flow charts that stipulate lines of authority. Rather, researchers have to examine how political leaders view the role and authority of such organizations.

The introduction of consensus-based legal norms into the body of international law challenges the volunteerist notion implicit in the concept of sovereignty by requiring states to accept some obligations that they may not have explicitly agreed to adopt and that may not reflect long-standing state practice. Of course, the international community does this to new states all

---

[55] On this last point, see Ian Hurd, "The Strategic Use of Liberal Internationalism: Libya and the UN Sanctions, 1992–2003," *International Organization*, vol. 59, no. 3, Summer 2005.

[56] There are currently 193 members of the United Nations, which includes all officially recognized states in the world. In addition, Kosovo and Taiwan are *de facto* independent entities that lack international recognition as sovereign states. The Holy See (Vatican) and Palestine have "permanent nonmember observer states" in the UN.

the time; governments and international organizations usually require newly formed states to accept the entire body of international law and diplomatic practices as the price of recognition and their acceptance into the international community. It is, however, more difficult to get established entities to agree to move beyond consent-based rules. Since there is a strong bias in favor of state sovereignty on the part of foreign policy officials, the integration of consensus-based norms into international law requires a deeper commitment by political leaders toward a set of common principles in specified issue areas, as well as the creation of legitimately accepted political processes through which a consensus can be reached.

Institutions for Consensus-Based Legal Norms

In order for a consensus-based legal norm to emerge, three conditions must be met: (1) a convergence of political values in those issue areas in which states seek to build consensus, (2) the existence of a widely accepted multilateral mechanism through which states can develop their collective understandings concerning which obligations are legally binding, and (3) some type of institution that is viewed by members of the international community as having the legitimacy to interpret and implement these consensus principles. I will examine the degree to which the first condition has been met in specific issue areas in the following empirical chapters. However, before examining specific issues, it is necessary to consider the next two conditions.

Over the past half-century, the international community has developed several multilateral institutions that collectively act as forums for forging legal norms based on international consensus. These institutions include (1) the ILC, which acts like a legislative committee with the mandate to conduct research, propose lawmaking treaties, and develop soft law norms; (2) UN-sponsored multilateral conferences, which mobilize large numbers of states to discuss, negotiate, draft, and ultimately sign said treaties and issue soft law declarations; (3) the United Nations Security Council, which acts as an interpretive community that determines what constitutes a legal consensus in a given case; and (4) multilateral treaty regimes, which provide a means for institutionalizing the legal norms and principles that are embedded in lawmaking treaties. While none of these institutions individually possesses any legislative authority, each plays a role in a broader process that, under the conditions articulated in Chapter 1, can lead to a consensus around specific binding principles of international law.

As I argued earlier, the development of a consensus-based legal norm requires processes that a wide range of states accepts as legitimate and authoritative. Each of the institutions that I discuss below contributes to this by embodying the key elements necessary for developing a consensus around the authority of a legal norm: (1) widespread participation by a broad section of states representing all of the world's regions, regime types, and legal systems; who engage in (2) extensive deliberation; (3) according to generally accepted operating procedures; (4) that rely on consensus decision-making.[57] This ensures that the outcome reflects a true consensus rather than either the will of a majority or the preferences of the most powerful states.

As I suggested in the previous chapter, the dramatic growth of multilateral institutions provides for extensive deliberation and participation according to broadly accepted standard rules of procedure and provides a permissive condition for developing consensus-based legal norms. Deliberation offers an opportunity for participants to determine the degree to which there is general agreement around a particular set of principles. It also gives government representatives a means of persuading each other that common areas of agreement may exist even though there may be conflicts in other interests.[58] Standard rules of procedure not only eliminate the need to engage in time-consuming debate over process; they also offer a method for legitimizing the process through which deliberation occurs by assuring the participants that the process is fair and that their individual concerns/interests have been taken into account.[59]

Over the past several decades, international institutions have adopted a common set of standard procedures for deliberation, debate, and decision-making in virtually all multilateral forums, in particular, those regarding the adoption of lawmaking treaties and other legal agreements. These processes

---

[57] For an extensive discussion of this process of collective decision-making in the development of lawmaking treaties, see Tommy Koh and Shannugam Jayakumar, "The Negotiating Process of the Third United Nations Conference on the Law of the Sea," in Myron H. Nordquist (ed.), *The United Nations Convention on the Law of the Sea, 1982: A Commentary*, vol. 1 (Martinus Nijhoff, 1985).

[58] This is a large literature on the connection between deliberation and legitimation. A number of scholars argue that deliberation dramatically increases the legitimacy of the outcome, even when the outcome of the deliberative process goes against the individual's interests. See Jürgen Habermas, *Between Facts and Norms: Contributions to a Discourse Theory of Law and Democracy* (MIT Press, 1998) and Jon Elster and Adam Przeworski (eds.), *Deliberative Democracy* (Cambridge University Press, 1998).

[59] See Robbie Sabel, *Procedure at International Conferences* (Cambridge University Press, 1997), p. 420.

incorporate the distributions of power that are present in the international system and, as such, provide for a level of consensus that echoes the political reality necessary for both strong and weak states to buy into the norms. Virtually all international organizations have both formal and informal mechanisms that enable the more powerful states to exercise a level of influence commensurate to their capabilities, even as it provides incentives for weaker powers to participate. This is the case with the United Nations, the African Union, the European Union, and other multilateral organizations.[60] Thus, even some institutions founded on the principle of sovereign equality and democratic decision-making reflect the distribution of resources among members as much as it does the collective will.

In order to ensure that decisions truly reflect the collective will of the individual participants, most multilateral institutions have adopted consensus—defined as the lack of a significant objection by the participants—as their decision-making rule. Jonathan Charney argues that one can measure the degree of consensus in such forums by the calculating the number of objecting states, the nature of their judgments, the importance of the interests such states seek to protect, and the degree to which support for the emerging norms encompasses all interest groups.[61] Unlike processes that rely on the aggregation of fixed preferences (such as voting), such decision rules are designed to integrate the individual concerns of each participant and avoid the use of majorities to impose outcomes that do not reflect common agreement.

International Law Commission

In practice, the ILC has emerged as one of the most important institutions for developing new legal norms. The ILC was established by the United Nations General Assembly in 1947 to promote the progressive development and codification of international law. According to Article 15 of the UN Charter, this involves "the preparation of draft conventions on subjects which have not yet been regulated by international law or in regard to which the law has not yet

---

[60] See Courtney B. Smith, *Politics and Process at the United Nations: The Global Dance* (Lynne Rienner Publishers, 2005); John Peterson and Elizabeth Bomberg, *Decision-Making in the European Union* (Palgrave, 1999); Institute for Security Studies, "Conference Report: Dynamics of Decision Making in Africa," Pretoria, 8–9 November 2010.

[61] Jonathan Charney, "Universal International Law," *The American Journal of International Law*, vol. 87, no. 4, 1993.

been sufficiently developed in the practice of States." Although the founding members of the UN consciously denied the General Assembly the authority to create or revise international law, there was broad support for them to establish a process for initiating and facilitating its progressive development. The ILC was one of the results of this.[62]

The ILC is composed of 34 legal specialists chosen according to a formula that guarantees representation from all of the world's principal legal systems and regions, as well as participation by legal scholars who are citizens of the five permanent members of the Security Council. Its work is based on extending the logic of existing rules rather than changing its underlying logic, and it therefore is designed to reflect the political will of the international community of states.[63] The composition of its membership, the political dynamics of its internal decision-making process, and the empirical record of its deliberations suggest that the Commission does indeed merge law with politics in a manner consistent with a process that reflect a form of international consensus.

The legitimacy of the ILC to represent the collective will of states in pursuing progressive development stems from several factors: its organizational and legal mandate, its thorough research process, and its ongoing active engagement and interaction with states and the General Assembly at all stages. A topic that fails to generate significant interest among states is unlikely to make it into its program of work, nor are topics that are perceived by states as mostly political or policy oriented.[64]

On paper, the Statute of the ILC requires the members to act in their professional capacities rather than as representatives of governments or regional blocs. To ensure this, its members are elected by the General Assembly using a process similar to that used to elect judges to the ICJ (although, unlike ICJ selection, Security Council approval is not required). Moreover, the ILC has independent control of its own agenda (that is, free from interference by the UN's political bodies in deciding which areas of international law they should promote). This makes it at least one important step removed from the

---

[62] See Pronto, "Codification and Progressive Development of International Law" and Jeffrey Morto, *The International Law Commission of the United Nations* (University of South Carolina Press, 2000).
[63] Allain Pellet, "Between Codification and Progressive Development of the Law: Some Reflections from the ILC," *International Law FORUM du droit international*, vol. 6, no. 1, 2004, p. 17.
[64] Charles C. Jalloh, "The International Law Commission's First Draft Convention on Crimes against Humanity: Codification, Progressive Development, or Both?," *Case Western Reserve Journal of International Law*, vol. 52, 2020, p. 343.

daily political whims of the United Nations and its members themselves. At the same time, although the members are required to act independently of any government, the involvement by states in their selection ensures that the Commission will at least partly reflect the political will of the primary units of the international community.[65]

This is reinforced by the fact that the individual members often reflect the political and legal philosophies (although not necessarily the immediate political interests) of their domestic legal systems. In fact, one of the few empirical studies of the Commission's work revealed internal political dynamics among the members that are similar to those of the General Assembly and other UN political bodies (for example, solidarity within regional blocs and ideological divisions among those from differing political systems).[66]

On one level, the ILC is charged with examining existing international law to determine its adequacy in addressing specific issues in international relations, but more important, it is also specifically charged with developing proposals for new law in areas where there is already a convergence of values.[67] The ILC's contribution toward the development of a consensus-based legal norm rests on two elements. First, its composition of independent specialists representing each of the world's legal systems without representing any particular states gives it a type of technocratic legitimacy.[68] Its breadth of membership enables the ILC to draw from general principles of law common to all legal systems (as defined in the Article 38 doctrine of sources), which can provide a foundation for a consensus around legal norms.

In this sense, the ILC, along with the UN Security Council (below), has emerged as a type of interpretive community, tasked with making pronouncements on legal norms that emerge from a variety of sources. While the ILC's interpretive declarations are not legally binding per se, they often generate an interpretive dialogue with states. This in turn creates a focal

---

[65] For a detailed history and analysis of the ILC, from the perspective of United Nations legal analysts, see United Nations, *The Work of the International Law Commission*, Office of Legal Affairs, 8th edition, vols. 1 and 2 (2012).

[66] Jeffrey S. Morton, *The International Law Commission of the United Nations* (University of South Carolina Press, 2000), chapter 5.

[67] See United Nations General Assembly Resolution 174(3) of 21 November 1947, article 15.

[68] Jean d'Aspremont and Eric De Brabandere argue that international legitimacy consists of two elements: the origin of their power and the way in which the actor exercises its power. Both elements are important for states to evaluate the legitimacy of the ILC. See their "The Complementary Faces of Legitimacy in International Law: The Legitimacy of Origin and the Legitimacy of Exercise," *Fordham International Law Journal*, vol. 34, no. 2, 2011.

point for state coordination and a subsidiary means for determining rules of law.[69]

Second, the process it employs in developing legal principles and ultimately draft treaties reflects the principles of consultation and deliberation. For example, in developing a proposed text for lawmaking treaties, the ILC circulates draft articles (accompanied by commentaries from legal specialists) to a wide variety of governments and members of the General Assembly's Sixth (International Law) Committee. The articles must be approved by a consensus within the Commission before they are distributed. The Commission in turn solicits comments and reservations from the recipients, which forms the basis of subsequent drafts that eventually become the foundation for new treaties.

The process by which the ILC progresses from topic consideration to final draft, therefore, is centered upon deliberation among Commission members. This consensus-driven debate enables Commission members to state their agreement or disagreement on the scope and content of each article under consideration, and statements made by Commission members are reported in the official record in paragraph form, with each paragraph consisting of statements relative to a particular article or topic.[70] Thus, even before the negotiations begin on such agreements, the ILC attempts to generate a general consensus around the core principles. Yet it remains only the first step in a longer process that ultimately requires the final input and approval of the vast majority of the world's states. Once again, the ILC's authority is limited to research, development, and proposal.

Over the past half-century, the Commission had been the central player in developing some of the most important and universally recognized multilateral conventions, for example, diplomatic and consular relations, the immunities of states, the nonnavigational uses of international watercourses, the succession of states, and state responsibility.[71] The creation and subsequent evolution of the ILC into a type of legislative committee (with the authority to gather information, hold hearings, interview experts, consult with key political leaders and diplomats, and draft proposals for new laws) within

---

[69] Danae Azaria, "'Codification by Interpretation': The International Law Commission as an Interpreter of International Law," *European Journal of International Law*, vol. 31, no. 1, February 2020.
[70] Morton, *The International Law Commission of the United Nations*, p. 79.
[71] For a complete overview of the treaties drafted by the International Law Commission, along with the process through which these drafts were developed, see United Nations, *The Work of the International Law Commission*, vols. 1 and 2. The most recent edition is the 9th (2017).

a universal body such as the United Nations suggest at least a general commitment to transform international law into a more coherent body of legal obligations.

More recently, the ILC has moved away from primarily drafting multilateral conventions to examining other ways to promote the progressive development of international law.[72] This reflects a decline in states' interest in developing new treaties, a product of rising nationalism and increased global tension among the major powers. As a result, the ILC has published a number of major studies and commentaries on issues of international law and focused on developing and expanding the use of soft law.

From the perspective of the ILC, soft law provides a more flexible environment for states to implement and adapt emerging norms. In this spirit, the ILC attempts to codify existing norms and promulgate new ones in pursuing progressive development, without halting the development process or discouraging engagement by states.[73] Indeed, some of the Commission's most important contributions, such as its work on the law of state responsibility, has not yet been transformed into a multilateral convention yet still stands as the most widely accepted legal statement of the general rules of responsibility of states for internationally wrongful acts.[74] This informal use of soft law has been widely accepted as a matter of consensus.

The ILC's work as a purveyor of international consensus in this area is legitimized by its direct and robust engagement with states, which have the opportunity not only to provide information to the ILC but also to discuss its drafts. Thus, while the ILC's soft law products do not always have the explicit agreement of states, they do possess the imprimatur of states' consideration, analysis, and input.[75]

Elena Baylis's research supports this contention, as she cites a number of empirical studies that suggest a fair degree of success in this endeavor, in particular the use of ILC Draft Articles as evidence of legal norms by the ICJ, the International Tribunal for the Law of the Sea, the World Trade Organization Appellate Body, the African Court on Human and Peoples' Rights, the

---

[72] Danae Azaria, "The International Law Commission's Return to the Law of Sources of International Law," *FIU Law Review*, vol. 13, no. 6, 2019 and Baylis, "The International Law Commission's Soft Law Influence."

[73] Baylis, "The International Law Commission's Soft Law Influence," p. 1011.

[74] Charles C. Jalloh, "Introduction: The Role and Contributions of the International Law Commission to the Development of International Law: A Symposium Celebrating the 70th Anniversary of the ILC," *Florida International University Law Review*, vol. 13, no. 6, 2019, p. 980.

[75] Baylis, "The International Law Commission's Soft Law Influence," p. 1014.

European Court of Human Rights, and the Inter-American Court of Human Rights.[76]

At the same time, the ILC has not abandoned its efforts to develop new multilateral lawmaking treaties. Indeed, its current work on two conventions addressing crimes against humanity is potentially groundbreaking and could represent its most important contribution to international law in decades.[77]

Lawmaking Conferences

Even with a shift away from multilateral agreements over the past decade, the most important source of consensus-based general international law is still the lawmaking treaty. These are usually initiated by the ILC and the UN General Assembly. Both work with the General Assembly's Sixth Committee to propose and even draft specific treaties or conventions for consideration by the UN membership. These reports have led to General Assembly resolutions that became the basis for organizing international lawmaking conferences where proposed treaties are negotiated. These conferences act as a quasi-legislative forum, a global town meeting among representatives of most, sometimes all, of the international community's legal subjects.

The practice of holding UN-sponsored conferences to discuss, negotiate, draft, and ultimately sign multilateral conventions increases the ability of the international community to create new principles of law. Since these conferences usually include representatives from most member states, it suggests an intention to develop legal obligations that apply broadly. Thus, while the United Nations itself lacks the legal authority to create new international law, it often acts as a vehicle for drafting legally binding multilateral treaties and conventions that does just that.

These conferences are based on the principle of multilateralism. As both John Ruggie and John Ikenberry argue, since World War II states have accepted multilateralism as the legitimate form of collective decision-making within the international community.[78] The historical record over the past half-century strongly suggests that this has been extended to the area of legal

---

[76] Baylis, "The International Law Commission's Soft Law Influence," pp. 1016–1017.
[77] See Jalloh, "The International Law Commission's First Draft Convention on Crimes against Humanity."
[78] John G. Ruggie, "Multilateralism: the Anatomy of an Institution," *International Organization*, vol. 46, no. 3, summer 1992. and G. John Ikenberry, *After Victory: Institutions, Strategic Restraint and the Rebuilding of Order after Major Wars* (Princeton University Press, 2000).

obligation. Even a cursory examination of the most important lawmaking agreements signed over the past generation clearly demonstrates that multilateral forums have become the preferred method for conceptualizing and creating general international law.

Charney argues that such forums provide the international community with the means to develop a type of legislative process without creating either a world legislature or even an equivalent. In doing so, the products of multilateral forums substantially advance and formalize the international lawmaking process.[79] When such a process is conducted within international organizations encompassing a broad membership, the outcome is legitimized by the fact that the members of these organizations have already committed themselves to this process by signing the organizational charters. In fact, Charney argues that multilateral organizations and treaty-negotiating conferences not only represent a different way of creating international law; they can provide more relevance to broad, multilateral consensus than state practice.[80]

Many of the most important lawmaking treaties have achieved widespread acceptance by following this extensive process. For example, the codification and expansion of diplomatic law—which is viewed by most political leaders to be universally binding—emerged from a proposal by the ILC, approved by the UN General Assembly, and drafted at the United Nations Conference on Diplomatic Intercourse and Immunities in Vienna in 1961. This conference brought together most UN members to adopt what became a universally accepted treaty, the Vienna Convention on Diplomatic Relations (EIF 1961). This treaty is a good example of how customary law merges with treaty law to create universal obligations, essentially a legislative act. Similarly, the Vienna Convention on the Law of Treaties was based on a document drafted by the ILC and confirmed at a UN-sponsored conference in 1966. (It entered into force in 1969.) Like the Diplomatic Convention, the Vienna Convention is considered the definitive document on the rules for creating all types of international legal agreements.

In addition to establishing rules on process, the international community has used these methods to enact several groundbreaking agreements that most states consider to be universally binding. These agreements reflect emerging principles of law in areas where there is growing consensus against

---

[79] See Charney, "Universal International Law," pp. 551 and 547.
[80] Charney, "Universal International Law."

the use of what I term "excessive state violence": genocide, violations of rules regarding internal armed conflicts, widespread systematic attacks on a civilian population, and the development of weapons designed to cause large-scale civilian casualties and suffering. Although legal positivists would surely argue that the resulting treaties are binding only on the signatories, the subsequent chapters of this book will demonstrate that most political leaders in fact consider these practices to be illegal, even for those states that have not specifically consented to them.

Viewed within a theory of consensus-based international law, the process of developing multilateral lawmaking treaties through multilateral forums— and expanding them to apply universally—can meet the conditions that I suggest are necessary for the creation of a universal legal norm. The legitimacy for considering lawmaking treaties as a virtual form of legislation is enhanced by the very lengthy process of conceptualization, research, discussion, debate, drafting, redrafting, consultation, and ultimately ratification that characterizes their adoption.[81] At each step, technical experts and state representatives develop and refine consensus principles into workable legal norms. By involving all or almost all states in the process, and by placing a minimum number of signatories necessary for a treaty to enter into force, the process provides for at least one element in achieving the status of general law.

United Nations Security Council

Over the past several decades, the United Nations Security Council has evolved from the enforcement body of a global collective security organization into an institution that makes authoritative decisions on a wide range of political and legal issues, including mass human rights violations. Since the early 1990s, the Council has expanded its Chapter VII authority well beyond its traditional role as guardians of international peace and security to taking action in the areas of humanitarian assistance (Somalia, 1992), racial equality and self-determination (South Africa, 1980s and, two decades earlier, Rhodesia), restoring democratic governance (Haiti, 1994), protecting populations from internal violence (Sudan, early 2000s; Syria, 2010s; Libya, 2011), and creating international tribunals to prosecute political leaders who

---

[81] For a good description of this process, see Szasz, "International Norm-Making."

are responsible for committing atrocities (former Yugoslavia, Rwanda, East Timor, 1990s).[82]

In fact the Council has gone so far as to create some new legal obligations for the UN member states (which means all states in the world) by essentially passing resolutions that assume the status of legislation. Council Resolution 1373 required all states to enact laws designed to suppress the financing and other forms of support for terrorist acts. Resolution 1540 required states to take legal action to prevent weapons of mass destruction from falling into the hands of terrorists. These were unprecedented acts of lawmaking by the Council, imposing binding obligations on all states under Chapter VII. Unlike traditional Chapter VII actions, they were neither directly related to a particular crisis nor limited in time. They do not seek to enforce a decision against a particular state but, rather, impose general obligations in a broad issue area for an indefinite period. This was qualitatively different from the Council's normal crisis management role.[83]

The significance of these resolutions for our understanding of how international law is created and enforced has been recognized by a wide range of international law scholars, some of whom refer to these acts as being akin to legislation.[84] Jose Alvarez, for example, describes the actions of the Council as "express attempts to make global law."[85]

Technically, the Council does not have the power to either create or enforce international law, and the scope of its authority is limited to the UN membership and to the organizational Charter. However, since every state in the world belongs to the UN, in practice the Council essentially acts as an executive committee for the international community, with the legal power to establish and implement global rules for the membership. The UN Charter invests considerable political and legal authority in the Council, and UN membership imposes a substantial level of obligation on the states to follow Council mandates.

The legitimacy of the Council to act as an interpreter of global rules stems from both its Charter authority and its internal organization. The

---

[82] See, for example, Security Council Resolutions 591, S/RES/591 (28 November 1986); 841, S/RES/841 (16 June 1993); 917, S/RES/917 (6 May 1994); 940, S/RES/940 (31 July 1994); 827, S/RES/827 (25 May 1993); 794, S/RES/794 (3 December 1992), and 1556, S/RES/1556 (30 July 2004).

[83] Ian Johnstone, "The Security Council as Legislature," in Bruce Cronin and Ian Hurd (eds.), *The UN Security Council and the Politics of International Authority* (Routledge, 2002).

[84] See, for example, Paul Szasz, "The Security Council Starts Legislating," *American Journal of International Law*, vol. 96, no. 4, 2002 and Johnstone, "The Security Council as Legislature."

[85] Jose Alvarez, *International Organizations as Law-Makers* (Oxford University Press, 2006), p. 198.

Charter gives the Council virtually unlimited authority in determining when and how to act. The UN Security Council has the authority under the Charter to act whenever there is a "threat to the peace, breach of the peace, or act of aggression," regardless of whether such a breach technically violates international law. It alone determines whether such a threat exists; there is no external check on its authority, nor are there any avenues of appeal.[86] However, the Council's internal organization, procedures, and rules facilitate a general acceptance by the membership that their decisions are legitimately reached.

First, in addition to including the five major powers, the Council also includes two states from each of the five regions of the world, representing the wide variety of legal systems and cultures. Passage of any resolution requires a positive vote from 9 of the 15 members, which means that even if all 5 of the major powers (permanent members, or P5) agree, they still need to garner support from at least 4 of the 10 elected members (known as the E10). Although it is rare for a resolution supported by P5 to be nullified by the E10, in practice Council resolutions are rarely passed by majority vote; they are usually approved by general consensus with few, if any, dissenters.[87]

Second, the Council is a deliberative body, meaning that decisions are made only after considerable discussion and debate according to a set of well-established procedures. (Of course, most of these deliberations are conducted in private.)[88] Moreover, since any positive outcome requires that there be no official dissent from any member of the P5, consensus rather than majority vote is the procedural rule, at least among the major powers. This principle of balance of power prevents any single member or combination from dominating the body.

Finally, since the ability of the Council to enforce its resolutions strongly relies on the cooperation of the other states (for example, in levying sanctions or providing peacekeeping forces), they must secure broad acceptance of both the procedure and the rule. This means that the Council's decisions and rulings need to be consistent with accepted international norms and precedents.

---

[86] United Nations, *Charter of the United Nations*, 24 October 1945, 1 UNTS XVI, article 39.

[87] For an in-depth study of the Council's decision-making process, see David Malone, *Decision-Making in the UN Security Council: The Case of Haiti, 1990–1997* (Clarendon Press, 1999).

[88] See UN Security Council, "Provisional Rules of Procedure," S/96; Security Council Report, *The UN Security Council Handbook: A Users Guide to Practice and Procedure* (United Nations, 2019); and Loraine Sievers and Sam Daws, *The Procedure of the UN Security Council*, 4th edition (Oxford University Press, 2014).

The existence of the Council and ILC as types of "interpretive community" provides the third condition necessary for a consensus-based legal norm. For the member states, the authority of the Council is derived not only from its formal power granted to it by the UN Charter but also from the process by which it makes its legally binding decision. In granting extensive authority to the Council, the member states have not accepted a set of legally binding *principles* as much as they agreed to the legitimacy of a legally binding political *process*.[89] The legitimacy of the Council to interpret consensus-based legal norms lies with its internal structure and its relationship to the general membership, as discussed above.

The Council creates new legal norms by acting as if such norms were in fact legal rules even in the absence of treaty or customary practice. Johnstone describes the process as follows:

> Operational activities occur against the backdrop of widely acknowledged but not well-specified norms; in carrying out those activities, international organizations do not seek to enforce the norms *per se* but typically act in a manner that conforms to them; these activities generate friction, triggering bouts of legal argumentation; the reaction of affected governments—and the discourse that surrounds the action and reaction—can cause the law to harden.[90]

Of course, the Council is a political body, not a legal one, and most of its decisions are guided by the interests of the permanent members and their interpretation of what constitutes a security threat. Its ability to act as a coherent interpretive community and facilitator of global norms rests on the relationships among its members. Council actions in this area, therefore, wax and wane depending upon the political dynamics of world politics at any particular time. When the Council can agree on particular issues, it can be an effective institution for the facilitation of consensus-based norms. When relations within the Council are frayed, it can be quite ineffective.

---

[89] See Johnstone, "Security Council Deliberations."
[90] Ian Johnstone, "Law-Making through the Operational Activities of International Organizations," *George Washington International Law Review*, vol. 40, no. 1, 2008, p. 88.

Treaty Regimes

Changes in the implementation of treaty rules have created strong institutional mechanisms for ensuring that such rules become a regular part of the daily interaction of states, even among those who are not parties to specific agreements. In this area, the evolution of multilateral treaty regimes is most significant. Shirley Scott argues that although multilateral treaties are the culmination of a long political process, both the process and the treaty itself are only the beginning. Once the treaty enters into force, it often provides the central focus for the creation of an even broader institutional process through the construction of an international treaty regime.[91]

Regimes are coherent sets of principles, norms, rules, and decision-making procedures that facilitate cooperation within a particular issue area.[92] States participate in regimes because they provide tangible benefits and because it is often costly for them to be left out. On a deeper level, however, regimes institutionalize the principles, norms, and rules within the international community. Thus, even states that do not formally agree to adopt particular international legal rules find that other states expect them to conform to the norms and expectations of a particular regime. For example, human rights regimes facilitate the expansion of many human rights norms, even among those states that have not formally ratified the Covenant on Civil and Political Rights or other such agreements. Treaty regimes are particularly important institutions inasmuch as they combine legal obligations with institutional rules that facilitate political cooperation.

These regimes help to extend the jurisdiction of treaties beyond the specific signatories by creating institutional structures, political pressure, and incentives for compliance among even nonsignatory states. Many modern multilateral treaties contain clauses that establish institutions that not only facilitate compliance but also promote a broad application of the treaty's goals to a wide variety of circumstances. Some also include provisions for regular formal meetings of the state parties, and some even create new organizations. Currently, the nine main human rights treaties, and one protocol,

---

[91] Shirley Scott, *International Law in World Politics* (Lynne Rienner Publishers, 2004), p. 161.
[92] For a discussion of regimes, see Stephen Krasner (ed.), *International Regimes* (Cornell University Press, 1983) and Andreas Hasenclever, Peter Mayer, and Volker Rittberger, *Theories of International Regimes* (Cambridge University Press, 1997).

have created 10 treaty bodies to monitor implementation of the legal norms created in the agreements.[93]

For example, the Nuclear Non-Proliferation Treaty (NPT), arguably one of the most successful agreements in modern international relations, contains provisions for inspecting the facilities of the party states and for making new regulations in pursuit of the treaty's goals. Toward this end, the treaty gives the International Atomic Energy Agency (IAEA) the authority to oversee compliance of the nonproliferation obligations. The treaty also contains a provision for convening a Review Conference of the Parties to the Treaty of Non-Proliferation of Nuclear Weapons every five years. In addition, a Preparatory Committee for the Review Conference holds sessions during the intermediate years. Although the treaty is technically binding only on the signatories, the regime has extended the nonproliferation obligation globally, and the IAEA often conducts inspections independently of the treaty. In this sense, the treaty not only articulates a set of legal obligations but also provides an institutional structure to monitor compliance and extend jurisdiction to nonparty states.

The degree to which the regime expanded its coverage to include nonparty states was tested in 1998 and 2006. Both cases involved two of the only three countries that failed to ratify the NPT (India, Pakistan, and Israel). Yet, although India and Pakistan were not parties to the treaty, the UN Security Council refused to recognize their legal right to continue developing nuclear weapons. Specifically, the Council expressed in a 1998 resolution "its firm conviction that the international regime on the nonproliferation of nuclear weapons should be maintained and consolidated" and that "in accordance with the Treaty on the Non-Proliferation of Nuclear Weapons, India or Pakistan cannot have the status of a nuclear-weapon State."[94]

In 2003, North Korea became the first (and only) state to officially withdraw from the treaty, an act that they could do legally under both the Vienna Convention and the NPT itself. Yet the Security Council indicated that they would still hold North Korea legally obligated to maintain its treaty

---

[93] See Office of the UN High Commissioner for Human Rights, "The Core International Human Rights Instruments and their monitoring bodies," at https://www.ohchr.org/en/professionalinterest/pages/coreinstruments.aspx.
[94] Security Council Resolution 1172 (1998), adopted at its 3890th meeting, on 6 June 1998, UN Doc. S/RES/1172.

commitments by unanimously passing a resolution declaring (among other things) that "the DPRK (North Korea) cannot have the status of a nuclear-weapon state in accordance with the Treaty on the Non-Proliferation of Nuclear Weapons."[95]

As another example, the antitorture regime, which grew out of the Convention Against Torture and Other Cruel, Inhuman or Degrading Treatment or Punishment, is grounded in the Committee Against Torture, the body of 10 independent experts that monitors implementation of the treaty. Yet this Committee does not limit its inspections to state parties; it also inspects places of detention run by nonparty states.[96]

In addition, a succession of multilateral treaties that address similar issues can form the basis for new institutions/regimes that may operate independently of the treaties themselves. For example, Kenneth Abbott discusses how an "atrocities regime" that provides for criminal responsibility for human rights abuses developed out of a number of interlocking human rights treaties, including the Genocide Convention, the Convention Against Torture, the Covenant on Civil and Political Rights, and the four Geneva Conventions.[97] In all three cases, the treaties established monitoring and implementation bodies through the United Nations, suggesting an intention to apply the principles of these agreements beyond the signatories. The principles embedded in these treaties collectively provided the foundation for the Security Council's decisions to establish international criminal tribunals to address what I call excessive violence in the former Yugoslavia and Rwanda.[98]

In this vein, Laurence Helfer argues that rulings by international courts, commissions, and expert committees established as part of a broad human rights regime have expanded the scope of existing human rights treaties and transformed nonbinding norms into legally binding obligations.[99]

---

[95] United Nations Security Council, Resolution 1718, adopted by the Security Council at its 5551st meeting, on 14 October 2006, S/RES/1718 (2006).

[96] See UN Third Committee, Meetings Coverage and Press Release, "Convention against Torture Only as Strong as States' Commitments, Support, Experts Tell Third Committee in Interactive Dialogues on Human Rights," GA/SHC/4139, 20 October 2015.

[97] Kenneth Abbott, "International Relations Theory, International Law, and the Regime Governing Atrocities in Internal Conflicts," *American Journal of International Law*, vol. 93, no. 2, 1999.

[98] See Security Council Resolutions 752 (15 May 1992), 764 (13 July 1992), 770 (13 August 1992), 771 (also of 13 August 1992), and 955 (8 November 1994).

[99] Laurence R. Helfer, "Nonconsensual International Lawmaking," *University of Illinois Law Review*, vol. 2008, no. 1, 2008, p. 87.

Testing the Theories

The degree to which states accept consensus-based international legal obligations is ultimately an empirical question. This chapter focused on the institutions and processes that have enabled the international community to create principles of international law that apply universally, even in cases where individual states fail to ratify a treaty and where there is a lack of state practice to create customary law. The following four chapters will examine how this applies—or fails to apply—to state practices that have met the standard of atrocities and are therefore considered by the international community to be illegitimate and illegal.

3
The Universal Ban on Extreme Internal State Violence

The 20th century was the most destructive and brutal period in history. Apart from the tens of millions of people killed during scores of armed conflicts, governments engaged in massive one-sided violence against their own populations on a grand and unprecedented scale.[1] According to one estimate, governments intentionally killed more than 84 million people in 201 distinct cases of mass killing between 1900 and the beginning of the 21st century. Other estimates range as high as 170 million.[2]

Prior to World War II, this type of aggression was not addressed in international law. Rather, the regulation of state violence was primarily limited to the means and methods through which states could conduct warfare or other applications of military force against other states. Between 1899 and 1907, for example, states drafted and ratified 13 Hague conventions regulating various aspects of international armed conflicts, including the treatment of prisoners, behavior on the battlefield, the types of weapons that belligerents may employ, the rights of neutrals, and the protection of certain types of civilian institutions such as hospitals.[3] States concluded another series of treaties following World War I, promoting arms control, the regulation of military force, and a ban on certain types of weapons in war.[4] These, too, dealt with interstate conflict and were signed by a limited number of states.

---

[1] One-sided violence is defined as military aggression directed at unarmed civilians that reaches a certain level of intensity. See Ralph Sundberg, "Revisiting One-Sided Violence: A Global and Regional Analysis," *Uppsala Conflict Data Program,* Paper No. 3, 2008, p. 3.

[2] See Charles Anderton, "Killing Civilians as an Inferior Input in a Rational Choice Model of Genocide and Mass Killing," *Peace Economics, Peace Science and Public Policy*, vol. 20, April 2014, p. 328 and R. J. Rummel, *Death by Government: Genocide and Mass Murder since 1900* (Routledge, 1997). For a more general discussion of mass killing in the 20th century, see also Benjamin Valentino, *Final Solutions: Mass Killing and Genocide in the Twentieth Century* (Cornell University Press, 2004).

[3] For a complete list with the text of the treaties, see Avalon Project: Documents in Law, History, and Diplomacy, "The Laws of War," at https://avalon.law.yale.edu/subject_menus/lawwar.asp) accessed 9 November 2020).

[4] For example, Protocol for the Prohibition of the Use of Asphyxiating, Poisonous or Other Gases, and of Bacteriological Methods of Warfare, Geneva, 17 June 1925; Limitation of Naval Armament (Five Power Treaty), Treaty signed at Washington, 6 February 1922; Treaty between the United

In each case, political leaders and legal analysts considered these agreements—and the other treaties that provided limitations on state violence—to reflect the principle that international law is based on verifiable state consent. The obligations of states stemmed from their explicit agreement to accept a specific set of legal norms that were binding only insofar as they reflected the text of a treaty. For example, Article 2 of the 1907 Hague Convention Respecting the Laws and Customs of War on Land states:

> The provisions contained in the Regulations mentioned in Article 1 are only binding on the Contracting Powers, in case of war between two or more of them. These provisions shall cease to be binding from the time when, in a war between Contracting Powers, a non-Contracting Power joins one of the belligerents.[5]

Thus, in and of itself, even a dramatic increase in the number and breadth of multilateral agreements designed to control the use of state violence did not challenge the traditional position that international law remained limited to voluntary consent.

This began to change in the second half of the 20th century. The experience of World War II forced political leaders to consider more general and universal approaches toward controlling internal state violence. The period surrounding the war (1933–1945) had seen unprecedented horrendous violence perpetrated by states against their own populations and those under their administration. Close to 15 million people perished in German concentration camps, Stalinist purges, and state terror campaigns waged by Italian and Spanish fascists.[6] Approximately 3.5 million more survived but were imprisoned, tortured, starved, and forced to work in the Nazi camps.[7] This does not include the millions of civilians killed, tortured, and held as sex slaves during the Japanese occupation of Korea, Malaysia, the Philippines, Singapore, and China.[8]

States and Other Powers Providing for the Renunciation of War as an Instrument of National Policy (Kellogg-Briand Pact), signed at Paris, 27 August 1928.

[5] "Hague Convention Respecting the Laws and Customs of War on Land," in Adam Roberts and Richard Guelff (eds.), *Documents on the Laws of War* (Oxford University Press, 2003), p. 67.

[6] There are still no definitive figures on the precise numbers of people killed during this period. I drew these numbers from Norman Davies, *Europe: A History* (Oxford University Press, 1996).

[7] Martin Gilbert, *The Routledge Atlas of the Holocaust* (Routledge, 2009), pp. 223–229.

[8] Like the war in Europe, there are no definitive numbers for civilian casualties in Asia and the Pacific attributed to the Japanese occupation. Estimates place the number between 3 million and 10 million. See Paul H. Kratoska and Ken'ichi Goto, "Japanese Occupation of Southeast Asia,

It was not only the level of brutality that caused such revulsion among political leaders and their populations; it was the fact that states had been able to amass so many coercive resources to implement it. This consolidation and centralization of state power combined with the increased destructiveness of military technology made for a lethal cocktail that surpassed the potential of even the most repressive regimes of previous years.

Largely in reaction to these events, the conclusion of World War II introduced several new trends that suggested a greater international commitment on the part of political leaders to regulate the level of internal violence that states may employ in the pursuit of national interest.[9] In particular, these leaders took two actions that demonstrated a collective effort to make these prohibitions universally binding regardless of whether states consented.

The first was the initiation of the Nuremberg war crimes trials, a series of judicial proceedings designed to hold German leaders and middle-level functionaries accountable for the extreme violence of the previous decade. Customary international law had long permitted states to prosecute enemy combatants for breach of the laws and customs of war, a practice viewed as a corollary to the principle of self-defense.[10] Certainly on one level Nuremberg represented this old tradition of "victor's justice"—a practice whereby the winners of a conflict prosecute the losers.[11] Indeed, the allies did not charge any of their own leaders with war crimes, despite themselves having engaged in massive, indiscriminate bombing of civilian areas. The Nuremberg Charter explicitly stated that the International Military Tribunal was limited to "the major war criminals of the European Axis."[12]

At the same time, although the four powers controlled all of the territory in Europe—and therefore could have imposed any type of tribunal

---

1941–1945," in Richard Bosworth and Joseph Maiolo (eds.), *The Cambridge History of the Second World War* (Cambridge University Press, 2015).

[9] There is a large literature on the connection between the Holocaust and the rise of human rights as an international issue after World War II; in fact most academics tend to take this as a given. For a good example, see Jack Donnelly, *International Human Rights* (Routledge, 2012), chapter 1 and Michael Ignatieff, "Human Rights as Politics," in Amy Gutman (ed.), *Human Rights as Politics and Idolatry* (Princeton University Press, 2001). For a contrary position, see Samuel Moyn, *The Last Utopia: Human Rights in History* (Harvard University Press, 2010).

[10] H. Lauterpacht and L. Oppenheim, *International Law: A Treatise, vol. 2: Disputes, War and Neutrality* (Longmans, 1952), p. 257.

[11] The International Military Tribunal for the Far East also charged Japanese leaders with war crimes, crimes against the peace, and crimes against humanity; however, the charges were not precedent-setting and are largely regarded as more reflective of victor's justice than Nuremberg. See Tim Maga, *Judgment at Tokyo: The Japanese War Crimes Trials* (University Press of Kentucky, 2001).

[12] Charter of the International Military Tribunal, Article 1.

they wished—they went through considerable lengths to establish a legal basis for the trials under international law. The legal principle of *nullum crimen nulla poena sine lege* (there can be no crime or punishment without law) is fundamental to any system based on the rule of law, and the Allies wanted their prosecution to have a legal foundation. Thus, the Charter of the International Military Tribunal (an annex to the London Agreement of 1945) outlined the charges under a mixture of customary and treaty law.[13] This required some creative reinterpretations of international law, since only one of the four charges (war crimes) was actually considered to be a criminal offense at the time. In the absence of a new approach to international law, the creation of new legal norms for the trials would have been a classic example of *ex post facto* justice.[14] In a further move to legitimize the trials, the four Allies sought to broaden support for the legal proceedings beyond the victors by inviting other countries to ratify the London Agreement. Nineteen did so.

Most important, Nuremberg moved beyond the moment by establishing precedents and principles that challenged our traditional notions of consent-based international legal norms. In the first place, the trials, and the subsequent adoption of its standards as elements of international law, institutionalized the principle that an international tribunal can judge the official acts of political leaders perpetrated within their own borders. Specifically, the Tribunal sought to prosecute those who committed political crimes "whose offenses have no particular geographical location whether they be accused individually or in their capacities as member of organizations" and "whether or not in violation of the domestic law of the country where perpetrated," a challenge to the concept of state sovereignty.[15]

Second, the Tribunal created a new category of international offense that was unrelated to the traditional definition of war crimes: crimes against humanity, which included "inhuman acts committed against any civilian population, before or during the war."[16] This expanded the scope of international

---

[13] Henry T. King Jr., "The Legacy of Nuremberg," *Case Western Reserve Journal of International Law*, vol. 34 (2002), pp. 336–339.

[14] For a critique of the trials as representing *ex post facto* justice written at the time, see Charles E. Wyzanski, "Nuremberg: A Fair Trial? A Dangerous Precedent," *The Atlantic*, April 1946.

[15] See Article 1 of the London Agreement of 8 August 1945 in D. Schindler and J. Toman, *The Laws of Armed Conflicts* (Martinus Nijhoff, 1988), pp. 912–919 and Charter of the International Military Tribunal, Agreement for the Prosecution and Punishment of the Major War Criminals of the European Axis, signed in London on 8 August, 1945, Article VI.

[16] Charter of the International Military Tribunal, "Agreement for the Prosecution and Punishment of Major War Criminals of the European Axis, signed at London on 8 August 1945," Article 6(3).

law from contracts between states to legal obligations owed to the international community itself. Such commitments are *erga omnes*, obligations that states owe to the international community as a whole and in whose protection all states have a legal interest.[17] As such they go beyond reciprocal relations among states based on mutual consent.

What is particularly important from the perspective of international law and human rights was that this specifically concerned the treatment of civilians within the territory of a state, regardless of whether such action was illegal under domestic law.[18] In pursuing this charge, the Tribunal established standards of international law that prevailed over national law. This was the first time that states claimed that international law could overwrite domestic law without the agreement of the state itself, a significant challenge to the doctrines of consent and sovereignty.

At the same time, although the Nuremberg tribunal was given the authority to prosecute atrocities that had occurred before the outbreak of the war, no one was actually convicted of any offense committed before 1939, even though the Holocaust began in 1933. In the end, Nuremberg held the Nazis to account for atrocities committed against their own nationals but only to the extent that those atrocities could be linked to the war of aggression and that they occurred after 1939. Clearly, officials from the allied states were still uncomfortable applying international law to acts of internal violence that were totally unconnected to an international armed conflict.[19] The reason for this was simple: while there was a long history of international law addressing armed conflict, there was virtually no international human rights law dealing with the way governments treated populations within their own borders. This limitation was rectified three years later with the conclusion of the Genocide Convention and Universal Declaration of Human Rights in 1948.

Taken together, this suggested a new approach toward the use of international law to regulate internal state violence. The United Nations General Assembly expressed the proposition that the law of Nuremberg should be part of general international law by unanimously approving Resolution 95(1)

---

[17] See International Law Commission, "Draft Articles on Responsibility of States for Internationally Wrongful Acts," Article 48 (1)(b); Report of the International Law Commission on the Work of Its 53rd Session, 2001; and ICJ Reports, 1970, *Barcelona Traction, Light and Power Company, Limited (Belgium v. Spain)* (1962–1970), Second Phase, Judgment, ICJ Reports 1970.

[18] Charter of the International Military Tribunal, London, 8 August 1945, Article 6.

[19] William A Schabas, "Origins of the Genocide Convention: From Nuremberg to Paris," *Case Western Reserve Journal of International Law*, vol. 40, nos. 1–2, 2007–2008, pp. 44–46.

on 11 December 1946.[20] This was subsequently affirmed by the ILC's restatement of the Nuremberg principles as general international law.[21] In fact the formulation of the "principles of international law recognized in the Charter of the Nuremberg Tribunal and in the Judgment of the Tribunal" was one of the ILC's first tasks given to it by the General Assembly.[22] Many legal scholars and government officials have since concluded these principles are indeed part of general international law, even though they appear to run counter to the doctrine of consent and were not a reflection of consistent state practice.[23]

A second trend begun during this period was initiated by the 1949 Convention on the Prevention and Punishment of the Crime of Genocide, discussed in Chapter 4. This was a groundbreaking treaty that introduced three innovative practices that constituted a significant change in the way political leaders and international lawyers viewed international law.

First, the Convention was first drafted and debated within the UN General Assembly, establishing a practice of using the universal-membership organization to develop multilateral agreements. This suggested an intention to develop a more general lawmaking treaty, as opposed to a traditional contractual one. In addition, it declared for the first time that a particular state practice would constitute an international crime, as opposed to a treaty violation.[24] Perpetrators would be violating general international law, not simply a legal obligation to other states.

Second, it stipulated that individual perpetrators would be held responsible for their acts whether they are constitutionally responsible rulers, public officials, or private individuals. This would entail even if they were acting in their official capacity as agents of the state.[25] Traditionally, the Act of State Doctrine and the customary principle of sovereign immunity protected state

---

[20] United Nations General Assembly, "Affirmation of the Principles of International Law Recognized by the Charter of the Nuremberg Tribunal," available at: https://legal.un.org/avl/pdf/ha/ga_95-I/ga_95-I_ph_e.pdf (accessed 1 September 2020).

[21] International Law Commission, "Principles of International Law Recognized in the Charter of the Nuremberg Tribunal and in the Judgment of the Tribunal," *Yearbook of the International Law Commission*, vol. 2, 1950, para. 97.

[22] UN General Assembly Resolution 177(II), 1947, para. A.

[23] See, for example, Elizabeth Borgwardt, "The Rise of the United Nations' 1948 'Nuremberg Principles': Consolidating and Destabilizing Wartime Reconfigurations of Sovereignty," paper presented at the 123rd Annual Meeting of the American Historical Association, New York City, 2–5 January 2009; Allan A. Ryan, "Nuremberg's Contributions to International Law," *Boston College International and Comparative Law Review*, no. 1, Winter 2007.

[24] United Nations Treaty Series, "Convention on the Prevention and Punishment of the Crime of Genocide," 1951, Article I.

[25] United Nations Treaty Series, "Convention on the Prevention and Punishment of the Crime of Genocide," 1951, Article IV.

leaders from being judged for their official acts in the courts of another state or by an international tribunal.[26] This had reflected the volunteerist notion that each state would decide for itself whether and how to deal with violations committed by its public officials. Holding individual violators (particularly state officials) accountable to the international community was a radical departure from customary practice. This universalized the notion of criminal responsibility.

Finally, the convention authorized individual states or international courts to prosecute such perpetrators even if they were nationals of states that were not parties to the convention.[27] This laid the groundwork for a universal law regarding the control of excessive state violence and the development of institutions to implement it.

Reviving and Expanding the Prohibition of Atrocities

For almost half a century after the conclusion of the Nuremberg trials and the Genocide Convention, these innovations appeared to be anomalies. During the Cold War, no one was prosecuted for perpetrating genocide or crimes against humanity by an international tribunal, although some individual states did prosecute Nazi war criminals who had escaped justice at Nuremberg and were subsequently captured. Moreover, the enthusiasm to regulate internal state violence on a universal basis was overshadowed by the political division of the world into East-West and North-South. The bifurcation of the world into these hostile camps made it difficult if not impossible to conceive of any form of political consensus, much less one that would lead to new legal obligations.

Indeed, the international community remained relatively silent in the face of genocide in East Pakistan in 1971, politicide in Cambodia in the late 1970s, and mass killings by the regime of Uganda's Idi Amin during the 1970s (although India, Vietnam, and Tanzania, respectively, intervened unilaterally in these situations).[28] This alone would challenge any argument that the

---

[26] This widely accepted doctrine in customary international law was articulated in a U.S. Supreme Court case, *Underhill v. Hernandez*, 168 U. S. 250, 18 Sup. Ct. 83, 42 L. Ed. 456, 1897.
[27] United Nations Treaty Series, "Convention on the Prevention and Punishment of the Crime of Genocide," Articles IV–VI.
[28] Rachel Kleinfeld, "The United States and the Future of Humanitarian Intervention," in William Schultz (ed.), *The Future of Human Rights* (University of Pennsylvania Press, 2008), pp. 54–55; John Salzberg, "UN Prevention of Human Rights Violations: The Bangladesh Case," *International*

prohibition of genocide or other crimes against humanity could be based on any form of state practice, a key requirement for customary law.

Two events in the early 1990s revived the movement that had begun and been stalled at the conclusion of the Second World War.

First, the end of the Cold War and the decline of the North-South conflict created opportunities for greater cooperation within the multilateral organizations that had been established after the Second World War. The changed political environment facilitated a major expansion of multilateralism into new areas of international politics. Within the United Nations, for example, the new political conditions fostered a significant growth in efforts to promote political stability and human rights within sovereign states. This was symbolized by the publication of *An Agenda for Peace* in 1992 (drafted at the request of the Security Council) and the adoption of the Responsibility to Protect principle by the members of the UN at the World Summit in 2005.[29] The latter endorsed the principle that sovereignty carried with it the obligation of the state to protect its own people, and that if the state was unwilling or unable to do so, the responsibility shifted to the international community.

The end of the division of Europe also resulted in the restructuring of the Organization for Security and Cooperation in Europe to include, among other things, the protection of domestic national and ethnic minorities and the promotion of human rights within a dozen new states and countries undergoing radical regime change.[30]

Second, the violent breakup of Yugoslavia and the brutal application of internal state violence in Eastern Europe, the former Soviet Union, and Africa in the 1990s shocked the international community, particularly the great powers.[31] More specifically, the lack of international action to stop atrocities in Bosnia, Rwanda, East Timor, and Liberia forced states to consider new mechanisms to deter and prevent such acts in the future. This was motivated not only by humanitarian concerns but also by a belief that extreme internal

---

Organization, vol. 27, no. 1, 1973; John-Mark Lyi, *Humanitarian Intervention and the AU-ECOWAS Intervention Treaties under International Law* (Springer, 2016), p. 50.

[29] United Nations, "An Agenda for Peace: Preventive Diplomacy, Peacemaking and Peace-keeping," Report of the Secretary-General pursuant to the statement adopted by the Summit Meeting of the Security Council on 31 January 1992; Resolution Adopted by the General Assembly on 16 September 2005; United Nations, "2005 World Summit Outcome" (A/RES/60/1), paras. 138 and 139.

[30] Jane Wright, "The OSCE and the Protection of Minority Rights," *Human Rights Quarterly*, vol. 18, no. 1, 1996.

[31] See Stephen Iwan Griffiths, *Nationalism and Ethnic Conflict: Threats to European Security*, SIPRI Research Report 5 (Oxford University Press, 1993), p. 90.

state violence could potentially threaten the stability of the international order through massive refugee flows, potential border changes, illegal arms trafficking, the rise of cross-border guerrilla armies, and external intervention by neighboring states and regional powers.

This resulted in the UN Security Council acting after the fact by establishing two Nuremberg-like tribunals to address serious war crimes, genocide, and crimes against humanity within Bosnia and Rwanda and hybrid courts to deal with atrocities committed in Cambodia and Sierra Leone.[32] Unlike Nuremberg, these tribunals were initiated by states that were not party to any of the conflicts that produced the violations. It is not only the creation of the tribunals that is significant, but the position taken by the Council that the Nuremberg principle established almost 50 years earlier could override sovereignty and state consent.

Extreme State Violence

Not all human rights violations are necessarily breaches of general international law, and even those that are accepted as such are often viewed differently than reciprocal legal obligations that states owe to each other, such as the freedom of navigation on the high seas. Traditionally, international law regulated the relations between states, while human rights violations were viewed as breaching the social contract between governments and their populations.[33] For hundreds of years, the latter was an internal matter protected by the principle of sovereignty. Although virtually all states have now accepted human rights as a legitimate concern in international relations and diplomatic practice, many of the obligations embedded in most human rights agreements are aspirational and political and subject to wide interpretation.

Over the past several decades, states and international organizations have made a sharp distinction between routine human rights violations (such as government censorship and denial of due process) and acts of mass state

---

[32] Security Council Resolutions 591, S/RES/591 (28 November 1986); 841, S/RES/841 (16 June 1993); 917, S/RES/917 (6 May 1994); 940, S/RES/940 (31 July 1994); 827, S/RES/827 (25 May 1993); 794, S/RES/794 (3 December 1992); and 1556, S/RES/1556 (30 July 2004).

[33] The foundation of human rights within the social contract paradigm is familiar to anyone with even a passing knowledge of basic political theory. See, for example, Thomas Hobbes, *The Leviathan*; John Locke, *Two Treatises of Government*; and Jean-Jacque Rousseau, *On the Social Contract: Or Principles of Political Right*.

violence perpetrated against a civilian population. This distinction does not appear in any treaty or organizational resolution, but has emerged over time through deliberation, as political leaders sought to regulate the means, methods, and limits of state violence against its own populations.

This position is confirmed by jurists who have considered the degree to which domestic courts can exercise universal jurisdiction in human rights cases. For example, in the Pinochet case (discussed below), British Lord Millett distinguished between "widespread and systematic use of torture as an instrument of state policy" and "isolated and individual instances of torture," recognizing only the former as a legitimate condition that would justify the prosecution of the former Chilean dictator in a British court.[34]

Mahmoud Cherif Bassiouni, vice chair of the Preparatory Committee on the Establishment of an International Criminal Court, argued that acts of internal state violence become international crimes only when they affect a significant international interest, constitute a threat to international peace and security, or represent egregious conduct deemed offensive to the commonly shared values of the international community, including conduct shocking to the conscience of humanity.[35]

While few political leaders consider human rights to be a significant factor in foreign policy, a general consensus has been slowly building that the entire international community has an interest in regulating internal state violence when it reaches the level of "a consistent pattern of gross, flagrant or mass violations" that "shock the conscience" of humanity.[36] Academics and political leaders have given these acts various names: atrocities, inhuman acts, crimes against humanity, mass killings, and actions of a heinous nature. As I will demonstrate in subsequent pages, there now appears to be a broad consensus within the international community that these practices violate general international law that overrides domestic law or state consent.

This leaves us with the task of determining which types of internal state violence are universally prohibited by consensus and which ones are not. A good place to start is the 1966 International Covenant on Civil and Political

---

[34] Devika Hovell, "The Authority of Universal Jurisdiction," *The European Journal of International Law*, vol. 29, no. 2, 2018, p. 447.

[35] Mahmoud Cherif Bassiouni, *Crimes against Humanity in International Criminal Law* (Kluwer Law International, 1999).

[36] These phrases are contained in United Nations General Assembly Resolution 96 (I) of 11 December 1946. Although most lawyers would likely find them to be too imprecise and subjective to constitute a legitimate legal standard, as a political concept it represents a useful benchmark for defining atrocities.

Rights, currently the world's most comprehensive human rights treaty. The Covenant codified the Universal Declaration of Human Rights into a legally binding agreement that was designed to transform what was an aspirational document into a set of legal obligations. At the moment, this multilateral agreement has 173 state parties plus six signatories.[37]

Although it does not state it in these terms, the Covenant implicitly defines which practices cross the threshold of harm that transfers a practice protected by sovereignty into an offense against the international community. The document enumerates a wide range of human rights protections; however, Article 4 explicitly permits states to derogate from most of these obligations "in time of public emergency which threatens the life of the nation," so long as it officially proclaimed.[38] The determination that such an emergency exists is made by the state itself and is not subject to external review.[39] Moreover, there is no time limit imposed on the length of the emergency; indeed, it can last indefinitely.[40] Similarly, Article 18 permits limitations on the free exercise of religion or the right to hold certain beliefs if they are "necessary to protect public safety, order, health, or morals or the fundamental rights and freedoms of others."[41] These loopholes have been evoked numerous times by many states, allowing them to legally suspend their obligations while remaining part of the Covenant.[42]

Moreover, the drafters decided that domestic implementation should be conducted through national legal institutions rather than international oversight, which is the principle means for realizing the rights articulated in the document.[43] From this we can deduce that the drafters were not prepared

---

[37] United Nations Treaty Collection, Multilateral Treaties Deposited with the Secretary-General, "International Covenant on Civil and Political Rights," Status of Treaties.

[38] International Covenant on Civil and Political Rights, entered into force 23 March 1976, Article 4(1).

[39] The treaty-based Human Rights Committee does assess reports submitted by states regarding their compliance; however, these reports are voluntary and the Committee lacks the authority or jurisdiction to rule on their legality.

[40] For example, Egypt has been under a continuous and semi-permanent state of emergency for almost 40 years. It was officially declared in 1967 and lasted until the 2011 Revolution. Following the coup against the new revolutionary government in 2013, however, the state of emergency was reimposed by coup leader Abdel Fattah el-Sisi, who later institutionalized it in 2017. See "Egypt Extends State of Emergency for Twelfth Time since 2017," *Al Jazeera*, 28 April 2020.

[41] International Covenant on Civil and Political Rights, entered into force 23 March 1976, Article 18(3).

[42] A typical example is the following declaration issued by the government of Peru to the United Nations on 21 February 2007: "During the state of emergency, the rights to inviolability of the home, freedom of movement, freedom of assembly and liberty and security of person ... will be suspended." For a complete list of all other such proclaimed "emergencies," see United Nations Treaty Collection, *Human Rights: International Covenant on Civil and Political Rights*, chapter 4, "Notifications under Article 4(3) of the Covenant (Derogations)."

[43] International Covenant on Civil and Political Rights, entered into force 23 March 1976, Article 2.

to unequivocally hold each other legally accountable for all types of human rights violations.[44]

However, at the same time, the treaty also enumerates some practices as so egregious that their prohibition cannot be suspended under Article 4, and therefore no derogation is permitted. These include genocide, torture, slavery, persecution, and denying the fundamental right to life.[45] We can deduce from this that these acts are considered by the signatories to be universally illegal on their face, regardless of context and circumstance. As we will see in the following pages, these exceptions are included in multiple documents, treaties, organizational charters, and soft law instruments, and can therefore be considered part of a body of international law that the international community considers to be universal by consensus.

This distinction between routine and extreme human rights violations is also embedded within the two primary institutions designed to hold perpetrators accountable for egregious violations of international laws restricting internal state violence: international criminal tribunals and humanitarian intervention. The two criminal tribunals created by the United Nations Security Council—the International Criminal Tribunal for the Former Yugoslavia (ICTY) and the International Criminal Tribunal for Rwanda (ICTR)—and the permanent International Criminal Court (formed through multilateral treaty) strictly limited the jurisdiction of these judicial bodies to three offenses deemed to be universal violations of international law: crimes against humanity, genocide, and grave breaches in the law of armed conflict.[46] Lesser offenses were excluded from their mandate.

Similarly, the special status given to crimes against humanity, ethnic cleansing, and genocide is demonstrated by their inclusion as the only practices that would legally justify external intervention by another state. The controversial "responsibility to protect" regime limits the conditions that would legitimize humanitarian intervention to these "extreme and exceptional cases . . . in which the very interest that all states have in

---

[44] For a discussion of the debate on this provision at the conference where the treaty was drafted, see Marc J. Bossuyt, *Guide to the Travaux Préparatoires of the International Covenant on Civil and Political Rights* (Martinus Nijhoff, 1987), pp. 81–103.

[45] International Covenant on Civil and Political Rights, entered into force 23 March 1976, Article 4(2).

[46] See Statute of the International Criminal Tribunal for the Former Yugoslavia, Articles 2–5; Statute of the International Criminal Tribunal for Rwanda, Articles 2–4; and the Rome Statute of the International Criminal Court, Article 5. The Rome Statute postponed and then activated a fourth offense, the crime of aggression, as a prosecutable offense with the conclusion of the Kampala Agreement in 2017.

maintaining a stable international order requires them to react when all order within a state has broken down or when civil conflict and repression are so violent that civilians are threatened with massacre, genocide or ethnic cleansing on a large scale."[47] This formulation was endorsed by 170 heads of state at the 2005 World Summit and validated by consensus in the UN General Assembly.[48]

This is not to say that the list will not be expended in the future; however, it provides us with a guide to how the international community distinguishes between different levels of human rights violations.

At the same time, the principle that political and military leaders could be individually culpable for violations of certain acts under international law has broadened into a general legal norm, beyond any particular treaty. The Nuremberg Charter (above) was the first legal document to articulate this principle, but it has since been further articulated and expanded in a variety of documents, charters, and judicial rulings (below).

In fact, criminal responsibility for stipulated acts of mass violence now applies beyond the individuals who actually commit the prohibited acts. The Statutes of the ICTY and ICTR both extend culpability to anyone who "planned, instigated, ordered, committed or otherwise aided and abetted in the planning, preparation or execution of a crime" covered under the statutes.[49] Similarly, the Rome Statute holds responsible anyone who "orders, solicits or induces the commission of such a crime . . . [or who] aids, abets or otherwise assists in its commission or its attempted commission, including providing the means for its commission . . . or in any other way contributes to the commission or attempted commission of such a crime by a group of persons acting with a common purpose.[50]

In addition, borrowing from the language of the Nuremberg Charter, the Genocide Convention stipulates that "persons committing genocide or any of the other acts enumerated in article III shall be punished, whether they are constitutionally responsible rulers, public officials or private individuals."[51] The ILC Draft Articles on Prevention and Punishment of Crimes Against Humanity also includes those "ordering, soliciting, inducing, aiding, abetting

---

[47] International Development Research Centre, "The Responsibility to Protect: Report of the International Committee on Intervention and State Sovereignty," December 2001, p. 31.
[48] United Nations, "2005 World Summit Outcome," Resolution adopted by the General Assembly on 16 September 2005 (A/60/1).
[49] ICTY, Article 7 and ICTR, Article 6.
[50] Rome Statute of the International Criminal Court, Article 25.
[51] Genocide Convention, Article IV.

or otherwise assisting in or contributing to the commission or attempted commission of such a crime."[52]

Probably the most important legal proceeding that established the universality of individual responsibility apart from the international tribunals is the Pinochet case. In 1996, Spanish judge Manuel Garcia Castellon began looking into atrocities committed in Chile during the early reign of General Augusto Pinochet, as well as those carried out by several Latin American leaders during Operation Condor. (Operation Condor was a coordinated effort by the South American militaries to assassinate and disappear opponents across borders in Latin America, Europe, and the United States.) Judge Baltasar Garzon subsequently followed up and issued an arrest warrant and request for extradition of General Pinochet when he arrived in London for medical treatment. The British House of Lords denied sovereign immunity for Pinochet and allowed the extradition case to proceed.[53] Significantly, the British court further ruled that there was no former head-of-state immunity for certain international crimes, including torture.[54]

Pinochet's detention was the first time a former head of state was arrested based on the principle of universal jurisdiction. This was a significant challenge to the Act of State Doctrine (which traditionally immunized top government officials when acting in their official capacities) and reintroduced the idea that political leaders could be prosecuted for international crimes under the principle of universal jurisdiction.

It is clear from these precedents that the question of individual responsibility for such acts is no longer subject to state consent, although there is still debate over the specifics of jurisdiction and enforcement.

Crimes against Humanity

The closest the international community has come to determining exactly where to draw the line between routine human rights violations and a level

---

[52] International Law Commission, "Draft Articles on Prevention and Punishment of Crimes Against Humanity," Article VI(2)c.

[53] Under the British system, the House of Lords is the highest court in the land and acts as the supreme court of appeal. It also is the final authority on points of law for the whole of the United Kingdom in civil cases and for England, Wales, and Northern Ireland in criminal cases. Its decisions bind all lower courts.

[54] See Diana Woodhouse, *The Pinochet Case: A Legal and Constitutional Analysis* (Hart Publishing, 2000).

of internal state violence that is universally banned under international law is its efforts to identify what constitutes a crime against humanity. The term itself dates back to the 1915–1922 Armenian genocide, although there is a long history in natural law designating some forms of government violence as so egregious that they transcend the territorial jurisdiction of the king, emperor, or state.[55] The term is regularly evoked in contemporary legal, political, and popular discourse, and to some degree it has become a catch-all to describe different types of extreme state violence involving a variety of nefarious practices. It therefore does not describe any particular offense or act as much as it defines a broad category of offenses. As such, it is not always easy to define exactly what types of practices rise to the level of a crime against humanity, apart from the use of the term as a rhetorical device.

Crimes against humanity are distinguished from other acts of state violence in that political leaders consider them to be offenses against humankind itself, an attack on the essential idea of humanness.[56] These actions are viewed as demeaning to all members of the human race, wherever they live and whatever their culture or form of political organization. Political leaders consider them to be universally abominable because it strikes at the heart of something fundamental to the notion of being human, which is by definition universal. While there may appear to be some degree of natural law in this formulation, the contemporary concept of crimes against humanity is derived from the fundamental values of the international community developed by states rather than an abstract principle derived from a deity or eternal sense of morality. This provides the foundation for claiming universality and legitimizes the contention that no state may derogate from the prohibitions even in times of national emergency and threat.

Beyond this, crimes against humanity are defined by the level and scope of violence perpetrated by states against their own populations or those under their administration. They go beyond isolated acts of state violence to encompass the most extreme types of atrocities perpetrated on a grand scale. The definition is reserved for the most heinous acts, committed repeatedly, and encompassing widespread violations of the international community's most fundamental notion of human decency. It is the ultimate breach of human

---

[55] See Robert Dubler and Matthew Kalyk, *Crimes against Humanity in the 21st Century: Law, Practice, and Threats to International Peace and Security* (Brill/Nijhoff, 2018), chapter 1 and Taner Akcam, *The Young Turks' Crime against Humanity: The Armenian Genocide and Ethnic Cleansing in the Ottoman Empire* (Princeton University Press, 2015).

[56] David Luban, "A Theory of Crimes against Humanity," *Yale Journal of International Law*, vol. 29, 2004, p. 90.

rights. Thus, once the abuse of civilians surpasses a particular threshold, the prescriptions of international law are activated and individual perpetrators are held internationally liable for the acts that qualify.[57]

The term itself is purposely loaded. It describes not only acts that are inhumane but also ones that are criminal by definition, placing them in a unique category of international offenses. (It is hard to imagine a more dramatic formulation than designating an act as a crime against the entire human race.) Of the many legal norms under international law, only grave breaches in the laws of armed conflict ("war crimes") also include the word "crime" in their name. For this reason, most political leaders and legal analysts believe that there is little need to consider, discuss, or debate the degree to which such acts are illegal under international law, or even whether those committing them have legal liability (although there is still an ongoing debate over details). By definition, a crime is a public offense that is punishable under the law. The purpose of this designation is to hold individuals accountable for violations.

On the surface, then, this seems to be an easy case for universal law. Few would challenge the proposition that crimes against humanity, however defined, are illegal under any and all circumstances in international law. But what is the basis for this position? What specifically allows the international community to override the doctrines of consent and sovereignty to declare that these practices are not only illegal on their face—even when perpetrated within a state's own borders—but are also grounds for prosecuting those perpetrating it by international courts? How is this determination made, and who gets to make it?

Over the past several decades, states and international organizations have engaged in ongoing deliberation that cumulatively established this principle. Its foundation is rooted in several conventions (discussed below), as well as the series of multilateral procedures through which these texts were developed. It is supported by numerous resolutions approved by the UN General Assembly, the UN Security Council, and regional security organizations. Taken together, they provide strong evidence of an international consensus that this category of human rights violations is universally binding. This has been confirmed in judgments issued by a number of international judicial bodies, tribunals, and regional human rights courts.

---

[57] See Beth Van Schaack, "The Definition of Crimes against Humanity: Resolving the Incoherence," *Columbia Journal of Transnational Law*, vol. 37, no. 3, 1999.

Treaties and Statutes

The evolution of crimes against humanity into a universal category of offenses was progressively developed by states over several decades. The consensus around both its definition and universality is represented in five documents: the 1945 Charter of the International Military Tribunal (Nuremberg); the Statutes of the ICTY (1993) and ICTR (1994); Article 7 of the 1998 Rome Statute of the ICC; and the 2019 ILC Draft Articles on Prevention and Punishment of Crimes Against Humanity.[58] Each of these instruments defines the concept in a slightly different way—and there is still debate over some of the details—but all encompass the same idea: that systematic, one-sided mass violence against civilians warrants a special category of offense.[59]

At the moment, the ICC Statute is the most important and authoritative of these instruments inasmuch as it best represents the will of the international community of states. The Nuremberg statute was created by the four victorious states of World War II, and the Yugoslavia and Rwandan tribunals by the 15 members of the UN Security Council. It was not the intention of these statutes to define crimes against humanity as an offense under general international law, but rather to outline the scope of the Tribunals' jurisdiction over specific offenses committed in a specific set of circumstances.[60]

On the other hand, the ICC conception, articulated in Article 7 of the statute, is not only the most detailed but also the product of several years of multilateral negotiations involving representatives from 160 states, with the intent of outlining universal offenses against the international community.[61]

---

[58] Charter of the International Military Tribunal, London, 8 August 1945, Article 6; Statute of the International Criminal Tribunal for the former Yugoslavia, UN Doc. S/25704, annex, Article 5 (1993); International Criminal Tribunal for Rwanda, SC Res. 955, annex (8 November 1994); Rome Statute of the International Criminal Court, United Nations Treaty System, vol. 2187, entered into force 1 July 2002, Article 7; United Nations International Law Commission, "Draft Articles on Prevention and Punishment of Crimes against Humanity," *Yearbook of the International Law Commission*, vol. 2, part 2, 2019.

[59] Three issues have dominated the debate over definition during the drafting of these documents: first, whether any link with an armed conflict should be required; second, whether the widespread or systematic test should be cumulative or disjunctive; and third, whether there is any requirement for a policy, plan, or level of organization. For a detailed examination of this debate, as well as other related controversies that animated this discussion, see Dubler and Kalyk, *Crimes against Humanity in the 21st Century*, pp. 159–186.

[60] See Phyllis Hwang, "Defining Crimes against Humanity in the Rome Statute of the International Criminal Court," *Fordham International Law Journal*, vol. 22, no. 2, 1998, p. 478.

[61] Darryl Robinson, "Defining Crimes against Humanity at the Rome Conference," *The American Journal of International Law*, vol. 93, no. 1, January 1999, p. 43.

The process began with the ILC, which drafted a preliminary text of 68 articles based on extensive consultation with legal experts from a variety of states. In 1995, the United Nations General Assembly passed a resolution convening the United Nations Preparatory Committee on the Establishment of an International Criminal Court based on this text. After 19 weeks of formal meetings to draft a comprehensive statute, the Preparatory Committee sent to Rome a draft convention of 116 articles with 1,700 brackets containing disputed language.[62]

The process through which states would discuss and debate the language of the Statute followed the General Assembly's established internal politics, traditions, parliamentary practices, rules of procedure, and institutional memory. The General Assembly's Sixth Committee (the organization's primary forum for the consideration of international law and other legal matters concerning the United Nations) prepared the resolutions authorizing the establishment and annual meetings of the Preparatory Committee and the convening of the Rome Conference, which gave governments an opportunity to review the progress of the negotiations. This procedure led delegations to combine their ideas, thus producing documents that included the proposals of many states.

The process was also facilitated by the active involvement of NGOs and an epistemic community of international lawyers. In 1995, a group of the 25 largest human rights organizations from around the world formed the Coalition for the International Criminal Court (CICC) to pressure governments within the United Nations to develop and strengthen the ICC. By 1997, the Coalition had grown to 450 organizations. The CICC participated in the six sessions of the Preparatory Committee on the Establishment of the ICC, and its members attended the Rome Conference. The CICC successfully mobilized and coordinated different NGOs throughout the negotiations, increasing their influence on the final document.[63]

According to a number of delegates to the conference, there were issues on which the NGO influence was crucial to the outcome of particular statute provisions. This influence seems to have been both direct (when states

---

[62] John Washburn, "The Negotiation of the Rome Statute for the International Criminal Court and International Lawmaking in the 21st Century," *Pace International Law Review*, vol. 11, no. 2, 1999, p. 364 and Hwang, "Defining Crimes against Humanity in the Rome Statute of the International Criminal Court."

[63] William R. Pace and Jennifer Schense, "Coalition for the International Criminal Court at the Preparatory Commission," in Roy S. Lee and Hakan Friman (eds.), *The International Criminal Court: Elements of Crimes and Rules of Procedure and Evidence* (Transnational Publishers, 2001), pp. 391–394 and Claude E. Welch Jr. and Ashley F. Watkins, "Extending Enforcement: The Coalition for the International Criminal Court," *Human Rights Quarterly*, vol. 33, no. 4, November 2011.

followed the advice of NGOs to advocate for particular wordings in statutory provisions) and indirect (such as providing information and advice to states lobbying for particular positions through position papers or seeking informal contact with delegates).[64] Many delegates believed that NGOs had made a large difference to the level of debate and the substantive content of the ICC negotiations, particularly since they had specialized knowledge that many of the delegates lacked.[65]

The influence of legal experts (who acted independently from the diplomats) was particularly important during the early preparatory work, especially in the development of the ILC's 1994 Draft Statute for an ICC, the report of the 1995 Ad Hoc Committee for an ICC, and the final draft of the 1996 Preparatory Committee.[66] Each of these bodies was comprised primarily of legal counsels and analysts from a wide variety of states; their job was to develop a consensus around both the structure of the Court and the principles of international law that would constitute international criminal violations.

John Washburn describes the long process through which the Rome Statute was completed—from ILC draft to the conference where the final document was approved—as a "very different kind of multilateral legislation by parliamentary diplomacy."[67] Roy Lee similarly characterizes the final product as part legislation and part constitution, creating a new system of international criminal law.[68]

As the Appeals Chamber of the Special Court for Sierra Leone stated, the definition of crimes against humanity in the ICC Statute "reflects the consensus reached by all of the States negotiating the Statute of the ICC at the Rome Conference, and therefore is a valuable indication of the views of

---

[64] Zoe Pearson, "Non-Governmental Organizations and the International Criminal Court: Changing Landscapes of International Law," *Cornell International Law Journal*, vol. 39, no. 2, 2006, p. 254.
[65] See Pearson, "Non-Governmental Organizations and the International Criminal Court," p. 273.
[66] See Mahmoud Cherif Bassiouni, *The Legislative History of the International Criminal Court, vol. 1: Introduction, Analysis and Integrated Text* (Hotei Publishing, 2005). For the text of the drafts, see "Text Adopted by the International Law Commission at Its Forty-sixth Session," *Yearbook of the International Law Commission*, vol. 2, part 2, 1994; Report of the Ad Hoc Committee on the Establishment of an International Criminal Court, General Assembly Official Records, 50th Session Supplement No. 22 (A/50/22); and Report of the Preparatory Committee on the Establishment of an International Criminal Court, vol. 1, General Assembly Official Records, 51st Session Supplement No. 22 (A/51/22).
[67] Washburn, "The Negotiation of the Rome Statute for the International Criminal Court and International Lawmaking in the 21st Century," p. 366.
[68] Roy Lee, "The Rome Conference and Its Contribution to International Law," in Roy Lee (ed.), *The International Criminal Court: The Making of the Rome Statute: Issues, Negotiations and Results* (Martinus Nijhoff, 1999).

States and the international community generally on the question of what constitutes a common purpose."[69]

Beyond the consensus generated through months of deliberation, the Rome Statute also represents universal values that had been accepted by virtually all of the states present at the meetings, regardless of cultural traditions. Leila Sadat, special advisor on crimes against humanity to the ICC prosecutor, observed at the time that beyond the Western values represented in the texts, Chinese, Islamic, and Hindu traditions underscore the universal values enshrined in the prohibition of crimes that shock the conscience of humanity. Due to the importance of the collective values they protect, they considered these crimes to be truly international.[70] As a result, a consensus emerged among the delegates on the universality of the core international crimes, irrespective of cultural differences between states.[71]

Even those states that ultimately declined to ratify the Statue never objected to the proposition that the practices defined as crimes against humanity were illegal under general international law. Rather, they objected to the authority, operation, and jurisdiction of the Court itself.[72]

The Statute extended the scope of the ICC's authority to prosecute atrocities to include the entire community of states, including those who refused to sign the treaty, by permitting the UN Security Council to refer cases to the Court that involve states that are not parties to Statute. The Council later exercised this option by referring the situation in Sudan, a state that had explicitly chosen not to ratify the Rome Statute, to the ICC for prosecution.[73] The Council, of course, is not bound by the doctrine of consent, nor is it limited by treaty law. It can take action against any state or individual—even

---

[69] Special Court for Sierra Leone, *Prosecutor v Brima, Kamara and Kanu* (Appeals Chamber Judgment), Case No SCSL-2004-16-A (22 February 2008), p. 79.

[70] Cited in Iris Haenen, "Classifying Acts as Crimes against Humanity in the Rome Statute of the International Criminal Court," *German Law Journal*, vol. 14, no. 7, 2013, p. 804.

[71] See Haenen, "Classifying Acts as Crimes against Humanity in the Rome Statute," fn. 46.

[72] For example, although the United States signed but never ratified the treaty, American opposition was based primarily on the charge (mistaken, in my view) that the Court would become politicized and target American peacekeepers and diplomats who were innocent of any crime as a way to embarrass the United States. See Jack Goldsmith, "The Self-Defeating International Criminal Court," *University of Chicago Law Review*, vol. 70, no. 1, 2003 and BBC News, "US Renounces World Court Treaty," 6 May 2002, available at: http://news.bbc.co.uk/2/hi/americas/1970312.stm. Additionally, the decision by the African Union to encourage its members to withdraw from the Court was not based on a challenge to the designation of its core crimes as being universal, but rather on the fact that up to that point the Court's only cases involved African leaders, even though atrocities had been perpetrated in other regions of the world. See Sascha-Dominick D. Bachmann and Naa A. Sowatey-Adjei, "The African Union–ICC Controversy before the ICJ: A Way Forward to Strengthen International Criminal Justice?," *Washington Law Review*, vol. 29, no. 2, 2020.

[73] See Security Council Resolution 1593, S/RES/1593 (2005).

those that do not accept the legal norm—simply by evoking the breach of the peace clause (Chapter VII) of the UN Charter. This raises the prohibitions against genocide, crimes against humanity, and grave breaches in the laws of armed conflict to the status of universal law.

If and when the ILC Draft Articles are eventually transformed into a multilateral convention, it will likely become the definitive lawmaking treaty that formally universalizes the principle. The ILC has already gone to considerable lengths to create a statute that reflects the wide breadth of the international community. During the debate on the annual report that developed the first draft of the proposed treaty, for example, 52 states, the Council of Europe, and the Community of Latin American and Caribbean States submitted "observations" on the document. As of early 2020, written comments were also submitted from 38 additional states, seven international and regional organizations, and 700 NGOs and individuals.[74] Ultimately, an international conference will be convened to develop the detailed text of an agreement.

Although all of these documents share similar conceptions of what constitutes a crime against humanity, the distinguishing characteristic that moves a particular act from the realm of domestic politics to international law has not always been entirely clear.[75] In the first place, it was not until the UN Security Council established the ICTR in 1994 that the necessary connection between crimes against humanity and an armed conflict was finally broken. Unlike the ICTY, its definition did not require any nexus with any armed conflict, signifying a significant expansion of international law in the prohibition of extreme internal mass violence.[76] Since that time, every official definition of crimes against humanity includes actions taken by states against their own populations even in peacetime.

Moreover, in establishing the legal foundation for the Rwanda tribunal, the Security Council chose to take a more expansive approach to the choice of the applicable law than the one underlying the statute of the Yugoslavia tribunal. It included within the jurisdiction of the ICTR international instruments regardless of whether they were considered part of customary

---

[74] International Law Commission, "Fourth Report on Crimes against Humanity," 71st Session Geneva, 29 April–7 June and 8 July–9 August 2019, A/CN.4/725, p. 4.

[75] See Charles Chernor Jalloh, "What Makes a Crime against Humanity a Crime against Humanity," *American University International Law Review*, vol. 28, no. 2, 2013, p. 385.

[76] See Article 3 of the Statute of the International Criminal Tribunal for the Prosecution of Persons Responsible for Genocide and Other Serious Violations of International Humanitarian Law Committed in the Territory of Rwanda and Rwandan Citizens Responsible for Genocide and Other Such Violations Committed in the Territory of Neighbouring States, between 1 January 1994 and 31 December 1994, adopted by Security Council Resolution 955 (1994).

international law or whether they had customarily entailed the individual criminal responsibility of the perpetrator of the crime.[77]

Second, the term "crimes against humanity" has been employed often by many people as a rhetorical device to describe a wide range of practices, and in many cases it has become as much a political as a legal label. As such, its overuse threatens to trivialize the significance of the crime, undermine the confidence that it will be applied correctly by courts, and dissuade states from supporting international institutions that attempt to enforce it.[78]

Thus, in developing a "threshold test" for crimes against humanity, political leaders have determined that not every inhumane act constitutes such an offense. The ICC statute, for example, lists 11 acts that qualify—including murder, imprisonment, sexual abuse, and forced disappearances—but these acts in and of themselves, though heinous and illegal, are not necessarily offenses against the international community. Rather, the statutes stipulate that such acts must be committed as part of a (1) widespread or systematic attack (2) against a civilian population (3) directed by public officials with knowledge of the attacks (4) in pursuit of a state goal.[79] In other words, a crime against humanity is not defined by specific acts, regardless of how heinous they may be, but rather requires a pervasive course of conduct that meets a threshold of harm as part of a general policy.[80]

Thus, while states have established judicial institutions for the prosecution and penal sanction for the most heinous forms of state violence, not all acts of extreme violence fall into the category of crimes against humanity. In international law, an act can be illegal without being criminal.[81] Indeed, over the past few decades, states have agreed that there are some domestic

---

[77] See United Nations Secretary-General, "Report of the Secretary-General Pursuant to Paragraph 5 of Security Council Resolution 955 (1994)," UN Doc. S/1995/134 (13 February 1995).

[78] See Dubler and Kalyk, *Crimes against Humanity in the 21st Century*.

[79] The International Law Commission defines "widespread" as "massive, frequent, large scale action, carried out collectively with considerable seriousness and directed against a multiplicity of victims" and "systemic" as "thoroughly organized and following a regular pattern on the basis of a common policy involving substantial public or private resources." Quoted in Simon Chesterman, "An Altogether Different Order: Defining the Elements of Crimes against Humanity," *Duke Journal of Comparative and International Law*, vol. 10, no. 2, 2000, p. 315.

[80] For an excellent discussion of this point, as well as a detailed breakdown of how each of the requirements is defined in practice, see Chesterman, "An Altogether Different Order."

[81] Both legal scholars and political scientists make a distinction between the Law of Nations (commonly referred to as international law) and international criminal law. The former imposes obligations on states, while the latter focuses on individuals who may be held personally accountable for violations. Such individuals usually include high-level political leaders and those with command responsibilities. For a good discussion of international criminal law, see William Schabas, *Unimaginable Atrocities: Justice, Politics, and Rights at the War Crimes Tribunals* (Oxford University Press, 2012), chapter 1.

practices that violate fundamental human rights law on their face, even if they are not sustained, persistent, or part of a broader systemic campaign of violence. These include torture, mass attacks on civilians, and persecution against defined groups. This determination has been expressed through an interlocking set of lawmaking treaties, declarations by the UN and regional organizations, and a wide variety of other soft law instruments, all of which moved through various multilateral processes. This is the focus of the next three chapters.

4
The Violent Persecution of Minorities

One of the oldest forms of internal state violence is persecution, defined as state action or policy designed to inflict upon an individual or group harassment, torment, suffering, or harm based on the victim's personal beliefs or membership in an identifiable group.[1] Like all forms of internal mass violence, it is directed primarily against a state's own population in the pursuit of official policy. Unlike other forms, however, it is targeted at individuals not for what they do but for who they are, based either on the innate or unchangeable characteristic of the particular social group of which they are a member (such as ethnicity or race) or on a shared collective characteristic or belief that is fundamental to one's identity or conscience (such as religion).[2] In either case, persecution is aimed at particular individuals precisely because they are part of a targeted group. This differentiates it from state violence aimed at political opponents who may engage in dissent or resistance.

When governments engage in violent persecution on a mass scale against national, ethnic, religious, or racial groups, they cross the threshold that designates the act as a universally illegal practice under all circumstances.

This chapter will focus on how the legal prohibition of mass violence against particular social groups became a universal principle under general international law, and how this reflects the special status that international human rights law extends to the integrity of certain defined groups and its members. In doing so, it will examine the special protection given to national, ethnic, religious, and racial minorities. I argue that this status favors groups possessing a definable social characteristic that is considered to be innate or cultural—such as ethnicity, race, or religion—rather than political beliefs or ideologies.

---

[1] Cherif Bassiouni developed this composite definition by surveying linguistic and legal formulations from 16 countries. See his *Crimes against Humanity in International Criminal Law* (Kluwer Law International, 1999), p. 327. The addition of "group" to this definition is mine.

[2] Joseph Rikhof and Ashley Geerts, "Protected Groups in Refugee Law and International Law," *Laws*, vol. 8, no. 4, 2019, article 25, at https://doi.org/10.3390/laws8040025.

Persecution as a Practice

Persecution had been an enduring practice by political authorities long before the rise of the nation-state system. Historically, the term referred almost exclusively to actions taken by authorities against religious groups, dating back to Roman attacks on Jews and early Christians in ancient Rome, and the persecution of Buddhists in Imperial China, particularly during the Tang dynasty.[3] This practice was also employed extensively by authorities within the Catholic Church, first against heretics (during the 13th-century Inquisition) and later against Protestants and Jews (during the 16th century).[4] While religious persecution continued long after these periods, over time the target groups expanded to include ethnic, racial, and national minorities. This reflected changes in the political organization of the state, a transformation that made these categories significant in defining the political community.

Like most human rights norms, persecution was not addressed in international law until after World War II, inspired not only by the Holocaust but also by the Armenian genocide and other 20th-century state violence against national minorities in Europe.

Much of the academic research and legal analysis on persecution in contemporary international law relates to the 1951 Refugee Convention and the 1967 Protocol. Under these treaties, a "well-founded fear of being persecuted" is the sole basis for claiming refugee status.[5] Such a claim is not based on an allegation that a particular type of state violence is itself a violation of international law. Rather it is based on an individual's fear of harm from the state, so long as such a claim is reasonable and sincere (thus, "well-founded"). Ever since the treaty entered into force, legal analysts, domestic courts, and political leaders have engaged in extensive debate over the subjective and objective elements necessary to establish this status within their own countries.[6]

---

[3] Jaakko Kuosmanen, "What's So Special about Persecution?," *Ethical Theory and Moral Practice*, vol. 17, no. 1 (February 2014), p. 131. See also Richard Smith, "Buddhism and the Great Persecution in China," in Kenneth Keulman (ed.), *Critical Moments in Religious History* (Mercer University Press, 1993).

[4] For one interesting account, see Christine Caldwell Ames, *Righteous Persecution: Inquisition, Dominicans, and Christianity in the Middle Ages* (University of Pennsylvania Press, 2008).

[5] 1951 Convention Relating to the Status of Refugees, Article 1A(2).

[6] The literature on the definition of persecution in the Refugee Convention and Protocols is far too numerous to cite. For a good overview of the debates on this matter, see José H. Fischel De Andrade, "On the Development of the Concept of 'Persecution' in International Refugee Law," *Brazilian Yearbook of International Law*, vol. 2, 2006. See also UN High Commissioner on Refugees, *Handbook*

Significantly, however, this aspect of international law is not concerned with persecution as a practice. The treaties not only fail to specify what kind of state action would constitute persecution; they do not even designate persecution as an illegal practice. In fact, there is still no universally accepted definition of "persecution" in refugee law, and various attempts to formulate such a definition have met with little success.[7]

Indeed, international refugee law does not even impose any obligations or restrictions on states regarding the treatment of those who are forced to flee their territory. Rather, the obligations are shifted to the receiving states, specifying the conditions under which they must accept refugees once they leave their country of origin. In refugee law, persecution is simply a label attributed to individuals who are victims, or potential victims, of targeted state violence. This individualized notion of persecution is similar to the concept found in the Universal Declaration of Human Rights, which simply holds that "everyone has the right to seek and to enjoy in other countries asylum from persecution."[8]

To understand the restrictions imposed on states regarding the practices that amount to persecution, we need to explore an entirely different area of international law, one that addresses those aspects of internal state violence that is directed specifically at what is known as "particular social groups."[9] This aspect focuses not on the rights of individuals to political asylum or refuge but on the legal restrictions imposed on governments regarding the specific actions and practices they may employ against targeted populations. This is the aspect that I discuss in this chapter.

This area of persecution law falls into the broad category of mass state violence perpetrated against its own population. The universal prohibition against such acts can be derived from a wide range of treaties, legal opinions, soft law, and organizational resolutions, even in cases where state practice does not conform to the legal norm. The documents that define persecution as an international crime include the 1950 Nuremberg Principles adopted by the UN General Assembly; the Statutes of the ICTY and ICTR; the 1998

on Procedures and Criteria for Determining Refugee Status under the 1951 Convention and the 1967 Protocol Relating to the Status of Refugees, reedited, 1992.

[7] UN High Commissioner on Refugees, *Handbook on Procedures and Criteria for Determining Refugee Status*, para. 51.
[8] Universal Declaration of Human Rights, Article 14.1.
[9] The term is used as a tag line in the Refugee Convention (Article 1, A2); however, it has since become a standard for determining who constitutes a protected class.

Rome Statute of the ICC; the Statute of the Special Court for Sierra Leone; the 2004 Law on the Extraordinary Chambers in the Courts of Cambodia; the 2015 Kosovo Law on Specialist Chambers and Specialist Prosecutor's Office; the 2019 International Law Commission Draft Articles on Prevention and Punishment of Crimes Against Humanity; and the 2014 Statute of the African Court of Justice and Human Rights (as amended by the Malabo Protocol).[10]

All of these documents list persecution as one element that could constitute a crime against humanity; however, not all consider it to be a crime unto itself. For some, such as the Rome Statute, it is only a predicate act when it occurs as part of a broader systemic campaign of mass violence involving at least one of the other elements (for example, mass murder).[11] For most, however, persecution does not require any connection to other state actions in order to be considered an international criminal act, so long as it is committed as part of a widespread or systematic attack against a civilian population. The debate over this "connection nexus" is the primary source of difference among the various documents, rulings, and agreements.[12] In all cases, however, there is a clear consensus that violent persecution is a universally illegal practice regardless of its context.

At its core, the concept of persecution has three necessary elements: (1) unwarranted discrimination against members of a particular social group; (2) an asymmetrical, systemic threat against this group; and (3) violent oppression perpetrated by the state or other authorities that follows this threat.[13] The target does not have to possess objective features that will easily identify it as a discernable social group (although it usually does). International

---

[10] Rome Statute of the International Court, Article 7; International Law Commission, "Principles of International Law Recognized in the Charter of the Nürenberg Tribunal and in the Judgment of the Tribunal," 1950; Statute of the International Criminal Tribunal for the Former Yugoslavia, Article 5(h); Statute of the International Criminal Tribunal for Rwanda, Article 3(h); Statute of the Special Court for Sierra Leone, established by an Agreement between the United Nations and the Government of Sierra Leone pursuant to Security Council Resolution 1315 (2000), Article 2(h); Law on the Establishment of the Extraordinary Chambers (Cambodia), as promulgated on 27 October 2004, Article 5; International Law Commission, "Draft Articles on Prevention and Punishment of Crimes against Humanity," *Yearbook of the International Law Commission*, vol. 2, part 2, 2019, article 2(h); Malabo Protocol, adopted by the 23rd Ordinary Session of the Assembly, Malabo, Equatorial Guinea, 27 June 2014, Article 28C(1)(h).

[11] In criminal law, a predicate act is one that provides the resources for, or contains some of the elements of, a more serious crime.

[12] Of the documents cited above, the Rome Statute, the ILC Draft Articles, and Nuremberg Principles require a connection between persecution and a broader campaign of state violence.

[13] See Michelle Foster, "The 'Ground with the Least Clarity': A Comparative Study of Jurisprudential Developments relating to 'Membership of a Particular Social Group,'" United Nations High Commissioner for Refugees, Legal and Protection Policy Research Series 25, Geneva, 2012.

law also encompasses acts taken against a collectivity of individuals who are perceived by the perpetrator to belong to such a group.[14]

Discrimination as the Foundation of Persecution

Discrimination is government policy or action that nullifies or impairs the enjoyment of rights and freedoms that are guaranteed to the general population, based on the characteristics of a targeted group.[15] It could also involve preferences or special rights provided to one group at the expense of another. It differs from other types of human rights violations in that it is motivated by a prejudicial distinction that distinguishes the targeted group from a dominant one based on certain generalized traits. Most people are familiar with such categorization as it pertains to characteristics such as nationality, religion, gender, ethnicity, and race.

On its face, basing public policy or state action on any of these categorizations is anathema to the fundamental concept of human rights inasmuch as it violates the principle that all individuals share these rights equally, and therefore they should apply to all persons without unwarranted exceptions.[16] However discrimination is a contested concept; there is no general agreement on who counts as a protected class and what constitutes "unwarranted" discrimination.

Indeed, discrimination is not only an enduring practice in human history; it continues to be widely employed in every region of the world. However, since the end of World War II, it has been legally prohibited, at least in general terms, in almost all major human rights agreements, mostly within the context of guaranteeing equality before the law "without distinction." In some cases this prohibition is aspirational—such as the United Nations Charter, which "promotes and encourages" nondiscrimination, and the Universal Declaration of Human Rights, which states that all persons "are entitled" without any discrimination to the equal protection of the law.[17] In

---

[14] Ken Roberts, "Striving for Definition: the Law of Persecution from Its Origins to the ICTY," in Hirad Abtahi and Gideon Boas (eds.), *The Dynamics of International Criminal Justice: Essays in Honour of Sir Richard May* (Martinus Nijhoff, 2005), p. 577.

[15] UN Human Rights Committee, General Comment 18 on Non-Discrimination, adopted at the 37th Session, 1989; UN Document HRI/GEN/1Rev.6, p. 146.

[16] Curtis Doebbler, *The Principle of Non-Discrimination in International Law* (DC Publishers, 2007), p. 1.

[17] See Article 1 of the UN Charter and Article 7 of the Universal Declaration of Human Rights.

other cases, resolutions passed by international organizations, multilateral conferences, and regional organizations condemning discrimination tend to be political statements rather than legal opinions.[18]

Some human rights treaties, however, include a general legal prohibition against discrimination against protected classes, for example the International Covenants on Civil and Political Rights (ICCPR) and Social, Economic, and Cultural Rights.[19] Importantly, although the ICCPR permits states to derogate from much of the treaty in times of "national emergency" (as discussed in Chapter 1), it may not do so if it involves "discrimination solely on the ground of race, color, sex, language, religion or social origin."[20]

In addition to these broad human rights agreements, there are conventions that focus on protecting specific groups from discrimination, such as the International Convention on the Elimination of All Forms of Racial Discrimination, the Convention on the Elimination of Discrimination against Women, and the International Convention on the Suppression and Punishment of the Crime of Apartheid (see below).

Discrimination is also prohibited in virtually all contemporary treaties regulating armed conflict. The first, third, and fourth Geneva Conventions of 1949 ban the practice on the basis of sex, race, nationality, religion, or political beliefs in the treatment of prisoners of war and in relation to the civilian population.[21]

At the same time, most discrimination is shielded from international law by the institution of sovereignty. In practice, international law treats some types of discrimination much differently than others. The principle of nondiscrimination does not prohibit states from making legal distinctions between groups in all forms, but rather requires a legal justification by the

---

[18] See, for example, the declaration issued by the World Conference against Racism, Racial Discrimination, Xenophobia and Related Intolerance, in Durban, South Africa, from 31 August to 8 September 2001 and the Beijing Declaration, issued by the Fourth World Conference on Women, September 1995.

[19] Article 2 of the ICCPR and part 2, Article 2 of the International Covenant on Economic, Social and Cultural Rights provide, in part, that "the rights recognized in the present Covenant" should be respected "without distinction of any kind, such as race, colour, sex, language, religion, political or other opinion, national or social origin, property, birth or other status." Similarly Article 26 of the International Covenant on Civil and Political Rights provides that "the law shall prohibit any discrimination and guarantee to all persons equal and effective protection against discrimination."

[20] UN General Assembly, *International Covenant on Civil and Political Rights*, 16 December 1966, United Nations, Treaty Series, vol. 999, articles.

[21] Geneva Convention for the Amelioration of the Condition of the Wounded and Sick in Armed Forces in the Field of 12 August 1949, Article 12; Geneva Convention Relative to the Treatment of Prisoners of War of 12 August 1949, Articles 25–27; Geneva Convention Relative to the Protection of Civilian Persons in Time of War of 12 August 1949, Article 13.

state for any discrimination against individuals belonging to a certain protected group.[22] Thus, many forms of discrimination are not only widely practiced but also tolerated.[23]

For example, virtually all countries in the world legally discriminate between citizens and noncitizens, and international law has no authority over immigration and citizenship. The overwhelming majority of states have an official language, which discriminates against those whose primary means of communication is not the native tongue. Virtually all societies legally restrict the enjoyment of certain rights based on age (at both ends). More subtly, many public institutions privilege the dominant culture over others, by discriminating in their favor in schools, literature and the arts, religious practices, media, and national holidays.[24]

In addition to prejudicial action against these groups, there are other forms of discrimination, such as those based on class, gender, or national origin. However, these are not universally condemned in international law, and there appears to be a lack of global consensus on the degree to which states may legally make such distinctions. Indeed, many countries' constitutions specifically discriminate on these grounds, particularly those that have a national religion or ethnic foundation for the state.[25]

This raises questions about how to define and classify a protected group under international law. Carola Lingaas, for example, argues that categories like gender and race are socially constructed rather than biologically given, and that they should therefore be studied in the context of the society in which they are used rather than by an objective standard.[26] Thus, there is a certain degree of subjectivity that is built into legal definitions of protected groups. At the same time, the degree to which a particular political distinction constitutes legitimate discrimination can be determined by whether

---

[22] See Mpoki Mwakagali, "International Human Rights Law and Discrimination Protections: A Comparison of Regional and National Responses, *Brill Research Perspectives in Comparative Discrimination Law*, vol. 1, no. 2, 2017, p. 2.

[23] See the most current reports by Amnesty International at https://www.amnesty.org/en/countries.

[24] See John Hutchinson, "Cultural Nationalism," in John Breuilly (ed.), *The Oxford Handbook of the History of Nationalism* (Oxford University Press, 2013).

[25] Currently, 43 countries have a state religion, 13 of which specify the national religion in their constitutions. Thirteen constitutions specify an ethnic foundation for the state. See Harriet Sherwood, "More Than 20% of Countries Have Official State Religions—Survey," *The Guardian*, 3 October 2017; Library of Congress, "Constitutional Provisions on National and Religious Identity," at https://www.loc.gov/law/help/national-religious-identity/constitutional-provisions.php#III-countries.

[26] Carola Lingaas, *The Concept of Race in International Criminal Law* (Routledge, 2020).

there is a sufficient connection between such distinction and the nature of the particular right itself, that is, whether the distinction is rationally related to the right or whether it is based on an arbitrary or prejudicial view of the group that is being excluded.

For example, the denial of certain rights to minors is premised on the proposition that they are not mature enough to assume the responsibilities attached to those particular rights. This may appear to be an easy case; however, not all societies define maturity in the same way and there is disagreement over which rights are rationally related to age.

One can conclude from this that in and of itself, nondiscrimination is not a universal norm under international law, although it is certainly widely condemned in diplomatic practice.

Persecution as Oppression

While discrimination is a necessary element in defining persecution as an illegal practice, it is a passive component. Absent coercive or violent action by the state, discrimination in and of itself is not considered an international crime, nor is it part of general international law. It is transformed into a crime of mass violence only when it is coupled with a general systemic threat against a target group followed by violent oppression. Thus, for example, the Rome Statute defines persecution as "the intentional and severe deprivation of fundamental rights contrary to international law by reason of the identity of the group or collectivity," which is essentially discrimination, but it does not constitute an international crime under the treaty unless it is committed as part of a widespread or systematic attack directed against a civilian population.[27]

By this conceptualization, discrimination alone covers circumstances where lesser harms occur, whereas persecution denotes harm that is severe and sustained.

Persecution can assume a variety of forms, some of which I discuss below. However, all types are focused on a target group that the state deems to be (1) undesirable, (2) a threat to the dominant institutions, or (3) one

---

[27] UN General Assembly, *Rome Statute of the International Criminal Court (as Amended 2010)*, 17 July 1998, Article 7, (1)h.

whose very existence is an obstacle to state policy or ideology.[28] All acts of persecution, then, involve serious violations of universally recognized fundamental rights that political authorities infringe on discriminatory grounds.

This raises two questions that are central to determining the degree to which persecution is universally banned under international law regardless of state agreement or consent.

First, where does international law draw the line between routine repression, which is present in many if not most countries, and a level of violence that transforms it into an international legal issue that extends beyond diplomatic concern? In general terms, the concept of persecution encompasses a broad set of state policies and actions aimed at harassing and depriving members of particular social groups basic rights enjoyed by the rest of the population. However, to reach the level of an international criminal act, the standard is much higher. The ICTY, for example, ruled that persecution involves acts that reach the same level of gravity and severity as crimes against humanity, including murder, extermination, enslavement, deportation, imprisonment, and torture.[29]

Similarly, in trying to determine what constitutes persecution for the definition of a refugee, the European Union delineates it as "those acts that are sufficiently serious by their nature or repetition as to constitute a severe violation of basic human rights, in particular the rights from which derogation cannot be made."[30] Simple discrimination, no matter how distasteful and unjust, is not enough, and there is no definitive list of what constitutes discrimination. At the same time, the reference to nonderogation in defining persecution suggests both the level of seriousness required and its universality, that is, its applicability beyond any specific legal commitments based on choice or consent. To be nonderogable, a legal norm must prevail under any and all circumstances, irrespective of protest, recognition, or acquiescence.[31]

---

[28] UN High Commissioner on Refugees, *Handbook on Procedures and Criteria for Determining Refugee Status*, para. 78.

[29] ICTY, *Prosecutor v. Krstić*, "Judgement," IT-98-33-T, 2 August 2001, para. 535; *Prosecutor v. Blakic*, Case No. IT-95-14-A, Judgment 135 (29 July 2004).

[30] International Association of Refugee Law Judges, European Chapter, "Qualification for International Protection" (Directive 2011/95/EU), December 2016. See also Council Directive 2004/83/EC of 29 April 2004 on the minimum standards for the status of third-country nationals or stateless persons as refugees.

[31] See International Law Commission, "Draft Articles on State Responsibility," *Yearbook of the ILC*, vol. 2, 1976, article 19, p. 73.

Second, how does international law determine what constitutes a protected class for the purpose of defining persecution? As mentioned above, the literature on persecution refers to "members of particular social groups" as constituting such a class. Such groups are those with an immutable or innate characteristic that is (1) beyond the power of an individual to change, (2) so fundamental to their individual identity or conscience that it ought not be required to be changed, or (3) defined by a former status and unalterable due to its historical permanence.[32] This collectivity must be clearly identifiable as a group in society, in which its members share a common characteristic (beyond simply being persecuted) that both unites them and distinguishes them from society at large.

Much of the work on designating these groups revolves around the question of how to define refugees. The 1951 Refugee Convention and the 1969 Convention Governing the Specific Aspects of Refugee Problems in Africa define a refugee as one with a well-founded fear of being persecuted "for reasons of race, religion, nationality, membership of a particular social group or political opinion."[33] This, however, applies only to the grounds on which a signatory is obligated to accept a refugee entering their country. The Nuremberg Charter and the Statutes of the ICTY and the ICTR were concerned with persecution as state action, but their list of persecuted groups was narrower, citing "political, racial, or religious" grounds.[34]

The Rome Statute of the ICC expanded the set to include "any identifiable group or collectivity on political, racial, national, ethnic, cultural, religious, gender ... or other grounds that are universally recognized as impermissible under international law."[35] The domestic laws of many states adopt an even broader list, including sexual orientation, gender, family, age, disability, economic or social class, and former status.[36]

Collectively, this demonstrates a firm prohibition against persecution against protected groups in international law. Defining persecution based on political belief or association as a universal criminal act, however, is trickier. Political persecution involves targeting those who hold particular views, are

---

[32] Foster, "The 'Ground with the Least Clarity.' "
[33] Convention and Protocol Relating to the Status of Refugees, Article 1(A)2; Organisation of African Unity Convention Governing the Specific Aspects of Refugee Problems in Africa, Article 1(1).
[34] Statute of the International Criminal Tribunal for the Former Yugoslavia, Article 5(h); Statute of the International Criminal Tribunal for Rwanda, Article 3(h).
[35] Rome Statute of the International Criminal Court, Article 7(1)h.
[36] Foster, "The 'Ground with the Least Clarity,' " pp. 20–23.

members of a particular political party or dissident group, or are associated with an opposition movement.[37] Many scholars do not view those being targeted for being dissidents or political opponents as being persecuted in the same sense as those who are members of particular social groups. Indeed, many distinguish between repression (physical violence or coercion against political targets to suppress certain types of actions and thought) and oppression (violence directed against groups who are primarily targeted for who they are rather than their political activities).[38] Titus Stahl, for example, argues that unlike political repression, the targets of oppression are members of disadvantaged social groups who are victimized in order to benefit dominant groups controlling the state.[39]

Although political grounds are included in virtually all legal definitions of persecution—and have been routinely cited by all of the international criminal tribunals—distinguishing political persecution from other forms of repression is often difficult. The term "repression" is not used in any of the legal documents or court rulings mentioned above. If the crux of persecution is discriminatory targeting based on some kind of group characteristic, then repression does not qualify as a form of persecution. This doesn't mean that political repression is not a serious violation of human rights, but it does challenge those who hold that it should be included in the definition of persecution.

Technically, political opinion or association as a reason for violent action by the state does not meet the three criteria listed above constituting a particular social group. While we can debate the degree to which one's political views are fundamental to one's individual identity or conscience, in practical terms those holding similar political views are rarely defined as a group or class in the same way that ethnicity and religion define a group. Moreover, political groups lack the homogeneity and stability necessary to grant eligible group status, and the threat to political groups is less when compared to other group types.[40]

---

[37] Roberts, "Striving for Definition," p. 593.
[38] James C Franklin, "Human Rights on the March: Repression, Oppression, and Protest in Latin America," *International Studies Quarterly*, vol. 64, no. 1, March 2020 and Charles Crabtree and Christian Davenport, "Contentious Politics in the Trump Era: Defining the Terms of Debate: Repression, Oppression, and Discrimination," *PS: Political Science and Politics*, vol. 51, no. 1, 2018.
[39] Titus Stahl, "Collective Responsibility for Oppression," *Social Theory and Practice*, vol. 43, no. 3, 2017.
[40] Jera White, "Genocide: New Understandings of an Age-Old Horror," unpublished manuscript.

Of course sometimes distinctions are not easy to make. The brutal repression/persecution of the Falun Gong movement by the Chinese government illustrates this problem. Falun Gong is difficult to characterize. It is not exactly either a religion or a political movement, although it has some characteristics of both. Falun Gong philosophy is spiritual and avows a path to salvation for the faithful through meditation and controlled physical movement/exercise. Adherents try to gain enlightenment by reading the works of founder Li Hongzhi—who advocates purifying one's body in another dimension and freeing one from bodily concerns—and following a moral code of truthfulness, benevolence, and forbearance.[41] There is a strong element of mysticism in the philosophy.

It is a relatively large movement; estimates are in the millions, making it the largest NGO in China, and some of its adherents are also members of the Chinese Communist Party. Its protest demonstration at the Communist Party headquarters in 1999 brought out 10,000 to 15,000 adherents, a very large political gathering for a nonsanctioned event.[42] The Chinese government has since banned the group and imprisoned and tortured thousands of its members. Still, at least some outside investigators consider Falun Gong to exhibit characteristics of a cult and suggest that they deliberately try to provoke violent action by the Chinese authorities.[43] This makes it difficult, at least conceptually, to determine whether the government reaction is a classic case of state repression against a potentially threatening political movement or oppression of a religious/spiritual body.

It is also ambiguous when considering state violence against an ethnic or national group seeking autonomy or secession (as in the case of the Kosovar Albanians in Serbia in the late 1990s) or when such violence is targeted against an adversary during an armed conflict or civil war (as in the case of the Bosniaks in Bosnia in the early 1990s). In both cases, violent action by state authorities could be related to the civil conflict rather than oppression of a minority group. Moreover, in cases such as these, ethnicity or religion is intertwined with designation as an enemy combatant.

---

[41] The best objective study of the movement I have found is Chang Maria Hsia, *Falun Gong: The End of Days* (Yale University Press, 2012).

[42] Benjamin Penny, "The Past, Present and Future of Falun Gong," National Library of Australia, Canberra, 2001.

[43] See, for example, James Lewis, *Falun Gong: Spiritual Warfare and Martyrdom: Elements in Religion and Violence* (Cambridge University Press, 2018).

Protection of Minority Groups

The targets of most persecution violence are minority groups, although there are a few cases (such as the Afrikaners in apartheid South Africa) where a minority used its power to oppress a majority. Like persecution in general, the oppression of minority groups predates the nation-state system. However the evolution of the centralized territorial state not only accentuated the categorization of various ethnic, racial, and religious characteristics within societies; it created minority groups as a category.[44] It also led to collective efforts to prohibit persecution of those designated as protected classes through international law.

The 1789 French Revolution largely institutionalized the ideas of both nationality and national citizenship in which the population shared an equal political status within the territory. So long as one was French, other physical, cultural, or historical characteristics did not matter.[45] However, in establishing what was then a radical democratic principle, it also inadvertently institutionalized the distinction between citizen and foreigner. Citizenship was linked to nationality (Frenchness). In theory, a nation-state is a nation's state, the state of and for a particular, bounded, sovereign nation, to which foreigners, by definition, do not belong.[46] This provided a clear separation between in-groups and out-groups. The institution of sovereignty further provided to each territorial state both autonomy from interference by other states and a national identity in which foreigners are not equal members. This, of course, raised the question of who constituted a foreigner.

The European nation-state was not built from scratch, but rather evolved over time from existing empires, kingdoms, principalities, and duchies in which the identities of the populations were largely irrelevant. In fact, the great empires of central, eastern, and southeastern Europe (Habsburg, Ottoman, Prussian, and Russian) contained many nationalities and

---

[44] Hannah Arendt argues that the creation of the "national minority" as a permanent institution—a *modus vivendi* between different ethnic groups living in the same territory—was not introduced until after World War I. See Hannah Arendt, "Concerning Minorities," *Contemporary Jewish Record*, vol. 8, no. 3, 1945, p. 359.

[45] This, of course, avoids the question of what it means to be "French." At the time, the nationalism of the French Revolution was based more on historic ties than on a sense of ethnic or linguistic solidarity; it included all of those living in France who were permanent residents of the country, regardless of social class or background. To be French was to be a French citizen. See Carlton J. Hayes, *The Historical Evolution of Modern Nationalism* (Russell and Russell, 1968), p. 69 and Eric J. Hobsbawm, *Nations and Nationalism since 1780* (Cambridge University Press, 1990), p. 86.

[46] This clever phrase is from William Rogers Brubaker, "The French Revolution and the Invention of Citizenship," *French Politics and Society*, vol. 7, no. 3, Summer 1989, p. 43.

ethnicities, all united by loyalty to the emperor or king. When these empires and smaller principalities transformed into territorial-based nation-states, state-builders inherited from the *ancien régimes* populations with diverse cultural, historical, religious, and ethnic backgrounds. This meant that although the ideal-type nation-state was one that theoretically merged a distinct nationality with a defined territory, in reality most states had large numbers of minorities.

This condition was exported to newly created developing countries following decolonization, particularly in Africa. The colonial powers created new states based on their former colonial boundaries rather than the traditional kinship or tribal distribution of the indigenous populations that existed within the kingdoms, city-states, and decentralized local political units prior to colonialization. Almost without exception, all African states had ethnically mixed populations, making it difficult for the newly formed states to build a unified citizenry based on the European concept of nationality.[47]

In theory, the liberal state (such as postrevolutionary France) addressed this problem by eschewing distinctions within the population, welcoming all citizens as political equals.[48] However the ideologies of nationalism, ethnocentrism, theocracy, and racism provide a justification for making just these distinctions. Within this environment, minorities become political outsiders whose identities do not fit the criteria defining political membership in the sovereign jurisdiction on whose territory they reside.[49] Under these circumstances, minority status becomes a liability and an easy target for state authorities who represent the dominant notion of nationality.

Seeing a threat to the stability and coherence of the state system, political leaders began to develop international legal and diplomatic rules against the persecution of religious, ethnic, and national groups within the units that formed out of the declining or collapsing empires in the late 19th and early 20th centuries. However, it was not until the mid- to late 20th century that these protections began to emerge as broad legal obligations based on general principles that applied to a wide range of states. Prior to this, specific

---

[47] T. A. Elliot demonstrates, for example, how tribal identities in Africa had to become reclassified as national when they became attached to a particular territory after decolonization. See his *Us and Them: A Study in Group Consciousness* (Aberdeen University Press, 1986). See also Robert Jackson, *Quasi-States: Sovereignty, International Relations and the Third World* (Cambridge University Press, 1993).

[48] See John Rawls's concept of the "veil of ignorance" in *A Theory of Justice* (Harvard University Press, 1971).

[49] See Jennifer Jackson Preece, "Minority Rights in Europe: From Westphalia to Helsinki," *Review of International Studies*, vol. 23, no. 1, 1997, p. 75.

minorities were afforded diplomatic and legal protection within target states in exchange for international recognition, usually following major wars or territorial reorganization. The primary purpose of these protections was to stabilize the newly created states, particularly in regions where large numbers of minority populations existed.[50]

For example, the 1878 Treaty of Berlin provided for the protection of religious minorities against persecution in the newly recognized states of Serbia, Montenegro, Bulgaria, and Romania; accepting these protections was the price of recognition.[51] However, these obligations were limited to the specific territories, and only religious minorities were protected. In some cases, the protection of religious minorities served a diplomatic purpose, such as the provisions in the bilateral 1829 Treaty of Peace between Russia and Turkey, providing for the protection of Christians within the Ottoman Empire.[52]

The focus shifted to national minorities following the conclusion of World War I. The end of the war and ensuing collapse of four empires had resulted in the creation of nine new states in central, eastern, and southeastern Europe, and all were required to accept legal protections for their minority populations as a precondition of diplomatic recognition. The minority rights agreements provided for full nationality and citizenship to all inhabitants, nondiscrimination in civil and political rights, and the right of all citizens to use their own language and maintain their own charitable and social institutions.[53]

In all, five states were compelled to sign minority rights treaties (Czechoslovakia, Yugoslavia, Greece, Romania, and Poland); four had to accept minority rights obligations as part of the general peace treaties (Austria, Hungary, Bulgaria, and Turkey); and five more were required to issue public declarations for the protection of minorities to the Council of the League of Nations as the condition of admission to the organization (Albania, Estonia, Iraq, Lithuania, and Latvia).[54] These protections were legal obligations; however, they were restricted only to newly created states in eastern and central Europe.

---

[50] Bruce Cronin, *Institutions for the Common Good: International Protection Regimes in International Society* (Cambridge University Press, 2003).

[51] See "Treaty of Berlin, July 13, 1878," in Fred L. Israel (ed.), *Major Peace Treaties of Modern History: 1648–1967* (Chelsea House Publishers, 2002), article 27, pp. 985–986.

[52] Treaty of Peace between Russia and Turkey, signed at Adrianople, 14 September 1829, BFSP XVI, p. 647, arts. V and VII.

[53] See Inis Claude, *National Minorities: An International Problem* (Harvard University Press, 1955), pp. 17–20.

[54] Oscar Janowsky, *Nationalities and National Minorities* (Macmillan, 1945).

Following the end of World War II, the international community expanded the protection of minorities from mass persecution to encompass all states. In particular, it stipulated three of the most extreme forms of persecution as constituting violations of general international law: genocide, ethnic cleansing, and apartheid.

Genocide

The violent persecution of minorities reached an apex during the 1933–1945 period in central and eastern Europe. Apart from the 6 million Jews whom the Nazis systematically enslaved, tortured, and killed during the Holocaust, the German state also murdered up to 5 million Roma (Gypsies), Jehovah's Witnesses, gays, Poles, and other minorities during this period.[55] In a 1941 radio broadcast, Winston Churchill referred to this as a "crime without a name."[56] Three years later, Raphael Lemkin gave it a name, "genocide," a term that has since evoked passion, emotion, debate, and outrage whenever it is employed.[57]

Genocide is presented in most human rights and international law literature as a distinct form of state aggression; indeed most people consider it to be the most heinous form of government violence. Nuremberg prosecutor Champetier de Ribes labeled it "the greatest crime of all," while the International Criminal Tribunal for Rwanda's final judgment declared it to be "the crime of all crimes."[58] Legal scholar Matthew Lippman referred to genocide as "the crime of the century" and posited that "genocide is the most elemental of human rights violations. . . . [Its costs] are not merely measured in the loss of human life; the killings extinguish culture and community and cosmopolitanism."[59] Daniel Feierstein argued that it is the "organisation,

---

[55] United States Holocaust Memorial Council, "Documenting the Numbers of Victims of the Holocaust and Nazi Persecution," United States Holocaust Memorial Museum, available at: https://encyclopedia.ushmm.org/content/en/article/documenting-numbers-of-victims-of-the-holocaust-and-nazi-persecution (accessed 11 June 2020).

[56] James E. Waller, "'A Crime without a Name': Defining Genocide and Mass Atrocity," in Charles H. Anderton and Jurgen Brauer (eds.), *Economic Aspects of Genocides, Other Mass Atrocities, and Their Prevention* (Oxford University Press, 2016).

[57] Raphael Lemkin, *Axis Rule in Occupied Europe: Laws of Occupation, Analysis of Government, Proposals for Redress* (Carnegie Endowment for International Peace, 1944).

[58] Ribes's statement is quoted in William A Schabas, "Origins of the Genocide Convention: From Nuremberg to Paris," *Case Western Reserve Journal of International Law*, vol. 40, nos. 1–2, 2007–2008, p. 42. For the other statements, see ICTR, *Prosecutor v. Akayesu*.

[59] Matthew Lippman, "The Drafting and Development of the 1948 Convention on Genocide and the Politics of International Law," in Harmen van der Wilt, Jeroen Vervliet, Göran Sluiter, and

training, practice, legitimation and consensus that distinguish genocide as a social practice from other more spontaneous or less intentional acts of killing and mass destruction."[60]

Reflecting this view, the Rome Statute of the International Criminal Court and the ICTY and ICTR separated genocide from the broader category of crimes against humanity (something that was not done in the Nuremberg Charter) and cited it as one of their three core crimes. The ICTR itself established a hierarchy in international human rights law by declaring genocide's primacy over other crimes in international criminal law and declaring it the most egregious of all human rights violations.[61] Although some convincingly argue that this special status has served to minimize other forms of mass state violence, in most political and legal circles genocide is treated as the most heinous of state crimes.[62]

In fact, political leaders and legal analysts consider genocide to be such a universal taboo that they spend much of their energy and resources debating whether the very use of the term should apply in particular cases. For example, the government of Turkey continues to vociferously deny that its Ottoman predecessors committed genocide against the Turkish Armenians (100 years ago!), even though they acknowledge that they killed thousands of them during and in the aftermath of World War I.[63] In 2004, despite a consensus that approximately 70,000 Black African civilians were targeted and killed by Arab militias in Sudan, much of the official debate in the United States and elsewhere focused not on how to stop the crisis but on whether or not it should be called a "genocide."[64] Similar debates were present in 2021 over whether the Chinese government's persecution of its Uyghur Muslim minority was genocide or just a violent campaign to combat a secessionist

Johannes Houwink ten Cate (eds.), *The Genocide Convention: The Legacy of 60 Years* (Brill, 2012), p. 24 and Matthew Lippman, "Genocide: The Crime of the Century: The Jurisprudence of Death at the Dawn of the New Millennium," *Houston Journal of International Law*, vol. 23, 2000–2001.

[60] Daniel Feierstein, *Genocide as Social Practice: Reorganizing Society under the Nazis and Argentina's Military Juntas* (Rutgers University Press, 2014), p. 14.
[61] *Prosecutor v. Jean Kambanda* (Judgment and Sentence), ICTR 97-23-S, 4 September 1998, available at: https://www.refworld.org/cases,ICTR,3deba9124.html (accessed 24 February 2021).
[62] Dirk Moses, for example, argues that creating a hierarchy of international criminal law, in which genocide is elevated to the top, blinds us to other types of atrocities, particularly those perpetrated on civilian populations during armed conflicts. See his *The Problems of Genocide: Permanent Security and the Language of Transgression* (Cambridge University Press, 2021).
[63] Tim Arango, "A Century after Armenian Genocide, Turkey's Denial Only Deepens," *New York Times*, 16 April 2015.
[64] Scott Straus, "Darfur and the Genocide Debate," *Foreign Affairs*, vol. 84, no. 1, January–February, 2005.

movement.⁶⁵ So too is the debate that raged in the United States for several years regarding the persecution of the Rohingya by the government of Myanmar.⁶⁶

So why do most legal analysts and political leaders consider genocide to be the crime of crimes, and how did it become a universal violation of international law that permits no derogation or exception, regardless of whether a state has ratified the Genocide Convention or joined the International Criminal Court?

It is neither the number of people killed nor the brutality of the acts that place genocide in a special category of universal law. Far more civilians died in the "killing fields" of Cambodia during the late 1970s as a result of actions that do not fit the legal definition of genocide than were killed in in either Rwanda or Sudan.⁶⁷ Indeed, even those who attach the label of genocide to the Chinese government's treatment of the Uyghurs acknowledge that few have actually been killed. Rather, what separates genocide from other atrocities is both its target and its intent. Its target is a designated minority group and its intent is to destroy that group. Genocide goes well beyond persecuting or killing individuals; its aim is the elimination of the social group itself.

As Lemkin argues, "genocide is directed against the national group as an entity, and the actions involved are directed against individuals, not in their individual capacity, but as members of the national group."⁶⁸ The goal of the actions is the destruction of the essential foundations of the life of these groups—through the disintegration of their political and social institutions, language and culture, national feelings, and economic existence—with the ultimate goal of group annihilation. Similarly, the United Nations General Assembly characterized genocide as "a denial of the right of existence of entire human groups."⁶⁹ For these reasons, the legal definition of genocide

---

⁶⁵ "Dutch Parliament: China's Treatment of Uighurs Is Genocide," Reuters, 25 February 2021.

⁶⁶ Conor Finnegan, "3 Years Later, US Pressed to Declare Rohingya Crisis 'Genocide,' Hold Myanmar Accountable," ABC News, 25 August 2020, at https://abcnews.go.com/Politics/years-us-pressed-declare-rohingya-crisis-genocide-hold/story?id = 72522830.

⁶⁷ Patrick Heuveline estimates that between 1.2 million and 1.8 million Cambodians were killed directly and indirectly by Pol Pot's regime in the late 1970s. See his "The Boundaries of Genocide: Quantifying the Uncertainty of the Death Toll during the Pol Pot Regime in Cambodia (1975–79)," *Population Studies*, vol. 69, no. 2, 2015. Marijke Verpoorten estimates approximately 500,000 to 600,000 Tutsi were murdered during the Rwandan genocide. See her "How Many Died in Rwanda?," *Journal of Genocide Research*, vol. 22, no. 1, 2020. Scott Straus estimates that 70,000 Black Africans were slaughtered in Sudan. See his "Darfur and the Genocide Debate," *Foreign Affairs*, vol. 84, no. 1, January–February 2005.

⁶⁸ Lemkin, *Axis Rule in Occupied Europe*, p. 79.

⁶⁹ United Nations General Assembly, Resolution 96(I), 1946.

is limited to campaigns of violence whose intent is to destroy a designated group "in whole or in part."

There is a general consensus within the international community that human collectivities have an inherent integrity that must be maintained, and that the unchangeable shared characteristic that constitutes such a group is fundamental to one's identity as a human being. The destruction of particular social groups is therefore a special kind of atrocity, much like the elimination of an endangered species. National, ethnic, racial, and religious groups are viewed as distinctive, unique, and having an inalienable right to exist and prosper. In this view, the eradication of such a collectivity deprives the world community of an irreplaceable part.[70] Moreover, since virtually all states have minority populations within them, sometimes in significant numbers, the potential for genocide is present throughout the world. At least partially for this reason, political leaders view genocide as radically destabilizing to a state, region, and international community.

The primary foundation for designating genocide as an international crime under international law is the 1948 lawmaking treaty, the Convention on the Prevention and Punishment of the Crime of Genocide. The Convention was initiated by the UN General Assembly as one of its first acts in 1946, when it unanimously adopted Resolution 96, calling on the Economic and Social Council to draft a treaty to this effect.[71] The Assembly passed it almost immediately after approving Resolution 95, which called for the adoption of the Nuremberg Principles into international law. These Principles did not specifically address genocide, since the Assembly wished to link genocide to the universal condemnation of atrocities. It therefore decided it needed a stand-alone treaty to embed its prohibition into general international law. In addition, Nuremberg's failure to recognize the international criminality of atrocities committed in peacetime prompted the first initiatives at codifying the crime of genocide.[72]

The process in which the Genocide Convention was conceived, debated, drafted, and ratified offers the classic example of how the international community builds a consensus around the creation of international legal norms as part of general international law. The Convention represented a collaborative effort within the United Nations involving the Secretariat, the Economic and

---

[70] Matthew Lippman, "A Road Map to the 1948 Convention on the Prevention and Punishment of the Crime Genocide," *Journal of Genocide Research*, vol. 4, no. 2, 2002, p. 177.

[71] UN General Assembly, *The Crime of Genocide*, 11 December 1946, A/RES/96.

[72] Schabas, "Origins of the Genocide Convention," p. 36.

Social Council (ECOSOC), the Committee on the Progressive Development of International Law and Its Codification (precursor to the International Law Commission), the Sixth (Legal) Committee of the General Assembly, and the General Assembly itself. It was the first international treaty prepared by the United Nations that was proposed for signature and ratification by the states of the world.

The process was messy and at times convoluted; various drafts were debated and vetted by a wide range of groups within the UN. At the same time, each step contributed to the eventual development of a document that declared genocide to be an international crime. After the General Assembly referred the question to ECOSOC, that body in turn asked the secretary-general to prepare a draft convention. He did so with the assistance of legal advisors and circulated it to member states for comment and revision. It then went to the Sixth Committee for further revision, and then it was sent back to ECOSOC. After they adopted the text, it was sent to the General Assembly, who debated the details over a period of weeks. It was ultimately unanimously adopted as a resolution on 9 December 1948. The entire process took approximately two years.[73]

The opening of the conference saw the delegates disagreeing on many key issues; indeed, they initially didn't even agree that genocide should be designated a crime unto itself, much less one that would have universal applicability. In fact some thought such a designation would be counterproductive and a violation of state sovereignty.[74] It was through months of deliberation and interaction that state representatives developed a consensus around the main principles that currently constitute the legal prohibition of genocide.[75]

Even then, however, the delegates were not prepared at that time to dispense with the legal doctrine of consent or the protection of sovereignty in enforcing the prohibition against genocide. In particular, they could not agree on the degree to which states should have the authority to punish genocide occurring on the territories of those who did not sign the treaty. They also could not reach a consensus over whether the treaty should designate the United Nations Security Council a competent body to enforce the

---

[73] For a detailed discussion of this process, based on the official records of the meetings, see Hirad Abtahi and Phillippa Webb, *The Genocide Convention: The Travaux Préparatoires* (Brill Nijhoff, 2008); Nehemiah Robinson, "The Genocide Convention, Its Origins and Interpretation," *Case Western Reserve Journal of International Law*, vol. 40, nos. 1–2, 2008; and William A. Schabas, *Genocide in International Law: The Crime of Crimes*, 2nd edition (Cambridge University Press, 2009), chapter 2.

[74] Lippman, "A Road Map to the 1948 Convention."

[75] See Schabas, "Origins of the Genocide Convention," p. 38.

convention against those who did not sign.⁷⁶ Attempts to generate a consensus subjecting genocide to universal jurisdiction—enabling individual states to prosecute genocide regardless of where it occurs—were also unsuccessful. While there was considerable support for this notion, the United States, France, and the Soviet Union, among others, took the position that the principle of sovereignty limited court jurisdiction to acts committed on a state's own territory.⁷⁷

At the same time, none of the delegates argued against declaring genocide a universal crime. The sovereignty debates focused on enforcement and jurisdiction rather than the degree to which the act would be a violation of international law.

Many of the issues that divided the conference have been revisited many times since, and the increased institutionalization of global politics enabled states to strengthen the universal ban on genocide over the past few decades. In 1978, UN Special Rapporteur on Genocide Nicodeme Ruhashyankiko issued a report concluding that the Convention in and of itself lacked effective international measures to prevent and punish genocide and therefore was not a sufficient obstacle to the perpetration of the practice. In the absence of an international criminal court, he advocated universal jurisdiction as a method for enforcing the Convention. In 1985, his successor, Benjamin Whitaker, echoed this sentiment, recommending that additional measures be incorporated into a supplementary convention or protocol, and opined that respect for state sovereignty and domestic jurisdiction should not take precedence over the protection against genocide.⁷⁸

These positions would soon become widely accepted. The expanded role of the UN Security Council (discussed in Chapter 2), the initiation of the international tribunals for the former Yugoslavia and Rwanda, and the creation of the International Criminal Court provided for the type of universal enforcement mechanisms that many delegates had unsuccessfully tried to implement in 1948. This was the beginning of a process that eventually led to the universalization of the genocide ban that did indeed permit universal

---

⁷⁶ Robinson, "The Genocide Convention," p. 13.

⁷⁷ In particular, the U.S. delegates argued that expanding jurisdiction to international institutions would infringe on U.S. sovereignty, promote world government, subject American citizens to trial abroad, and interfere with segregation laws in the southern United States. See N. Kaufman, *Human Rights Treaties and the Senate: A History of Opposition* (University of North Carolina Press, 1990), pp. 37–62. See also William A. Schabas, "National Courts Finally Begin to Prosecute Genocide, the Crime of Crimes," *Journal of International Criminal Justice*, no. 1, April 2003, p. 42.

⁷⁸ Lippman, "A Road Map to the 1948 Convention," p. 177; Schabas, *Genocide in International Law*, chapter 8.

jurisdiction.[79] This was confirmed in 2006 and 2007, when the ICTR became the first international court to deliver verdicts against individuals responsible for committing genocide. Equally significant, it authorized the transfer of suspects for trial on the basis of universal jurisdiction with the approval of the United Nations Security Council. This provided further evidence of a growing broad acceptance of universal jurisdiction over genocide.

At the same time, there is still some debate over whether to expand the list of groups that must be targeted in order for the genocide label to be legally applied.

Many countries have broadened the inclusion of more protected groups. The most frequently included groups were political and social groups, but some countries also included groups defined by class, ideology, resistance to occupation, age, disability, health, gender, and sexual orientation. In total, according to a study by Tamas Hoffman, more than 100 counties altered the international legal definition of genocide when adopting the crime in their domestic law.[80]

Those countries that are parties to the Genocide Convention are clearly bound by its provisions, and both domestic and international legal institutions use the Convention as its source when adjudicating cases involving those accused of the crime.[81] However, as of 2021, 42 countries are not parties to the Convention. Of those, 19 are in Africa, 17 in Asia, and 6 in the Americas. Does this mean that they may legally commit genocide under international law?

Clearly, few if any political leaders or legal analysts would take this position, at least not publicly. The sheer volume of resolutions by international and regional organizations, multiple charters, and rulings by international tribunals and domestic courts alone support this. Thus, the International Court of Justice, for example, opined that "the principles underlying the [Genocide] Convention are principles which are recognized by civilized nations as binding on States, even without any conventional obligation.... [Moreover] the origins of the Convention show that it was the intention of the United Nations to condemn and punish genocide as 'a crime under international law.'"[82]

---

[79] See Schabas, "National Courts Finally Begin to Prosecute Genocide," p. 42.

[80] Tamas Hoffman, "The Crime of Genocide in Its (Nearly) Infinite Domestic Variety," in Marco Odello and Piotr Łubiński, ed., *The Concept of Genocide in International Criminal Law: Developments after Lemkin*, (Routledge, 2020), pp. 67–97.

[81] See, for example, Schabas, *Genocide in International Law*, chapter 9.

[82] See "Reservations to the Convention on the Prevention and Punishment of the Crime of Genocide, Advisory Opinion," ICJ Report, 1951, p. 23.

The prohibition of genocide is arguably one of the few legal norms that appears to have achieved the status of *jus cogens*. According to the Vienna Convention on the Law of Treaties, in order for a legal norm to be considered as such it must be "accepted and recognized by the international community of States as a whole."[83] They must also embody general and universalizable principles that are public, clear, feasible, consistent with other, similar norms, relatively stable over time, and prospective rather than retroactive.[84] Their purpose is to protect overriding interests and values of the international community of states and prohibit what has come to be seen as intolerable because of the threat it presents to the survival of states, their peoples, and the most basic human values.[85]

The prohibition of genocide meets these standards. In particular, genocide is unique in the canon of human rights norms inasmuch as national, ethnic, religious, and racial groups provide much of the foundation of human society. More specifically, their preservation is absolutely necessary to the stability of nation-states, almost all of which are cosmopolitan, with large numbers and varieties of minorities.

As discussed in Chapter 1, the only way to determine whether a *jus cogens* norm exists is through widespread consensus. This basic agreement has been reached in contemporary international society inasmuch as it is supported by a wide variety of different sources, including both international courts and the legal institutions of numerous states.[86] In 1951 the ICJ opined:

> The origins of the Convention show that it was the intention of the United Nations to condemn and punish genocide as a crime under international law.... The first consequence arising from this conception is that the principles underlying the Convention are principles which are recognized by civilized nations as binding on States, even without any conventional obligation. A second consequence is the universal character both of the condemnation of genocide and of the cooperation required 'in order to liberate mankind from such an odious scourge' [T]he Genocide Convention was

---

[83] Vienna Convention on the Law of Treaties, concluded at Vienna on 23 May 1969, United Nations, Treaty Series, vol. 1155, article 53.

[84] Evan J. Criddle and Evan Fox-Decent, "Deriving Peremptory Norms from Sovereignty," *American Society of International Law Proceedings*, vol. 103, 2009.

[85] International Law Commission Report, Draft Articles on Responsibility of States for Internationally Wrongful Acts, with Commentaries, 2001, Article 40, Commentary 3, p. 112.

[86] For a sample of the numerous legal opinions declaring the prohibition against genocide to have the character of *jus cogens*, see Amnesty International, "Genocide: The Legal Basis for Universal Jurisdiction," 31 August 2001, AI Index: IOR 53/010/2001, particularly pp. 3–6.

therefore intended by the General Assembly and by the contracting parties to be definitely universal in scope.[87]

At the same time, legal analysts and jurists overwhelming hold the view that genocide is a crime under international law over which any state may exercise universal jurisdiction.[88] Few would challenge this proposition; it has been endorsed by governments and regional and international organizations, and it has led to the prosecution of thousands of Nazis in domestic courts over the past 70 years.[89] Indeed, genocide is specifically mentioned as one of the four practices that would justify multilateral humanitarian intervention, as articulated in both the seminal document, *The Responsibility to Protect*, and, more important, the final resolution passed by 170 heads of state at the 2005 World Summit and subsequent endorsement by consensus by the UN General Assembly.[90] Nowhere was this conditioned on an offending state being a party to the Genocide Convention.

Thus, although the Genocide Convention is an important source for both articulating the legal prohibition of genocide and legitimizing domestic and international efforts to enforce it, being a party to the treaty is not necessary to bind states to its provisions.

Ethnic Cleansing

Another form of group persecution that has emerged in discussions of international law and diplomatic practice is ethnic cleansing, defined as a "purposeful policy designed by one ethnic or religious group to remove by violent and terror-inspiring means the civilian population of another ethnic or religious group from certain geographic areas."[91] Unlike genocide, its objective is not to eliminate or destroy the target group but rather to create a

---

[87] International Court of Justice, "Reservations to the Convention on the Prevention and Punishment of the Crime of Genocide," Advisory Opinion of 28 May 1951, p. 23.

[88] See Amnesty International, "Genocide," p. 8, fn. 10.

[89] Michael Bazyler, *Holocaust, Genocide, and the Law: A Quest for Justice in a Post-Holocaust World* (Oxford University Press, 2016), chapter 4.

[90] International Commission on Intervention and State Sovereignty, "The Responsibility to Protect: Report of the International Committee on Intervention and State Sovereignty," International Development Research Centre, December 2001; United Nations, "2005 World Summit Outcome," Resolution Adopted by the General Assembly on 16 September 2005 (A/60/1).

[91] UN Security Council, "Final Report of the Commission of Experts Established Pursuant to Security Council Resolution 780," 27 May 1994 (S/1994/674), p. 33, para. 130.

homogeneous population in a given geographic area by expelling individuals associated with a particular social group through violence and intimidation. This differs from other types of mass forced eviction—such as the deportation of immigrants, the expulsion of adversaries in the wake of defeat in an armed conflict, and the imposition of exile for political reasons—in that its purpose is to render an area ethnically homogeneous in favor of the dominant group.[92]

Like persecution in general, there is a long history of public authorities uprooting and expelling groups they consider to be undesirable or a threat to their political power or social policies. Corporate expulsion—the banishment of an entire category of subjects beyond the physical boundaries of a political entity—has been a characteristic of Western civilization dating back to the Middle Ages, although it was also present in ancient Assyria, Greece, and Rome.[93] Jewish populations were often the target, although Lombards and Cahorsins (Christian usurers), Moriscos (Spanish Muslims converted to Christianity), Protestants, Jesuits, and Mormons were all expelled at one time or another between the 13th and 19th centuries in Europe.[94]

In the 20th century, ethnic cleansing was widely practiced during the process of new state formations, particularly in the wake of the breakup of existing states and in the process and aftermath of armed conflicts.[95]

Part of the problem in characterizing the practice as a specific form of mass violence is distinguishing it from genocide and war crimes. The line between ethnic cleansing and genocide is sometimes blurred, particularly when both are pursued simultaneously by the same perpetrator against the same targeted group. One of the most odious aspects of ethnic cleansing as it was practiced in 1990s Bosnia, for example, was the systematic mass rape of Bosniak women by Serbian militias. The perpetrators committed this act with the intent of impregnating the victims, thereby changing the group's ethnic genetic pool (which would be a form of genocide), and terrorizing them, their families, and their communities into fleeing the territory (which would fulfill the goals of ethnic cleansing).[96] Rape also had the objective of

---

[92] See Benjamin Z. Kedar, "Expulsion as an Issue of World History," *Journal of World History*, vol. 7, no. 2, Fall 1996, p. 166.
[93] Andrew Bell-Fialkoff, *Ethnic Cleansing* (St. Martin's Griffin, 1999).
[94] See Kedar, "Expulsion as an Issue of World History."
[95] Jennifer Jackson-Preece, "Ethnic Cleansing as an Instrument of Nation-State Creation: Changing State Practices and Evolving Legal Norms," *Human Rights Quarterly*, vol. 20, no. 4, 1998.
[96] See Amnesty International, "Rape and Sexual Abuse by Armed Forces," January 1993, AI Index: EUR 63/01/93, p. 12.

preventing births within the group by inflicting psychological damage on women that would drive them to refuse future sexual contact or to give birth (another characteristic of genocide). The rape of wives and mothers was also designed to disrupt family relations (a form of terrorism).[97]

Similarly, the U.S. government engaged in both practices in relation to various indigenous tribes and nations in North America during the 19th century.[98] For example, in addition to ordering the systematic killing of thousands of Native Americans, President Andrew Jackson oversaw the forced removal of 20,000 Cherokees from their lands in Oklahoma in what has informally been labeled "the Trail of Tears."[99]

At the moment, there is no official definition of ethnic cleansing in international law, and it has yet to be listed as an independent crime in any treaty or in the statutes of the ICTY, ICTR, or ICC. Moreover, although the term has been used in a number of resolutions of the UN Security Council, the General Assembly, and in judgments and indictments of the ICTY, these references have tended to be rhetorical descriptions rather than legal pronouncements.[100] Indeed, some legal scholars argue that the very use of the term corrupts observation, interpretation, ethical judgment, and decision-making, and bleaches the atrocities of genocide, leading to inaction in preventing current and future genocides.[101]

For these reasons, many legal scholars doubt that ethnic cleansing, as a category of state violence, is in and of itself a violation of international law.[102] Rather, many political leaders and judicial officials have usually considered ethnic cleansing to be an element of a crime against humanity and/or a grave breach in the laws of armed conflict (when conducted during wartime).

---

[97] For a discussion of this practice, see Drazen Petrovic, "Ethnic Cleansing—An Attempt at Methodology," *European Journal of International Law*, vol. 5, no. 3, 1994, p. 357.

[98] Gary Clayton Anderson, "The Native Peoples of the American West: Genocide or Ethnic Cleansing?," *Western Historical Quarterly*, vol. 47, no. 4, Winter 2016.

[99] See, for example, Gary Clayton Anderson, *Ethnic Cleansing and the Indian: The Crime That Should Haunt America* (University of Oklahoma Press, 2014).

[100] UN resolutions citing ethnic cleansing include Security Council Resolution 771, 13 August 1992, UN Doc. S/RES/771; Security Council Resolution 780, 6 October 1992, UN Doc. S/RES/780; Security Council Resolution 787, 16 November 1992, UN Doc. S/RES/787; Security Council Resolution 808, 22 February 1993, UN Doc. S/RES/808; Security Council Resolution 819, 16 April 1993, UN Doc. S/RES/819; Security Council Resolution 827, 25 May 1993, UN Doc. S/RES/827; Security Council Resolution 836, 4 June 1993, UN Doc. S/RES/836; and Security Council Resolution 859, 24 August 1993, UN Doc. S/RES/859.

[101] See, for example, Rony Blum, Gregory H. Stanton, Shira Sagi, and Elihu D. Richter, "'Ethnic Cleansing' Bleaches the Atrocities of Genocide," *European Journal of Public Health*, vol. 18, no. 2, 2008.

[102] See, for example, Robert Hayden, "Schindler's Fate: Genocide, Ethnic Cleansing and Population Transfers," *Slavic Review*, vol. 55, no. 4, 1996.

For example, the United Nations Commission of Experts, created by the Security Council to investigate violations of international humanitarian law (IHL) in the former Yugoslavia, concluded:

> Based on many reports describing the policy and practices conducted in the former Yugoslavia, ethnic cleansing has been carried out by means of murder, torture, arbitrary arrest and detention, extra-judicial executions, rape and sexual assaults, confinement of civilian population in ghetto areas, forcible removal, displacement and deportation of civilian population, deliberate military attacks or threats of attacks on civilians and civilian areas, and wanton destruction of property. Those practices constitute crimes against humanity and can be assimilated to specific war crimes.[103]

Similarly, international organizations and tribunals have also viewed the practice as violations of IHL, a euphemism for the laws of armed conflict as they pertain to the protection of civilians and other noncombatants. This is largely because most of the major cases of ethnic cleansing over the past two decades have occurred during internal armed conflicts. The first mention of ethnic cleansing as a violation of international law by an official body was by the UN Security Council in Resolution 771 in 1992. The Council expressed "grave alarm at continuing reports of widespread violations of international humanitarian law occurring within the territory of the former Yugoslavia and especially in Bosnia and Herzegovina including reports of mass forcible expulsion and deportation of civilians.... [The Council] strongly condemns any violations of international humanitarian law, including those involved in the practice of 'ethnic cleansing.'"[104] The Council subsequently approved a half-dozen more resolutions that specifically mentioned ethnic cleansing in relation to IHL.[105]

Apart from any action by the Security Council, the 1977 Second Protocol to the Geneva Conventions, which covers internal/noninternational armed conflicts, prohibits the "displacement of the civilian population" and stipulates that "civilians shall not be compelled to leave their own territory

---

[103] UN Security Council, "Final Report of the Commission of Experts Established Pursuant to Security Council Resolution 780," 27 May 1994 (S/1994/674), p. 33, para. 130.
[104] UN Security Council, Resolution 771, adopted on 13 August 1992, S/RES/771.
[105] See footnote 79.

for reasons connected with the conflict."[106] This protocol is examined in greater detail in Chapter 6.

As a crime against humanity, the prohibited acts associated with ethnic cleansing (as defined in the Rome Statute of the ICC) include mass rape and "deporting or forcibly transferring a population" "by expulsion or other coercive acts from the area in which they are lawfully present, without grounds permitted under international law," when committed as part of a widespread or systematic attack directed against a civilian population.[107]

As discussed earlier in regard to genocide, ethnic cleansing is specifically mentioned as an act that would justify the use of multilateral humanitarian intervention. Significantly, unlike the Rome Statute of the ICC, it is not folded into the broad definition of crimes against humanity, but rather "large scale 'ethnic cleansing,' actual or apprehended, whether carried out by killing, forced expulsion, acts of terror or rape," is listed along with genocide and war crimes as a "just cause" that alone would trigger such an intervention.[108]

Based on all of these factors, there appears to be an international consensus that the prohibition of ethnic cleansing is a universal legal norm. However, the lack of any specific mention of ethnic cleansing as an international crime in any treaty, ruling from an international tribunal, or resolution of an international organization means that unlike genocide it is considered an act that would constitute a crime against humanity or a grave breach of the laws of armed conflict. In this capacity, its prohibition does qualify as part of general international law that is binding on all states regardless of whether they have agreed to it. Moreover, the use of the term also serves a useful diplomatic purpose in helping states and international organizations to sanction those practicing it.

Apartheid

Another form of persecution that has been discussed in legal circles as potentially constituting an international crime under general international law is apartheid. Unlike other forms of persecution, apartheid is focused

---

[106] Protocol Additional to the Geneva Conventions of 12 August 1949 and Relating to the Protection of Victims of Non-International Armed Conflicts (Protocol II), adopted on 8 June 1977, Article 17. This article is identical to the First Protocol, which covers international armed conflicts.

[107] See Rome Statute of the International Criminal Court, Article VII(d) and (g).

[108] International Development Research Centre, p. 32, part 4.18.

solely on race, although obviously the line between race and ethnicity is not always easily drawn.[109] The term "apartheid" is an Afrikaans word derived from the French term *mettre à part*, literally "separating" or "setting apart." It is a policy to segregate the population based on racial criteria in order to facilitate the legal domination of one racial group over another. In doing so, the rights of the target group are severely limited, and the policy is enforced through draconian laws, coercive sanctions, and systemic state violence. The separation is largely exercised though the creation and maintenance of defined geographical zones. The persecuted population is restricted to designated areas (known in South Africa as "homelands") and denied access to other parts of the country.[110] The system was developed in South Africa in 1948, when it became the official policy of the state, and was enacted through a series of discriminatory laws. It officially ended in 1990.

What defines apartheid as a particular form of persecution, then, is the institutionalization of racial domination through territorial segregation and legal restrictions that extend to all areas of civil society, including employment, housing, marriage, association, and travel. It has similarities with the racial caste system that prevailed in the American South between 1877 and the early 1960s.[111] However, apartheid goes well beyond systemic discrimination and the segregation of public facilities to include the denial of even the most basic rights to the oppressed group and the regulation of every aspect of their lives. Indeed, the Black African population of South Africa did not have the constitutional protections that were legally extended to African Americans in the United States in 1868.[112] During the apartheid era in South Africa, the actions and opportunities of the population were tightly regulated through identity cards issued at birth that identified and registered all residents of the country as belonging to one of four distinct racial groups. One's rights were defined by these categories.[113]

---

[109] The most recent scholarship in genetics holds that as a matter of science, "race" does not exist as a distinct biological category inasmuch as there is no gene that can identify it. See Natalie Angier, "Do Races Differ? Not Really, Genes Show," *New York Times*, 22 August 2000.

[110] See Saul Dubow, *Apartheid, 1948–1994* (Oxford University Press, 2014).

[111] For a classic analysis of the system in the American South, see C. Vann Woodward, *The Strange Career of Jim Crow* (Oxford University Press, 1955).

[112] The 14th Amendment to the U.S. Constitution guarantees equal protection under the law for all citizens. Several decisions by the U.S. Supreme Court ruled that Jim Crow laws violated this protection and nullified them, the most famous being *Brown v. Board of Education of Topeka* (1954).

[113] See Geoffrey C. Bowker, *Sorting Things Out: Classification and Its Consequences*, Inside Technology (MIT Press, 2000), chapter 6.

For decades, apartheid was treated by states as a political and diplomatic matter rather than a legal issue. While a number of states and international organizations issued numerous statements and resolutions condemning apartheid and calling for sanctions against South Africa, few designated it as a violation of general international law.[114] This changed in 1984, when the Security Council referred to apartheid as a crime against humanity.[115] While this mention in and of itself is not a legal pronouncement, it was an important step in the development of a broad consensus regarding the illegality of the practice.

The first coordinated attempt to address apartheid in the context of international law was the 1974 International Convention on the Suppression and Punishment of the Crime of Apartheid (the Apartheid Convention). The Convention declared apartheid to be an illegal practice under international law based on three principles. First, the practice violated the UN Charter's principle of equal rights and self-determination of peoples, articulated in Chapter 1, Article 1. Since all recognized states (except at the time Switzerland) were members of the UN, the Charter was essentially a universal treaty. Second, apartheid is a "crime against humanity and . . . inhuman acts resulting from the policies and practices of apartheid and similar policies and practices of racial segregation and discrimination . . . are crimes violating the principles of international law."[116]

Third, individuals, organizations, and governments within states that are parties to the Convention are legally liable for "inhuman acts" in which they may become involved "resulting from the policies and practices of apartheid." The Convention designates "those organizations, institutions and individuals committing the crime of apartheid" to be criminal entities, much as the Nuremberg Charter did with the various organizations that upheld the Nazi regime. This was based on the legal concept of criminal conspiracy.[117]

---

[114] See Newell M. Stultz, "Evolution of the United Nations Anti-Apartheid Regime," *Human Rights Quarterly*, vol. 13, no. 1, February 1991. The General Assembly did refer to the practice as a crime against humanity in its 1966 resolution; however, it is clear from the wording and context that they did not attach any legal significance to this designation; it was more of a rhetorical device. See UN General Assembly, "The Policies of Apartheid of the Government of the Republic of South Africa," 16 December 1966, A/RES/2202. See also United Nations Security Council Resolutions 418 (1977), 421(1977), 473 (1980), 558 (1984), and 591 (1986).

[115] UN Security Council Resolution 556 (1984).

[116] International Convention on the Suppression and Punishment of the Crime of Apartheid, 1015 UNTS 243, entered into force 18 July 1976, Article I(1).

[117] United Nations, *Charter of the International Military Tribunal—Annex to the Agreement for the Prosecution and Punishment of the Major War Criminals of the European Axis ("London Agreement")*, 8 August 1945, article 6.

In addition, the Convention suggests that states can enforce the prohibition even against those who refuse to be party to the treaty through domestic courts exercising universal jurisdiction. Specifically, it encourages state parties to prosecute nonnationals for violating the treaty even when committed in the territory of a nonstate party where the accused is physically within the jurisdiction of a state party.[118]

Twenty-six member states abstained on the vote in the General Assembly that adopted the Apartheid Convention (91 voted in the affirmative). This falls far short of a consensus under any definition of the term, and the transcripts from the drafting conference do not indicate that the representatives believed they were creating a lawmaking treaty. Even now, there are only 110 parties to the treaty, a large but not overwhelming number. Indeed, three of the five members of the Security Council (United States, United Kingdom, and France) have not ratified it.

At the same time, a review of the debates leading up to the adoption of the Apartheid Convention—including the statements of country representatives explaining their votes—indicates that those who withheld their support for the document by abstaining did so on mostly technical grounds. The classification of apartheid as a crime against humanity was generally not a controversial issue.[119] But a number of countries were uncomfortable with the provisions granting jurisdiction to extradite and prosecute individuals for violating the treaty and the extension of authority to the UN Human Rights Commission.[120]

At the same time, 182 states (about 94%) did ratify the International Convention on the Elimination of All Forms of Racial Discrimination (ICEARD), which declares that all parties "condemn racial segregation and apartheid and undertake to prevent, prohibit and eradicate all practices of this nature in territories under their jurisdiction." But like similar treaties, ICEARD is written more like an aspirational document declaring a state's position than one intended to create new international law. Thus, ICEARD should be viewed as just one piece that contributes to the overall body of treaties, resolutions, soft law, and judicial rulings creating a general legal prohibition of apartheid.

---

[118] International Convention on the Suppression and Punishment of the Crime of Apartheid, articles 4 and 5.

[119] Ronald C. Slye, "Apartheid as a Crime against Humanity: A Submission to the South African Truth and Reconciliation Commission," *Michigan Journal of International Law*, vol. 20, no. 2, 1999, p. 293.

[120] Slye, "Apartheid as a Crime against Humanity," p. 294.

Most recently, the Rome Statute of the ICC listed apartheid as one of 11 acts that could constitute a crime against humanity when such acts are committed in the context of an institutionalized regime of systematic oppression and domination by one racial group over another with "the intention of maintaining that regime."[121] Thus, the three primary elements that define the practice as a crime are (1) an intent to maintain a system of domination by one racial group over another, (2) systematic oppression by one racial group over another, and (3) inhuman acts carried out on a widespread or systematic basis in pursuit of those policies. All three elements are necessary for the criminalization of apartheid.

Additionally, the First Protocol to the Geneva Conventions of 1949 recognized the imposition of a system of apartheid as a "grave breach," without designating any geographical limitation, prohibiting "practices of 'apartheid' and other inhuman and degrading practices involving outrages upon personal dignity, based on racial discrimination."[122] However, this applies only during an armed conflict and only to a party in the conflict rather than to a state against its own population.

Over the past few decades, then, there appears to be a growing and broadening body of hard and soft law declaring apartheid to be an illegal practice under general international law. At the same time, designating apartheid as a universal crime under general international law raises several challenges.

First, the Rome Statute does not actually designate apartheid itself an international crime. Rather it refers to the "inhumane acts" (such as murder, torture, and persecution) that are committed "in the context of an institutionalized regime of systematic oppression and domination by one racial group over any other group or groups and committed with the intention of maintaining that regime."[123] Yet any one of these acts committed as part of a widespread or systematic attack on a civilian population, regardless of who the targets are, already constitutes a crime against humanity. From this perspective, it is not the system of apartheid itself that constitutes a universal violation of international law, but the practices that create and sustain it. This may be a technical point, but it is one that must be considered.

---

[121] Rome Statute, article 7(1)h.
[122] Protocol Additional to the Geneva Conventions of 12 August 1949, and relating to the Protection of Victims of International Armed Conflicts, Article 85, para. 4(c).
[123] UN General Assembly, *Rome Statute of the International Criminal Court (as Amended 2010)*, 17 July 1998, Article 7(2)h.

Although the Convention refers several times to "inhuman acts" as the predicate violations, at least some of the specific practices cited in the Convention that comprise apartheid are not generally considered to be "atrocities" outside of the context of an apartheid system, such as arbitrary arrest, segregation, discriminatory legislation, the prohibition of interracial marriages, the illegal imprisonment of members of a racial group, and the persecution of persons opposed to apartheid.[124] These are all clearly serious human rights violations, but they fall below the threshold that has come to define atrocities. As discussed earlier in the chapter, in and of itself discrimination is not illegal under all circumstances under general international law. It must be coupled with an asymmetrical, systemic threat against a particular social group and, most important, violent oppression perpetrated by the state or other authorities that follows this threat.

Still, some legal bodies have opined that widespread racial discrimination itself is universally banned under general international law. Referring specifically to the case of South Africa and its colonization of Namibia, the International Court of Justice ruled that race-based distinctions constitute a denial of fundamental human rights and are therefore prohibited under general international law by constituting a "flagrant violation of the purposes and principles of the [UN] Charter," and that the "norm of non-discrimination or non-separation on the basis of race has become a rule of customary international law."[125]

This would presumably apply directly to apartheid. However, the UN Charter does not actually mention nondiscrimination in either its purposes (Article 1) or the main text. Moreover, in its ruling, the ICJ asserts customary law without providing any evidence of a widespread, consistent practice. While many political leaders, diplomats, and officials from international organizations have regularly condemned South Africa's policies, few at the time referred to apartheid as a violation of international law. Moreover, the lack of overwhelming support for the Apartheid Convention challenges the presumption that the prohibition of apartheid was recognized as a customary practice.[126]

---

[124] International Convention on the Suppression and Punishment of the Crime of Apartheid, 1015 UNTS 243, entered into force 18 July 1976, Article II.

[125] South West Africa Cases (*Ethiopia v. S. Africa*; *Liberia v. S. Africa*), Second Phase, 1966, ICJ 6, p. 293.

[126] See Paul Eden, "The Role of the Rome Statute in the Criminalization of Apartheid," *Journal of International Criminal Justice*, vol. 12, no. 2, May 2014.

Second, to some extent apartheid is *sui generis* in that the only official case is South Africa, although some human rights organizations charge Israel with maintaining such a system in the West Bank.[127] While some legal analysts have argued that the practice of apartheid violates general international law apart from the practices of any particular state, even when the Convention was being drafted there was a division among the delegates concerning its scope. Although some delegates took the position that the Convention would cover other states that engaged in systemic racial discrimination, most saw it as an instrument to be employed solely against South Africa.[128] The final draft referred to situations of similar policies and practices of racial segregation and discrimination "as practiced in southern Africa."[129]

Third, apropos of the above, there are few judicial rulings from international courts that can help legal analysts interpret the standing of apartheid in general international law. This is in part because apartheid has never been prosecuted in an international court.

Yet despite these questions, there appears to be general agreement among legal analysts, international law scholars, and political leaders that apartheid is in fact prohibited under general international law regardless of whether or not a state has signed the Apartheid Convention. In general, this proposition is derived from the consensus that (1) persecution is specifically mentioned as a crime under general international law in multiple treaties, charters, and court rulings, including the Rome Statute, the Statute of the ICTY, and the Statute of the ICTR;[130] (2) apartheid is not only a form of persecution but an extreme one; (3) as such, it is considered to be a crime against humanity by a wide range of political and legal bodies;[131] and (4) the very nature of the apartheid system means such persecution and oppression is widespread and systematic.

---

[127] See Amnesty International, "Israel's Apartheid against Palestinians: Cruel System of Domination and Crime against Humanity," 1 February 2022, MDE 15/5141/2022 and Human Rights Watch, "A Threshold Crossed: Israeli Authorities and the Crimes of Apartheid and Persecution," April 2021.

[128] Summary Record of the 2004th Meeting of the Third Committee, 28th session of the General Assembly, held on 23 October 1973 (A/C.3/SR.2004), para. 4.

[129] International Convention on the Suppression and Punishment of the Crime of Apartheid, 1015 UNTS 243, entered into force 18 July 1976, Article II.

[130] See *Statute of the International Tribunal for the Prosecution of Persons Responsible for Serious Violations of International Humanitarian Law Committed in the Territory of the Former Yugoslavia since 1991*, UN Doc. S/25704, article 5; UN Security Council, *Statute of the International Criminal Tribunal for Rwanda*, 8 November 1994, UN Doc. S/955.

[131] See the discussion concerning apartheid as an extreme form of persecution in Slye, "Apartheid as a Crime against Humanity."

Summary

The violent persecution of minorities is an old and enduring practice, but it is also one that is now universally prohibited under general international law. As a broad category, it includes widespread, systemic violence targeted at specific ethnic, racial, religious, or national groups. This has been confirmed by a wide range of treaties, judicial opinions, soft law, and resolutions by numerous international and regional organizations, even in cases where state practice does not conform to the legal norm. All of the documents were produced within multilateral organizations and conferences after considerable deliberation among a wide range of diplomats, legal analysts, and political leaders. The principles have also been confirmed through soft law resolutions in regional security organizations.

Of the various forms violent persecution of minorities takes, genocide is considered the most serious; it is the only practice specifically mentioned as a core crime in the Rome Statute and the statutes of the ICTY and ICTR. Ethnic cleansing also has a status of its own as a result of its inclusion as a precipitating act that could legitimize humanitarian intervention in the Responsibility to Protect document.

At the same time, the widespread persecution of various groups around the world, often justified by the need to maintain social order, challenges the proposition that its prohibition is part of customary international law. Rather, there is a general consensus among political leaders and legal analysts in international and regional organizations, judicial bodies, and NGOs that the practice is illegal regardless of how widespread it may be or whether it reflects widespread, consistent practice.

5
Torture

Between 2015 and 2020, intelligence agents, police officers, and security officials acting in an official capacity in 140 countries engaged in various forms of torture.[1] The practice was not necessarily widespread in all of these countries, but it occurred in all regions of the world and by all types of regimes, including both authoritarian systems and democracies. Lest one assume that this was simply a response to the increase in terrorist attacks after 11 September 2001, from 1997 to mid-2000 state officials in more than 150 countries committed torture.[2] The most common victims were criminal suspects abused by police, although a fair number of political prisoners were also targets.

At the same time, the prohibition against torture is also one of the most cited and broadly accepted legal norms in international law. Virtually all legal analysts agree that torture and other forms of cruel, inhuman, or degrading treatment violate the most fundamental principles of human rights. It is inconsistent with a global legal order based on recognition of the basic dignity and bodily integrity of all people. As a practical matter, torture conducted with official sanction sends a social message of intimidation and reveals the scope, character, and strategies of official social control. As such, it can provoke or intensify social conflict and, in its tacit claim to unlimited social control, challenge the rule of law itself.[3]

Few international legal norms are as entrenched as the prohibition against torture. The ban on torture is included in a wide range of treaties, charters, and judicial judgments spanning several areas of international law. Torture is considered to be a gross human rights violation, a grave breach in the laws of armed conflict, a crime against humanity (when widespread), and a form of state terrorism. Its ban imposes obligations on both states and public

---

[1] Amnesty International, *Ending the Torture Trade: The Path to Global Controls on the "Tools of Torture,"* 2020, Index: ACT 30/3363/2020, p. 5.
[2] Amnesty International, *Take a Step to Stamp Out Torture*, 2000, AI Index: ACT 40/13/00, p. 1.
[3] Winston P. Nagan and Lucie Atkins, "The International Law of Torture: From Universal Proscription to Effective Application and Enforcement," *Harvard Human Rights Journal*, vol. 14, 2001, p. 90.

officials. Of the many human rights violations proscribed in the Universal Declaration, it is one of the only practices that is prohibited by its own convention. It is also one of the few nonderogable acts enumerated in Article 4(2) of the International Covenant on Civil and Political Rights. In contrast to other forms of repression, it cannot be legally justified on security grounds, nor can it be legitimately viewed as necessary for the maintenance of social order.

Like genocide, torture is so taboo that few political leaders publicly admit to practicing it, even in the face of extreme security threats. Indeed, even authoritarian regimes usually find it necessary to publicly renounce its use, even if they employ it privately.[4] Unlike most crimes against humanity, it constitutes an atrocity even if it is not practiced as part of a broader campaign of widespread or systematic violence.

Support for the prohibition is so widespread that many legal scholars and jurists argue that it is firmly established as a legal norm in customary international law binding on all states regardless of whether they consent to it.[5] However, if international custom is based on state practice that is "widespread, representative, and consistent,"[6] clearly one would be hard-pressed to argue that the ban on torture reflects such practice. Moreover, although the vast majority of states have signed the Convention Against Torture and Other Cruel, Inhuman or Degrading Treatment or Punishment, as of 2021, 25 states have not.[7] Under the generally accepted understanding of customary law, this explicit refusal to sign constitutes a persistent objection, thereby releasing these states from the norm.

Yet few would argue that state officials from nonsignatory states are free to legally engage in torture, and virtually all courts and tribunals that have

---

[4] James R. Hollyer and B. Peter Rosendorff argue that by accepting the legal norm prohibiting torture by signing the Convention Against Torture, authoritarian states reduce their vulnerability to domestic unrest and international scrutiny. See their "Why Do Authoritarian Regimes Sign the Convention Against Torture? Signaling, Domestic Politics and Non-Compliance," *Quarterly Journal of Political Science*, vol. 6, nos. 3–4, 2011.

[5] This belief is prevalent. For a sample, see American Law Institute, Restatement (Third) of the Foreign Relations Law of the United States, 702(d) (1986); David Weissbrodt and Cheryl Heilman, "Defining Torture and Cruel, Inhuman, and Degrading Treatment," *Law and Inequality*, vol. 29, no. 2 (Summer 2011); and Bruno Simma and Philip Alston, "The Sources of Human Rights Law: Custom, Jus Cogens, and General Principles," *Australian Yearbook*, 1992, p. 82.

[6] International Law Commission, "Text of the Draft Conclusions on Identification of Customary International Law Adopted by the Commission," Report of the International Law Commission at Its 68th Session, UN Doc. A/71/10 (2016), Conclusion 8, p. 77.

[7] United Nations Treaty Collection, Chapter IV, Human Rights, Convention against Torture and Other Cruel, Inhuman or Degrading Treatment or Punishment, New York, 10 December 1984, Status as AT: 28 August 2022, at: https://treaties.un.org/pages/ViewDetails.aspx?src = IND&mtdsg_no = IV-9&chapter = 4&clang = _en.

addressed the issue in specific cases have ruled that all states are bound by the prohibition. Rather, the universal prohibition against torture is a clear case of *opinio juris* not only preceding state practice but being accepted *in spite* of it. This suggests a *prima facie* case supporting the authority of international consensus over state consent.

As I demonstrate below, the universality of the ban on torture is reflected in the sheer volume and authority of international and regional treaties, conventions, organizational charters, judgments by domestic, regional, and international tribunals, and soft law. The increasing number and breadth of legal sources prohibiting torture has led to a cross-fertilization, creating a rich, detailed, and increasingly consistent body of general international law. It is one of the few legal norms that one could credibly claim has achieved the status of *jus cogens*. The absolute prohibition of torture in all circumstances is a universal standard that applies irrespective of agreement or acquiescence by any state.[8]

This chapter will examine how the prohibition of torture became a universal legal norm in international law despite its widespread practice, and explore the way this influences how political leaders attempt to reconcile this with the commonality of its use. It will also discuss how the torture ban developed from a violation of international law of states to an international crime of public officials that could be prosecuted through international tribunals and domestic courts through universal jurisdiction.

The Practice of Torture

The use of torture by public officials for political repression and law enforcement dates back millennia in all parts of the world. For hundreds of years it was legal, morally accepted, and commonplace in most ancient, medieval, and early modern societies.[9] From ancient times to the present, it was used to determine guilt or innocence, force confessions, obtain information, and as punishment and a deterrent to maintain social order. Often it was

---

[8] See Association for the Prevention of Torture and the Center for Justice and International Law, *Torture in International Law: A Guide to Jurisprudence*, 2008, p. 180.

[9] The first known use of torture to prove guilt or innocence (known as "trial by ordeal") dates back the Sumerian Code of Ur-Nammu in the 21st century BCE and the Babylonian Code of Hammurabi in the 18th century BCE. See Museum of Torture, "History of Torture," at https://tortureum.com/history-of-torture/ (accessed 22 March 2021).

carried out in public as a form of state terrorism and humiliation.[10] In addition to governments, other types of public authorities, such as the European Catholic Church, used torture extensively to coerce confessions and intimidate nonbelievers and heretics during the height of its political power in Europe.[11]

Torture usually involves several types of perpetrators, all of whom are culpable for the act: the individuals who inflict the pain, the supervisors or commanders who order the act, and the public officials who may not be directly involved but have knowledge of it and choose to either permit or ignore it.[12] The typical torturer tends to be a law enforcement official or member of the security or intelligence services; a torturer may also be someone with no official status acting in collusion with, or to advance the purposes of, a public official. In some cases, perpetrators include medical personnel who supervise torture to ensure that the victim does not die during the assaults and psychologists who provide assistance in determining the most effective methods of torture.[13]

Unlike most other forms of mass state violence, torture is not exclusively employed for political purposes. Police and other security agencies torture criminal suspects and even witnesses to extract confessions, gather information, impose punishment, or exact revenge against an unpopular detainee. Soldiers torture prisoners of war and civilians during armed conflicts for similar purposes. Still, agents of the state frequently employ torture to immobilize and intimidate political opponents and induce a sense of terror and fear within a population. They often target those for whom they have contempt and wish to purge from society, for example, marginalized populations, foreigners, migrants, and ethnic, racial, or religious minorities.[14]

International law does not make distinctions between these categories. Torture is prohibited under any and all circumstances regardless of whether

---

[10] See Brian Inne, *The History of Torture* (Amber Books, 2017) and Christopher J. Einolf, "The Fall and Rise of Torture: A Comparative and Historical Analysis," *Sociological Theory*, vol. 25, no. 2, 2007, p. 104.

[11] See, for example, Joseph Perez, *The Spanish Inquisition: A History* (Yale University Press, 2006), particularly chapter 4.

[12] Nigel S. Rodley, "The Definition(s) of Torture in International Law," *Current Legal Problems*, vol. 55, no. 1, 2002, p. 485.

[13] See Giovanni Maio, "History of Medical Involvement in Torture—Then and Now," *The Lancet*, vol. 357, 19 May 2001.

[14] James Welsh and Mary Rayner, "The 'Acceptable Enemy': Torture in Non-Political Cases," Amnesty International Report, 1996, AI Index: ACT 40/01/96; Einolf, "The Fall and Rise of Torture."

it is to control the population, maintain social order, extract information, punish criminal suspects, or humiliate and break down political opponents.

What all of these cases have in common is that the victims are powerless to defend themselves or even resist, because they are in the custody and under the control of the people responsible for their detention, treatment, or punishment.[15] Aside from the blatant assault on the dignity and bodily integrity of an individual, this is the element that makes torture so objectionable in both international law and public discourse. There is a long history in international law forbidding violence against defenseless victims, regardless of who they are. Soldiers have been prohibited from attacking an undefended town or abusing enemy combatants who are *hors de combat* or in their custody.[16] Political leaders, security agencies, and law enforcement officers are proscribed from engaging in one-sided violence against individuals who are unarmed and do not pose a threat to them.[17]

The generally accepted legal definition of torture, drawn from the Convention Against Torture and Other Cruel, Inhuman or Degrading Treatment or Punishment (discussed below), is fairly specific:

> any act by which severe pain or suffering, whether physical or mental, is intentionally inflicted on a person for such purposes as obtaining from him or a third person information or a confession, punishing him for an act he or a third person has committed or is suspected of having committed, or intimidating or coercing him or a third person, or for any reason based on discrimination of any kind, when such pain or suffering is inflicted by or at the instigation of or with the consent or acquiescence of a public official or other person acting in an official capacity.[18]

---

[15] J. Herman Burgers and Hans Danelius, *The United Nations Convention Against Torture: A Handbook on the Convention Against Torture and Other Cruel, Inhuman or Degrading Treatment or Punishment*, (Martinus Nijhoff, 1988), p. 149.

[16] For example, Article 25 of the 1899 Hague Regulations states that "the attack or bombardment of towns, villages, habitations or buildings which are not defended, is prohibited." Convention (IV) respecting the Laws and Customs of War on Land, and its annex, Regulations concerning the Laws and Customs of War on Land, The Hague, 18 October 1907. Article 3 of the Convention (I) for the Amelioration of the Condition of the Wounded and Sick in Armed Forces in the Field, Geneva, 12 August 1949, prohibits violence to life and person, in particular murder of all kinds, mutilation, cruel treatment, and torture of any soldier who is in the power of an adverse party, expresses an intention to surrender, has been rendered unconscious, or is otherwise incapacitated by wounds or sickness, and is therefore incapable of defending himself or herself.

[17] One-sided violence is distinguished from armed conflict in that it involves attacks by a government or formally organized group against defenseless civilians rather than combat. See: Therese Pettersson, Uppsala Conflict Data Program, One-sided Violence Codebook vol. 19, no. 1, 2019.

[18] UN General Assembly, *Convention Against Torture and Other Cruel, Inhuman or Degrading Treatment or Punishment*, 10 December 1984, United Nations, Treaty Series, vol. 1465, Article 1(1).

The key elements include the type of abuse (severe pain and suffering); intentionality (deliberately inflicted rather than an incidental result of lawful sanctions); the identity or status of the perpetrator (a public official or agent of the state acting in an official capacity); and the purposes of the act (extracting a confession, obtaining information, punishment, political intimidation and coercion, or discrimination). The status of the perpetrator has subsequently been interpreted by jurists and legal analysts to include those acting in an official capacity on behalf of *de facto* nonstate authorities who hold comparable governmental powers, for example, members of paramilitary organizations who have effective control over a territory and its administration.[19]

The Rome Statute of the ICC is the other major document that defines torture. Its approach is similar but less specific and with fewer required elements: "the intentional infliction of severe pain or suffering, whether physical or mental, upon a person in the custody or under the control of the accused; except that torture shall not include pain or suffering arising only from, inherent in or incidental to lawful sanctions."[20] Unlike the Convention Against Torture (CAT), the ICC does not require that the perpetrator be an agent of the state, nor is it required that torture have a specific purpose; the act is itself a violation regardless of its purpose.

These differences are ones of focus rather than principle. While the CAT was designed to establish state obligations under international human rights law, the Rome Statute is concerned with establishing judicial standards to prosecute the individual violators under international criminal law.[21] Because state parties to the CAT are legally obligated to incorporate its provisions into their national legal systems and enforce them through their executive and judicial institutions, the definition of torture is very detailed and specific. Indeed, the Convention requires that state parties assert criminal jurisdiction over acts of torture, prosecute or extradite its offenders, and exclude any statements obtained through torture in future legal proceedings. These are serious obligations not required for inhuman acts that fall below the threshold of torture.

According to the *travaux préparatoires* of the conference where the CAT was drafted, the delegates to the conference sought to distinguish suffering

---

[19] See Committee on Civil and Political Rights, *Elmi v. Australia*, Communication 120/1998, 14 May 1999, cited in Office of the UN High Commissioner on Human Rights, "Interpretation of Torture in the Light of the Practice and Jurisprudence of International Bodies," 11 December 2012, p. 5.

[20] Rome Statute of the International Criminal Court, United Nations Treaty System, vol. 2187, entered into force 1 July 2002, Article 7(2)(e).

[21] Rodley, "The Definition(s) of Torture in International Law," p. 469.

that might result from the disproportionate use of force against criminal suspects and the deliberate infliction of pain for specific purposes, such as obtaining information or intimidating a population.[22] On the other hand, as a document detailing criminal acts, the Rome Statute is more concerned with the nature of the acts by individual perpetrators rather than their motives.

At any rate, governments hold the primary responsibility to prevent torture. Under international law, all states are required to take effective legislative, administrative, judicial, or other measures to prevent acts of torture, particularly those regarding their public officials. According to the ICTY, for example:

> States are obliged not only to prohibit and punish torture, but also to forestall its occurrence: it is insufficient merely to intervene after the infliction of torture, when the physical or moral integrity of human beings has already been irremediably harmed.... It follows that international rules prohibit not only torture but also the failure to adopt the national measures necessary for implementing the prohibition.[23]

Sources of the Universal Prohibition

The widespread use of torture, along with the occasional defense of the practice by public officials in certain circumstances, suggest that its ban is not reflected in consistent state practice. At the same time, the prohibition is included in a wide range of treaties, conventions, and judicial judgments spanning several areas of international law. It is also one of the few acts over which states may exercise universal jurisdiction and one of the few legal norms that may have achieved the status of *jus cogens*. Although the use of torture was not included as a specific offense in the Nuremberg Charter, it has been prominently mentioned in every international human rights treaty since: the Universal Declaration of Human Rights; International Covenant on Political and Civil Rights; Convention on the Rights of the Child; Convention on the Rights of Persons with Disabilities; International Convention on the

---

[22] Burgers and Danelius, *The United Nations Convention Against Torture*, p. 149.
[23] International Criminal Tribunal for the Former Yugoslavia, "Prosecutor v. Anto Furundzija, Judgement," 10 December 1998, para. 148.

Elimination of All Forms of Racial Discrimination; and the International Convention on the Suppression and Punishment of the Crime of Apartheid.[24]

It is also included in all regional human rights charters. Torture is explicitly prohibited in the European Convention for the Protection of Human Rights and Fundamental Freedoms; the African Charter on Human and Peoples' Rights (Bangui Charter); American Convention on Human Rights; Arab Charter of Human Rights; and the Cairo Declaration of Human Rights in Islam.[25] Indeed, the African Charter lists torture and cruel, inhuman, or degrading punishment and treatment as a "form of exploitation and degradation of man" alongside slavery and the slave trade. The European Convention (Article 15/2), American Convention (Article 27), and Arab Charter (Article 8) specifically list the prohibition of torture as nonderogable.

In addition to human rights agreements, torture is one of the very few acts that constitute a "grave breach" in all modern agreements outlining the laws of armed conflict.[26]

Like genocide, the ban on torture is institutionalized primarily through a multilateral lawmaking treaty initiated by the United Nations. And like the genocide convention, the treaty was concluded after considerable deliberation among the member states over a long period of time. It began with the 1975 "Torture Declaration," by the General Assembly, the first formal

---

[24] United Nations, Universal Declaration of Human Rights, Article 5; UN General Assembly, International Covenant on Civil and Political Rights, 16 December 1966, United Nations, Treaty Series, vol. 999, Article 7; Convention on the Rights of the Child, United Nations, Treaty Series, vol. 1577, Article 37; Convention on the Rights of Persons with Disabilities, General Assembly Resolution A/61/611 (2006), Article 15; International Convention on the Elimination of All Forms of Racial Discrimination, United Nations, Treaty Series, vol. 660, p. 195, Article 5; and International Convention on the Suppression and Punishment of the Crime of Apartheid General Assembly Resolution 3068 (XXVIII)), Article 2(a)II.

[25] Council of Europe, European Convention for the Protection of Human Rights and Fundamental Freedoms, as amended by Protocols Nos. 11 and 14, 4 November 1950, Article 3; Organization of African Unity, African Charter on Human and Peoples' Rights ("Banjul Charter"), 27 June 1981, Article 5; Organization of American States, American Convention on Human Rights, "Pact of San Jose", Costa Rica, 22 November 1969, Article 5; Arab Charter of Human Rights, Article 8; Organization of the Islamic Conference, Cairo Declaration on Human Rights in Islam, 5 August 1990, Article 20.

[26] Convention (I) for the Amelioration of the Condition of the Wounded and Sick in Armed Forces in the Field, Geneva, 12 August 1949, Articles 12 and 50; Convention (II) for the Amelioration of the Condition of Wounded, Sick and Shipwrecked Members of Armed Forces at Sea, Geneva, 12 August 1949, Articles 12 and 51; Convention (III) relative to the Treatment of Prisoners of War, Geneva, 12 August 1949, Articles 17, 87, and 130; Convention (IV) relative to the Protection of Civilian Persons in Time of War, Geneva, 12 August 1949, Articles 32 and 147; Protocol Additional to the Geneva Conventions of 12 August 1949, and relating to the Protection of Victims of International Armed Conflicts (Protocol I), 8 June 1977, Article 75 (2a and e); Protocol Additional to the Geneva Conventions of 12 August 1949, and relating to the Protection of Victims of Non-International Armed Conflicts (Protocol II), 8 June 1977, Article 4 (2a and h).

statement declaring the practice to constitute a violation of international law.[27] Prior to this resolution, the protection against abusive treatment was an aspirational right purportedly held by individuals rather than an obligation imposed upon states.[28] For example, the only mention of torture in the Universal Declaration of Human Rights and the International Covenant for Civil and Political Rights was a short statement saying, "No one shall be subjected to torture or to cruel, inhuman or degrading treatment or punishment."[29]

The Torture Declaration initiated a process spanning almost a decade that led to one of the world's most consequential international human rights lawmaking treaties. Following its Declaration, the General Assembly specifically requested that the Commission on Human Rights draft a convention against torture and other cruel, inhuman, or degrading treatment.[30] After six years of contentious negotiations, the Assembly adopted Resolution 39/46 on 10 December 1984, which approved the draft and opened it up to all states for ratification. As of mid-2021, the Convention has 170 parties. The international convention is reinforced by similar regional treaties in Europe and South and North America.[31]

Significantly, the Convention does not specifically designate torture as an international crime, nor does it create liability for individuals engaging in it. These designations developed over the subsequent decades. Rather, it requires the state parties to use their domestic political and legal systems to prevent and punish torture. Article 10 of the Convention requires states to educate their "law enforcement personnel, civil or military, medical personnel, public officials, and other persons who may be involved in the custody, interrogation or treatment of any individual subjected to

---

[27] United Nations, "The Protection of All Persons from Being Subjected to Torture and Other Cruel, Inhuman or Degrading Treatment or Punishment," General Assembly Resolution 3452 (XXX), 9 December 1975.

[28] See, for example, General Assembly Resolution 3059, which simply "rejects" the practice of torture and calls on states to join existing instruments that contain provisions renouncing torture. UN General Assembly, "Question of Torture and Other Cruel, Inhuman and Degrading Treatment or Punishment," 28th session, 2 November 1973.

[29] United Nations, Universal Declaration of Human Rights, Article 5; UN General Assembly, International Covenant on Civil and Political Rights, 16 December 1966, United Nations Treaty Series, vol. 999, Article 7.

[30] United Nations General Assembly, "Draft Convention Against Torture and Other Cruel, Inhuman or Degrading Treatment or Punishment," Resolution 32/62, 8 December 1977.

[31] See the Organization of American States, Inter-American Convention to Prevent and Punish Torture, 9 December 1985, OAS Treaty Series, No. 67; and Council of Europe, European Convention for the Prevention of Torture and Inhuman or Degrading Treatment or Punishment, 26 November 1987, ETS 126.

any form of arrest, detention or imprisonment" about the prohibition against torture. Article 11 mandates that states "keep under systematic review interrogation rules, instructions, methods and practices, as well as arrangements for the custody and treatment of persons subjected to any form of arrest, detention or imprisonment." Article 12 requires the parties to the Convention to "promptly and impartially" investigate allegations of torture.

Although the parties are obliged to punish acts of torture that are committed on their territories, under the terms of the Convention they are not also obliged to criminalize acts amounting to torture as a separate offense in their domestic laws. This increases the importance of international law in establishing a global ban on the practice. At the same time, the Convention established three bedrock principles that now define the obligations of states (and their agents) and establish the foundation for criminalizing the practice internationally. These principles are now firmly rooted in general international law.

First, the prohibition of torture is absolute. According to Article 2, "no exceptional circumstances whatsoever, whether a state of war or a threat of war, internal political instability or any other public emergency, may be invoked as a justification of torture." The language is unambiguous; the obligation is nonderogable, a position endorsed by virtually all domestic and international courts and repeated in all subsequent regional and international treaties addressing the practice.

Second, the principle of non-refoulement ensures that states cannot evade their obligations by sending detainees to another county in order to be tortured there, nor can they favorably respond to a request from another state to extradite a suspect if they believe that he or she will likely be subjected to torture or mistreatment. According to Article 13, "no State Party shall expel, return [*refouler*] or extradite a person to another State where there are substantial grounds for believing that he would be in danger of being subjected to torture." To make such a determination, the CAT requires states to examine all relevant factors, including whether there exists a consistent pattern of gross or flagrant violations of human rights in the country in question. This prohibition is also unambiguous and, like torture itself, does not permit any exceptions.

Third, the Convention expands the prohibition to include "other acts of cruel, inhuman or degrading treatment or punishment which do not amount to torture . . . when such acts are committed by or at the instigation of or with the consent or acquiescence of a public official or other person acting in an official capacity."[32] This was designed to prevent violators who engage in highly abusive practices to claim that their actions fall short of torture and are therefore legal. However the Convention did not define what constitutes cruel, inhuman, or degrading treatment, and therefore it fell to political institutions and judicial bodies to do so in subsequent years. This continues to be a source of controversy, as public officials attempt to redefine which acts fall within this standard and how this is distinguished from torture (see below).

In addition to the formal legal agreements, the prohibition against torture has been incorporated into soft law. For example, following lengthy and intense negotiations, the UN General Assembly unanimously adopted a resolution in 2015 (including all 193 member states) declaring that the prohibition against torture is not only absolute and nonderogable; it is a peremptory norm of international law without territorial limitation. It further held that legal and procedural safeguards against such acts must not be subject to measures that would circumvent this right.[33] Finally, the resolution "welcomed" the Convention against Torture Initiative introduced by Denmark, Chile, Ghana, Indonesia, and Morocco designed to achieve universal ratification of the CAT by 2024.

Searching for Loopholes

The prohibition against torture is so firmly rooted in international law that many public officials wishing to circumvent the prohibition have been forced to develop various legal machinations.

Some have sought to exploit the distinction between torture (which is absolute and defined in treaty law) and cruel, inhuman, and degrading treatment (which is more ambiguous and mentioned but not defined in either the CAT or the Rome Statute). Both are forms of abusive treatment, and as such, the distinction between the two categories requires some interpretation. Generally, the difference lies with the severity of the mistreatment,

---

[32] Convention Against Torture and Other Cruel, Inhuman or Degrading Treatment or Punishment, adopted and opened for signature, ratification and accession by General Assembly Resolution 39/46 of 10 December 1984, Article 16.
[33] General Assembly Resolution on December 17, 2015, A/RES/70/146.

the cumulative effect of the abuse, the vulnerability of the victim, and the degree to which the abuse is committed in pursuit of a purpose outlined in the CAT.[34]

At the same time, the line that divides the two forms of abuse is not one between prohibited and permissible conduct—both are violations of international law—but rather between categories of prohibited conduct that are subject to different implementation regimes.[35] For example, although both forms are prohibited in the CAT, the provisions in the treaty that refer to state obligations for prevention, non-refoulement, extradition, domestic criminalization, and the exercise of universal jurisdiction specifically apply only to torture, not to cruel or inhuman treatment.[36] For some legal scholars, this provides flexibility, allowing forms of physical or psychological pressure that fall short of torture during interrogation under extreme circumstances.[37]

Of course, human rights law has expanded significantly since the Convention was drafted during the early 1980s, and the development of international criminal law, global and regional judicial institutions, regional treaties, and a robust torture regime has greatly expanded the scope of the torture ban. This is one of the principal reasons those who are not party to the Convention are still expected to adhere to its provisions.

Still, the distinction between torture and inhuman treatment has both legal and political value. To some degree, it mirrors the conceptual distinction raised when trying to determine if a pattern of atrocities against a civilian population rises to the level of genocide (discussed in the previous chapter). Like genocide, torture is viewed both politically and legally as a distinct form of mistreatment perpetrated by public officials against defenseless victims. Just as many people view genocide as the "crime of crimes" against human collectivities, torture is seen as the ultimate abuse of the individual.

---

[34] Manfred Nowak and Elizabeth McArthur, *The United Nations Convention Against Torture: A Commentary* (Oxford University Press, 2008), p. 73; Office of the UN High Commissioner on Human Rights, "Interpretation of Torture in the Light of the Practice and Jurisprudence of International Bodies," 11 December 2012, pp. 6–8; Human Rights Committee, General Comment No. 20 on Prohibition of Torture, or Other Cruel, Inhuman, or Degrading Treatment or Punishment, UN Doc. HRI/GEN1/Rev.7 (2004), p. 4; Manfred Nowak, "What Practices Constitute Torture," *Human Rights Quarterly*, vol. 28, no. 4, November 2006, p. 809; Manfred Nowak, "Mind the Gap: Purpose, Pain, and the Difference between Torture and Inhuman Treatment," *Human Rights Brief*, vol. 14, no. 2, 2007.

[35] See Brad R. Roth, "Just Short of Torture: Abusive Treatment and the Limits of International Criminal Justice," *Journal of International Criminal Justice*, vol. 6, 2008.

[36] Convention Against Torture and Other Cruel, Inhuman or Degrading Treatment or Punishment, Articles 2–9.

[37] See, for example, Yuval Shany, "The Prohibition Against Torture and Cruel, Inhuman, and Degrading Treatment and Punishment: Can the Absolute Be Relativized under Existing International Law?," *Catholic University Law Review*, vol. 56, no. 3, Spring 2007.

For this reason, some public officials and legal advisors try to avoid the torture label by arguing that their actions may be cruel and degrading but don't rise to the level of torture. This certainly suggests that governments view torture as universally taboo, but it also raises the question of whether states can circumvent their obligations by relabeling their actions as something less than torture.

The term "cruel, inhuman, or degrading" is widely used in both human rights and criminal law, and therefore states are legally proscribed from committing abuses that fail to meet the technical definition of torture. However the degree to which a particular interrogation or punishment meets even this standard can be more difficult to determine than identifying torture. This has been a source of controversy, particularly within states that operate under the rule of law and are subject to oversight by independent courts.

The Trial Chamber of the ICTY held that in assessing the seriousness of the acts charged as torture, one must take into account all the circumstances of the case, including the nature and context of the infliction of pain, the premeditation and institutionalization of the ill treatment, the physical condition of the victim, the manner and method used, and the position of inferiority of the victim.[38]

This issue was also addressed by the European Court of Human Rights in a case involving the United Kingdom's abusive treatment of suspects from the Irish Republican Army. In *Ireland v. United Kingdom*, the court held that treatment is inhuman if it constitutes a deliberate infliction of severe suffering, mental or physical, which, in the particular situation, is unjustified. This is determined, at least in part, by the duration of treatment, the physical and mental effects, and the sex and state of health of the victim.[39] It is degrading if it grossly humiliates a person before others or drives him or her to act against his or her will or conscience.[40]

The same court opined that torture deserved a "special stigma" that is not merited by other forms of inhuman or degrading treatment. They ruled that forcing detainees to stand for long periods of time in a "stress position," hooding (covering the head with a bag), subjection to continuous loud

---

[38] William A. Schabas, "The Crime of Torture and the International Criminal Tribunals," *Case Western Reserve Journal of International Law*, vol. 37, 2006, p. 362.

[39] European Court of Human Rights, *Ireland v. United Kingdom*, para 162.

[40] Omer Ze'ev Bekerman, "Torture: The Absolute Prohibition of a Relative Term: Does Everyone Know What Is in Room 101?," *The American Journal of Comparative Law*, vol. 53, no. 4, Fall 2005, p. 753.

noises, sleep deprivation, and deprivation of food and drink constituted inhuman and degrading treatment, but not torture.[41] However, from a legal standpoint, this was a distinction without a difference since the court also found that inhuman and degrading treatment was still illegal under regional and international law even if it does not meet the threshold of torture.[42]

The distinction between torture and inhuman treatment offered by the European Court has been much criticized by many legal analysts and other human rights bodies; most international tribunals have declined to follow their interpretation.[43] At any rate, the court subsequently challenged its own narrow approach, ruling in a subsequent case that "certain acts which were classified in the past as 'inhuman and degrading treatment' as opposed to 'torture' could be classified differently in the future."[44]

Legal analysts and political leaders have also considered the degree to which certain types of punishments and other coercive acts constitute torture as opposed to other forms of state violence. For example, rape that is perpetrated at the behest of a commander is considered an element of a crime against humanity, but only if it is part of a widespread or systematic attack against a civilian population on national, political, ethnic, racial, or religious grounds. However, according to Special Rapporteur on Torture Manfred Nowak, "it is widely recognized, including by former Special Rapporteurs on torture and by regional jurisprudence, that rape constitutes torture when it is carried out by or at the instigation of or with the consent or acquiescence of public officials."[45] Thus, no connection to a broader systemic attack is required for it to be considered a criminal act under international law.

This position was also taken by the ICTR, which held that rape violated the prohibition against torture where it is used for such purposes as intimidation, degradation, humiliation, discrimination, punishment, control, or destruction of a person, and when inflicted by or at the instigation of or with the consent or acquiescence of a public official or other person acting in an official capacity.[46]

---

[41] Bekerman, "Torture," p. 754.

[42] Louis-Philippe Rouillard, "Misinterpreting the Prohibition of Torture under International Law: The Office of Legal Counsel Memorandum," *American University International Law Review*, vol. 21, no. 1, 2005, p. 24.

[43] Schabas, "The Crime of Torture and the International Criminal Tribunals."

[44] Cited in Office of the UN High Commissioner on Human Rights, "Interpretation of Torture in the Light of the Practice and Jurisprudence of International Bodies," 11 December 2012, p. 8.

[45] Special Rapporteur on Torture report before the Human Rights Council, 15 January 2008, A/HRC/7/3, para 36.

[46] International Criminal Tribunal for Rwanda, "The Prosecutor v. Jean-Paul Akayesu," Trial judgment, Case No. ICTR-96-4-T, para. 597.

Other practices, such as corporal punishment, flogging, severing limbs, and prolonged solitary confinement, are more controversial.[47] In *Osbourne v. Jamaica* the UN Human Rights Committee opined, "Irrespective of the nature of the crime that is to be punished, however brutal it may be, it is the firm opinion of the Committee that corporal punishment constitutes cruel, inhuman and degrading treatment or punishment contrary to article 7 of the Covenant."[48] Although the Committee is not a legal body, its opinion does carry weight with both political leaders and legal analysts.

The most audacious and blatant attempt to circumvent the universal ban on torture has been the redefinition of the term "severe pain and suffering" by political leaders justifying what they term "enhanced interrogation" and other techniques that appear on their face to be acts of torture. This approach was employed by some democratic states operating under the rule of law after 11 September 2001.

In 2002, for example, U.S. Attorney General Alberto Gonzales asked the Office of Legal Counsel at the Justice Department to prepare legal opinions on how much flexibility there was in the interrogation standards under the CAT, federal statute, and other binding international law instruments. In particular, he wanted to legally justify the use of waterboarding, a technique that uses towels soaked with water to suffocate detainees and provoke the sensation of drowning. The effect results within a few seconds or minutes and leaves no external injuries, thereby eluding a criminal definition of torture, which often requires proof of injury, bleeding, or other physical harm.[49]

John Yoo, the second-ranking official at the Office, drafted a memo providing such a justification, which was then submitted to Gonzales by Assistant Attorney General Jay Bybee. Their legal opinion was creative, to say the least: "The victim must experience intense pain or suffering of the kind that is equivalent to the pain that would be associated with serious physical injury so severe that death, organ failure or permanent damage resulting in a loss of significant body functions will likely result." Moreover, "severe mental pain requires suffering not just at the moment of infliction but it also requires

---

[47] For a good discussion of these issues, see Manfred Nowak, *Torture: An Expert's Confrontation with an Everyday Evil* (University of Pennsylvania Press, 2018), chapters 7–10.

[48] United Nations Human Rights Committee, "Osbourne (George) v Jamaica: Merits," Communication No 759/1997, UN Doc CCPR/C/68/D/759/1997.

[49] Cristián Correa, "Waterboarding Prisoners and Justifying Torture: Lessons for the U.S. from the Chilean Experience," *Human Rights Brief*, vol. 14, no. 2, 2007.

lasting psychological harm, such as seen in mental disorders."[50] Thus, according to memo, the enhanced interrogation techniques might constitute some form of inhuman or degrading treatment, but not torture.

Not surprisingly, few legal analysts outside of the George W. Bush administration found this to be a serious interpretation of the law, much less persuasive. It has been the general consensus that the definition of torture under international law is unambiguous and that simply relabeling it "enhanced interrogation" does not release public officials from the universal legal obligation prohibiting the practice.[51] This position is supported by the fact that Yoo's theories were subsequently quietly withdrawn by the U.S. government and have never resurfaced.

Finally, some states have attempted to skirt the universal ban on refoulement by relying on written diplomatic assurances from the receiving state that the suspects would not be subject to torture, in cases where there may be reason to believe that they would otherwise face this outcome. The purpose of such assurances is to exact guarantees of compliance from states that are known to violate established human rights obligations or have a history of its agents engaging in torture. Thus, the *de facto* function of a diplomatic assurance is to elevate the circumstances to a case of diplomatic significance or personal trust between senior state officials.[52]

The degree to which this provides a legitimate legal loophole is questionable. Since the prohibition against refoulement is already absolute and nonderogable, diplomatic assurances do not increase the legal obligation of the receiving state. However, they may increase the political costs of a violation, since they directly affect the credibility of the commitments to another state and therefore the receiving state's reputation and credibility.

At the same time, many human rights experts and lawyers clearly believe that the use of these assurances threatens to create a dangerous loophole in the prohibition against torture, even if the sending state is sincere in wanting to comply with its legal obligations. Rather than enhancing human

---

[50] Jay S. Bybee, Assistant Attorney General at the U.S. Department of Justice, Office of Legal Counsel, Memorandum for Alberto R. Gonzales, Counsel to the President, Re: Standards of Conduct for Interrogation under 18 U.S.C. §§2340–23, 1 August 2002.

[51] The literature on this is too extensive to cite. For a sample, see Rouillard, "Misinterpreting the Prohibition of Torture under International Law"; Jose A. Alvarez, "Torturing the Law," *Case Western Reserve Journal of International Law,* vol. 37, 2006; Michael P. Scharf, "International Law and the Torture Memos" (2009), Faculty Publications. Case Western University School of Law Commons, 2009; Harold Koh, "Can the President Be Torturer in Chief?," *Indiana Law Journal,* vol. 81, 2006.

[52] Nina Larsaeus, "The Use of Diplomatic Assurances in the Prevention of Prohibited Treatment," University of Oxford Refugee Studies Center, Working Paper No. 32, October 2006.

rights protection, one legal scholar argues, diplomatic assurances serve as a fig leaf for torture.[53] Thus, international officials firmly believe that diplomatic assurances are not an adequate means to satisfy the principle of non-refoulement in relation to countries where torture is systematically practiced.[54] If officials from the sending state believe that there is a reasonable chance that the suspect could be subjected to torture or mistreatment, the use of diplomatic assurance would violate the legal norm of non-refoulement that is embedded not only in international law but, in many cases, domestic law as well.

In extreme cases, governments try to circumvent their own domestic laws and international obligations prohibiting torture by relying on another state to interrogate and torture on its behalf. This is known as "extraordinary rendition" and involves the extrajudicial transfer of a suspect to another country for detention and abusive interrogation outside the normal legal system. This practice was used extensively by democratic states seeking to avoid public scrutiny and legal liability after the attacks on 11 September 2001.[55] These practices are unambiguously illegal under any and all circumstances, and the fact that it almost always occurs in secret suggests that those practicing it are well aware of this.[56]

The biggest challenge to the universality of the torture ban is the metaphor of the ticking bomb. The ticking bomb scenario—in which interrogators believe that they must use extreme measures to force a person to reveal the location of a bomb that could kill thousands of people—became popular in the aftermath of the 11 September 2001 attacks in the United States.[57] The

---

[53] See Benjamin Ward, "A Fig-Leaf for Torture: The Use of Diplomatic Assurances in the OSCE Region," Institute for Peace Research and Security Policy, *OSCE Yearbook,* 2005, pp. 181–183 and Human Rights Watch, "Still at Risk: Diplomatic Assurances No Safeguard against Torture," vol. 17, no. 4(D), April 2005.

[54] See, for example, United Nations Commissioner for Human Rights, "Statement of the Special Rapporteur on Torture, Manfred Nowak, to the 61st Session of the UN Commission on Human Rights," Geneva, 4 April 2005.

[55] From 2001 to 2005 the United States ran a global network to transfer terrorism suspects to secret detention sites across the world, where they were interrogated and tortured. This was done with close cooperation of U.S. allies in Western Europe. For a comprehensive study documenting this practice, see Rebecca Cordell, "Measuring Extraordinary Rendition and International Cooperation," *International Area Studies Review,* vol. 20, no. 2, June 2017.

[56] See Association of the Bar of the City of New York and Center for Human Rights and Global Justice, *Torture by Proxy: International and Domestic Law Applicable to "Extraordinary Renditions"* (ABCNY and NYU School of Law, 2004); David Weissbrodt and Amy Bergquist, "Extraordinary Rendition: A Human Rights Analysis," *Harvard Human Rights Journal,* vol. 19 (2006).

[57] For a discussion of the moral debate around this scenario, see Rory Stephen Brown, "Torture, Terrorism, and the Ticking Bomb: A Principled Response," *Journal of International Law and Policy,* vol. 4, no. 1, 2008.

purpose of this hypothetical scenario is to propose a situation in which the use of torture would be the lesser evil, so that the prohibition against torture is not in fact absolute. Of course, this line of argument does not challenge the proposition that torture is illegal under any and all circumstances; it merely proposes that there are circumstances under which it is morally justified to violate the prohibition. Still, few legal scholars or public officials actually claim the prohibition against torture can be suspended in these circumstances.[58]

Jus Cogens and Universal Jurisdiction

More than a few legal scholars confidently hold that the prohibition of torture has achieved the status of *jus cogens,* and therefore imposes obligations that are *erga omnes* (owed to the international community as a whole) on all states.[59] This claim is obviously difficult to verify. *Jus cognes* relies on a collective belief that is not easy to document in a systematic and objective way. For a legal norm to be a peremptory norm, it must reflect a value of the international community that is so fundamental to its identity that it supersedes individual will.

The prohibition against torture could reasonably be seen to meet this standard inasmuch as its use by public officials undermines the legitimacy of government and severely breaches the social contract that binds the population to the state, a tie that legitimizes the state itself. Unlike other human rights norms (such as freedom of expression), its prohibition is absolute under all circumstances, leaving no flexibility in its interpretation.

This position is supported by an increasing number of international organizations and domestic and international courts. For example, the International Law Commission, in its Draft Articles on state responsibility, posits that torture is one of only seven legal norms that are currently "clearly

---

[58] For one who does, see former civil liberties advocate Alan Dershowitz, Alan Dershowitz, 'The Case for Torturing the Ticking Bomb Terrorist' in James E. White ed., *Contemporary Moral Problems: War, Terrorism, Torture and Assassination* (Wadsworth Publishing Co., 2011). Countless legal scholars have challenged his position. See, for example, Matthew Kramer, "Alan Dershowitz's Torture-Warrant Proposal: A Critique," *University of Cambridge Faculty of Law Research Paper,* no. 2, 2015 and Jeremy Waldron, "Torture and Positive Law: Jurisprudence for the White House," *Columbia Law Review,* vol. 105, no. 6, October 2005, especially pp. 1713–1717.

[59] See, for example, Robert K. Goldman, "Trivializing Torture: The Office of Legal Counsel's 2002 Opinion Letter and International Law Against Torture," *Human Rights Brief,* vol. 12, no. 1 (2004) and Erika de Wet, "The Prohibition of Torture as an International Norm of and Its Implications for National and Customary Law," *European Journal of International Law,* vol. 15, no. 1, 2004, pp. 105–112.

accepted and recognized" as having *jus cogens* status, placing it on par with the prohibitions against slavery and genocide.[60] Similarly, the International Court of Justice has explicitly mentioned only three norms having this status: the prohibition of the use of force, the prohibition of genocide, and the prohibition of torture.[61] The International Court for the Former Yugoslavia based part of its rulings on the presumption that the crime of torture attained this status, holding:

> [The] major feature of the principle proscribing torture relates to the hierarchy of rules in the international normative order. Because of the importance of the values it protects, this principle has evolved into a peremptory norm or jus cogens, that is, a norm that enjoys a higher rank in the international hierarchy than treaty law and even "ordinary" customary rules.... The most conspicuous consequence of this higher rank is that the principle at issue cannot be derogated from by States through international treaties or local or special customs. The prohibition has now become one of the most fundamental standards of the international community.[62]

Another indication that the ban on torture is a general legal norm binding on all states is the broad acceptance among legal analysts and many public officials that it can be enforced through universal jurisdiction. This allows states to prosecute individuals accused of torture even if they are not citizens of states who are signatories to international treaties banning the practice, and even if they committed the act outside the territorial jurisdiction of the prosecuting state. The principle of universal jurisdiction is based on the idea that some acts of states are so severe that they affect all humankind, and therefore the perpetrators should not be given safe haven or impunity. States exercising universal jurisdiction are regarded as agents of the international community with a universally accepted obligation of enforcing international

---

[60] International Law Commission, "Draft Articles on Responsibility of States for Internationally Wrongful Acts, with Commentaries 2001," text adopted by the International Law Commission at its 53rd session, 2001, Article 26, Commentary (5).

[61] International Court of Justice, "Democratic. Republic of Congo v. Rwanda, Armed Activities on the Territory of the Congo (Dem. Rep. Congo v. Rwanda), Jurisdiction and Admissibility," 3 February 2006, p. 32, para. 64; "Application of the Convention on the Prevention and Punishment of the Crime of Genocide (Bosnia and Herzegovina v. Serbia and Montenegro)," Judgment, 26 February 2007, p. 111; and "Belgium v. Senegal," Questions relating to the Obligation to Prosecute or Extradite (Belgium v. Senegal), Separate Opinion (Judge Abraham), 20 July 2012, para. 99.

[62] International Criminal Tribunal for the Former Yugoslavia, "Prosecutor v. Anto Furundzija," Case No. IT-95-17/1, Trial Chamber Judgment, 10 December 1998, paras. 153 and 154.

law.⁶³ This principle regarding torture is embedded in both international conventions and the domestic law of a number of states.

Although the CAT does not explicitly *require* states to exercise universal jurisdiction to prosecute violators engaging in torture outside their territory, it does encourage it and, in doing so, provides legal cover for those states that wish to act on it. According to Article 2, "Each State Party shall likewise take such measures as may be necessary to establish its jurisdiction over such offences in cases where the alleged offender is present in any territory under its jurisdiction and it does not extradite him pursuant to article 8 [concerning extradition] to any of the States mentioned."⁶⁴ This is not limited to individuals from states who have signed the Convention; it applies to all. In addition, states are required to detain individuals present in their territory alleged to have committed torture so that they can either be tried locally or extradited to another state for trial.⁶⁵

Lawmaking treaties that authorize states to pursue universal jurisdiction not only significantly increase the legitimacy of the practice; they also suggest a broad international consensus around the legal norm represented in the agreement. Most important, they provide an opportunity for domestic lawyers and judges to pursue an expanded notion of jurisdiction, particularly in cases where their own laws do not specifically provide for it. Thus, states that accept treaties as self-executing (that is, that they can be directly applied in the courts, without the need of enabling legislation) can draw directly from the CAT to justify their use of this tool. Very few human rights conventions contain such provisions; in fact the CAT is the only one aside from the Apartheid Convention that does.⁶⁶ This suggests the importance the delegates at the drafting conference placed on universalizing the prohibition against torture.

As of 2012, 85 states have provided for universal jurisdiction over torture through legislation and their judicial systems.⁶⁷ In most cases, it is not limited to nationals of states who have ratified the CAT. This does not mean that

---

⁶³ Beth van Schaack and Ronald C. Slye, *International Criminal Law and Its Enforcement: Cases and Materials* (Foundation Press 2015), p. 53.
⁶⁴ Convention Against Torture and Other Cruel, Inhuman or Degrading Treatment or Punishment, Article 5(2).
⁶⁵ Convention Against Torture and Other Cruel, Inhuman or Degrading Treatment or Punishment, Article 6.
⁶⁶ Darren Hawkins, "Universal Jurisdiction for Human Rights: From Legal Principle to Limited Reality." *Global Governance*, vol. 9, no. 3, July–September 2003, pp. 350–351.
⁶⁷ Amnesty International, "Universal Jurisdiction: A Preliminary Survey of Legislation Around the World—2012 Update," p. 13.

most or even many of them have exercised this legal option in practice; enforcement of international law is a topic that is beyond the scope of this book. It does, however, mean that they recognize torture as a universal legal norm under international law.

International courts have recognized this as well. According to a ruling from the International Court for the Former Yugoslavia:

> The legal basis for States' universal jurisdiction over torture bears out and strengthens the legal foundation for such jurisdiction found by other courts in the inherently universal character of the crime. It has been held that international crimes being universally condemned wherever they occur, every State has the right to prosecute and punish the authors of such crimes.... This legal basis for States' universal jurisdiction over torture bears out and strengthens the legal foundation for such jurisdiction found by other courts in the inherently universal character of the crime.[68]

Anti-Torture Regime

The international legal prohibition against torture is facilitated by a large network of intergovernmental bodies and NGOs that collectively constitute a robust anti-torture regime. This regime plays an important role in institutionalizing the ban and promoting the recognition that the legal norm is deeply embedded in international law and diplomatic practice. The degree to which it also increases compliance with the norm is mixed; however, this question is beyond the scope of this chapter.

International Organizations

The primary international institution promoting the ban on the use of torture as a universal legal norm is the office of the UN Special Rapporteur on Torture and Other Cruel, Inhuman and Degrading Treatment or Punishment. The rapporteur is one of several "special procedures" created by the UN Commission on Human Rights. (The Commission has since

---

[68] International Criminal Tribunal for the Former Yugoslavia, "Prosecutor v. Anto Furundzija," paras. 156 and 126.

been replaced by the Human Rights Council.)[69] "Special procedures" refers to the independent experts and working groups created by the UN's political bodies. Their purpose is to promote human rights law and norms with member states; investigate, monitor, and report on violations; and recommend ways to improve compliance.[70]

The rapporteurs serve a three-year term. Once appointed, they are independent from both the Council and the UN member states. They promote the universalization of the torture ban through monitoring, advocacy, fact-finding, and standard-setting. As such, they visit select countries, communicate with states regarding allegations of torture, and submit annual reports on their activities to the Human Rights Council and the UN General Assembly. These reports are a primary tool to record and analyze information, present findings of investigations, express concern about particular problems, promote dialogue with authorities, and propose recommendations for corrective action.[71]

Although rapporteurs do not have coercive authority to enforce or punish violations, their independence, background, expertise, training, and prestige enables their office to promote the prohibition without being tainted by political interests. In their independent capacity, they act as a watchdog for the international prohibition against torture and help to ensure that governments and other political actors remain aware of their obligations under international law. They also serve as an authority for addressing controversies regarding the application of the CAT and defining the degree to which state practices might constitute torture or cruel, inhuman, and degrading treatment. This reinforces the power of the legal norm internationally.

The special rapporteur is empowered to examine questions of torture in all UN member states, which essentially means all states in the world, regardless of whether they signed the CAT. However, like all UN independent monitors, the work of rapporteurs is often limited by a lack of adequate cooperation from many states and the failure of some governments to implement the recommendations rapporteurs make in their reports and private

---

[69] UN Commission on Human Rights, *Torture and Other Cruel, Inhuman or Degrading Treatment or Punishment*, 13 March 1985, E/CN.4/RES/1985/33.

[70] The mandate and working procedures of the rapporteurs are articulated in detail in United Nations Human Rights Council, "Institution-Building of the United Nations Human Rights Council," Resolution 5/1, 2007, Section II.

[71] Office of the High Commissioner on Human Rights, "Human Rights Reporting," in *Manual on Human Rights Monitoring* (2011), p. 4.

communications.[72] Rapporteurs cannot visit a country without agreement from its government, something which involves considerable negotiation and which obviously limits the rapporteurs' ability to monitor some of the most egregious cases.

The other UN body that specifically addresses torture is the United Nations Committee Against Torture, a 10-person body of independent specialists established by the CAT to monitor the implementation of the Convention for the large majority of states who are parties to the treaty.[73] All parties are legally obliged under the Convention to submit regular reports to the Committee on how the rights and standards enshrined in the Convention are being observed in their country. The Committee examines each report and expresses its concerns and recommendations to the state party in the form of "concluding observations."

In developing these observations, the members of the Committee are not limited to the information provided by the state; they may utilize data from NGOs, domestic sources, and other interested parties that may be able to validate or refute the claims made by the states in their reports. The Committee makes public these reports, along with its conclusions and observations.

Requiring countries to submit reports on their compliance with human rights law is a common practice within the United Nations. These reports are supposed to describe the legal, administrative, and judicial measures taken by the state that give effect to the treaty. The reporting requirement is a compromise that compels states to account for their behavior, without giving the monitoring bodies the authority or ability to verify their accuracy through on-site inspection, except by invitation. Obviously this limits the credibility of reports that are submitted by the very governments that are being asked to account for their behavior. The Committee is a monitoring, not an enforcement, body. However, in adopting its "observations" and "conclusions," the Committee does reinforce the prohibition against torture as a universal legal norm and evaluates compliance, even if it lacks coercive authority to enforce it.

These reports—and the extensive consulting process surrounding their evaluation—facilitate public participation and scrutiny of state policies,

---

[72] See Ted Piccone, "The Contribution of the UN's Special Procedures to National Level Implementation of Human Rights Norms," *The International Journal of Human Rights*, vol. 15, no. 2, 2011.

[73] UN General Assembly, Convention Against Torture and Other Cruel, Inhuman or Degrading Treatment or Punishment, Article 17.

laws, and programs to advance compliance with each state's commitment.[74] Moreover, domestic human rights groups within civil society often take advantage of the process to promote their own evaluations and observations. This provides an additional opportunity to mobilize domestic action and pressure their governments.

The most effective element of the anti-torture regime's ability to universalize the ban on abusive treatment is the monitoring process created by the Optional Protocol for the Convention Against Torture (OPCAT), which entered into force in 2006. OPCAT establishes an international inspection system for domestic detention facilities run by states that are party to the Protocol and creates a 10-person Subcommittee on the Prevention of Torture comprised of independent specialists to oversee the process. Under OPCAT, states not only agree to allow international inspections by the Subcommittee; they must establish an independent national prevention mechanism within their countries to conduct inspections of all detention facilities and closed environments.[75] The mechanism often works with domestic NGOs regarding how OPCAT should be implemented in their country.

The OPCAT provides an important link between the legal ban on torture and the ability of international institutions to enforce it. This reinforces the universality of the ban inasmuch as it shifts the focus from national compliance to international implementation and enforcement. While the CAT itself establishes a strict legal standard for defining and prohibiting torture and other cruel and humiliating treatment under all circumstances, it does not include any instruments or procedures for verifying compliance beyond analyzing the self-reports submitted by the parties to the treaty. The special rapporteurs often negotiate visits to detention centers with national governments, but they lack the authority to conduct inspections without permission from the state. The protocol has no such limitations.

As of 2021, only a little more than half of the CAT state parties have ratified the Protocol, limiting the scope of its authority.[76]

---

[74] Office of the High Commissioner on Human Rights, "Reporting Compliance by State Parties to the Human Rights Treaty Bodies," 15 May 2020.
[75] UN General Assembly, Optional Protocol to the Convention Against Torture and Other Cruel, Inhuman and Degrading Treatment or Punishment, 9 January 2003, A/RES/57/199, especially Parts I and IV.
[76] United Nations High Commissioner on Human Rights, "Status of Ratification, Optional Protocol to the Convention against Torture and Other Cruel, Inhuman or Degrading Treatment or Punishment," at https://indicators.ohchr.org (accessed 30 March 2021).

NGOs

The institutionalization of the prohibition against torture as a universal legal norm is also facilitated by a large network of international NGOs.

The decades-long effort by NGOs to stigmatize, expose, and de-legitimize torture as a political practice began in 1972, when Amnesty International launched its Campaign for the Abolition of Torture. The campaign was designed to raise awareness of the practice and advocate for a total international legal ban, even before there was an international convention prohibiting the act. Amnesty's chair Sean McBride declared at the time that the goal of the campaign was to make torture as "unthinkable as slavery" by rendering it universally prohibited.[77] On 10 December 1972, Amnesty held the Conference for the Abolition of Torture in Paris, ushering in a new era of anti-torture activism.

Amnesty's pressure campaign is credited with influencing the UN General Assembly to pass its resolutions declaring torture to be a heinous practice and, subsequently, declaring it to be a violation of international law. In fact, it was Amnesty's subsequent reports on the global practice of torture that raised the practice as an international issue and helped to facilitate the growing belief that its use constituted a fundamental violation of human rights under all circumstances.[78]

Since then many other human rights and humanitarian organizations have mobilized the public, coordinated the activities of civil society organizations, and provided a presence at meetings of intergovernmental organizations. Two organizations/coalitions of note are the Swiss-based Association for the Prevention of Torture (formerly the Swiss Committee Against Torture) and the World Organization Against Torture (Organisation Mondiale Contre la Torture).

The Association for the Prevention of Torture was originally founded to promote an international convention creating a universal system of visits to places of detention. Its initial focus was on the adoption of the European Convention for the Prevention of Torture in 1987, but it later shifted toward the expansion of the CAT. It provides legal advice to institutions and individuals involved in torture-prevention activities, operates training and

---

[77] Renata Meirelles, *State Violence, Torture, and Political Prisoners: On the Role Played by Amnesty International in Brazil during the Dictatorship (1964–1985)* (Routledge, 2020), p. 71.

[78] Ann Marie Clark, *Diplomacy of Conscience: Amnesty International and Changing Human Rights Norms* (Princeton University Press, 2001), p. 38.

capacity-building programs, conducts research and analysis on the causes of torture, and acts as a resource.

The World Organization Against Torture is a global network based in Geneva comprising 300 local, national, and regional organizations fighting against arbitrary detention, torture, summary and extrajudicial executions, and forced disappearances. It was founded in 1985.

The degree to which these organizations and networks help to institutionalize the prohibition against torture as part of general international law is an empirical question that requires more intensive study; however, as part of the broader anti-torture regime, they play an important role in maintaining the prohibition against torture as nonderogable in any circumstances.

Summary

The prohibition against torture has emerged as a universal legal norm since the latter part of the 20th century. Even if not committed as part of a widespread or systematic attack against a civilian population, it is a violation of international law on its face regardless of whether states consent to the ban. Regardless of whether the consistent and frequent practice of torture by states excludes its prohibition from customary law, states are still universally held to the basic rule. Additionally, it has emerged as one of the few practices cited under international criminal law, making its perpetrators liable for prosecution. This is a relatively recent development and is the culmination of decades of deliberation among a wide range of institutions.

This is all reflected in the growing number of countries ratifying the CAT. In 2006, there were 141 parties to the Convention; by 2022, there were 173.[79] This is still 25 states short of universal ratification, but it indicates that the trend is moving quickly toward that goal. At any rate, it has been established that all states are still bound by the legal norm regardless of their ratification status.

---

[79] United Nations Treaty Collection, Chapter IV (Human Rights), Status as of 3 August 2022.

6
Civilian Immunity in Domestic Armed Conflicts

Internal state violence and international armed conflicts have been traditionally regulated by two distinct legal regimes. The former falls within the broad category of human rights, while the latter are covered under the laws and customs of war. Each regime evolved along a different path, shaped by their distinct histories and the roles that the state typically performs in maintaining security and order. Human rights law has a relatively short history and is designed to protect the population from arbitrary and excessive state violence. It applies in circumstances closely associated with governance and power rather than combat with an enemy force.[1] The laws of armed conflict (LOAC) date back hundreds of years and are concerned with national security and international relations. They are considered to be *lex specialis*, a body of law that is distinct and prevails over other obligations whenever the country is at war because the condition of armed conflict poses a unique challenge to both the state and society at large.

Under international law, a state of war provides a much wider set of options for governments to engage in violent, deadly action that would be otherwise be prohibited, including killing, forcibly detaining, and destroying the property and resources of one's adversaries without any form of due process.[2]

---

[1] See Kenneth Watkin, "Controlling the Use of Force: A Role for Human Rights Norms in Contemporary Armed Conflict," *The American Journal of International Law*, vol. 98, no. 1, January 2004, p. 2.

[2] A classic example of this distinction is the 1985 bombing of row houses occupied by members of a community organization, MOVE, by the City of Philadelphia. After failing in their attempt to storm the compound and arrest its occupants, the police dropped an explosive device from a helicopter onto the bunker of the MOVE house. When the bomb exploded it ignited a gas tank, destroying 61 homes and killing the 11 members of the organization, including five children. Had this been done during an armed conflict, it could have been a legal act, assuming that the members of MOVE were considered to be combatants. However, in the context of a domestic law enforcement effort, it was an act of summary execution, a violation of due process and basic human rights. See John Ismay, "35 Years after MOVE Bombing That Killed 11, Philadelphia Apologizes," *New York Times,* 13 November 2020.

Moreover, unlike human rights law, humanitarian concerns in the LOAC are balanced against military necessity, a principle that permits a range of aggressive measures that are necessary to accomplish a legitimate military purpose.

At the same time, the LOAC limit the means and methods through which this can be accomplished. Traditionally, this focused primarily on the behavior of combatants on the battlefield. Thus, for example, the four Geneva Conventions of 1949 provide few protections to civilians during combat, focusing mostly on the treatment of those under the control of its armies, such as prisoners of war. The protection of civilians is addressed only in the Fourth Convention, and even there it focuses primarily on the treatment of populations in occupied territories.[3]

Over the past half-century, however, the international community has progressively increased the protection of civilians, creating a category of legal norms that has been termed "international humanitarian law" (IHL). IHL amends the LOAC by expanding its focus from regulating combat to protecting civilians and other individuals who do not directly participate in hostilities. It represents an attempt to limit the means and methods of warfare that parties to a conflict may employ to ensure the protection and humane treatment of noncombatants. Its purpose is to establish minimum standards of humanity that must be respected in any situation of armed conflict.[4] Principally, it aims to protect both those who are not combatants (mainly civilians, but also medical and religious personnel) and those who are *hors de combat* (literally "out of the fight," that is, combatants who no longer are able to participate in hostilities as a result of being wounded or in the custody of the adversary).[5]

IHL does not address whether a decision to use military force is legal or justified. It is concerned only with the means and methods of military operations and how it affects noncombatants. In this sense, IHL provides

---

[3] Many legal scholars make a distinction between what is termed Hague Law and Geneva Law. The former is derived from the Hague Conventions of 1899 and 1907 and addresses the means and methods of warfare, while the four Geneva Conventions of 1949 focus primarily on what has been termed the "humanitarian" aspects, such as protecting prisoners of war and the sick and wounded. The 1977 law can be viewed as a merger of the two. See, for example, Richard John Erickson, "Protocol I: A Merging of the Hague and Geneva Law of Armed Conflict," *Virginia Journal of International Law*, vol. 19, no. 3, 1979.

[4] Nils Melzer, "International Humanitarian Law: A Comprehensive Introduction," International Committee of the Red Cross, 2016, p. 17.

[5] Hans-Peter Gasser, *International Humanitarian Law: An Introduction* (Henry Dunant Institute, 1998).

a link between the legal regimes covering human rights and armed conflict. Thus, the evolution of IHL created a new area of international law that attempts to humanize warfare (to the extent that an institution based on violence and destruction can be humanized) by limiting its effects on noncombatants.[6]

At the same time, international law also distinguishes between international armed conflicts (those fought between recognized states) and those that involve at least one nonstate actor (known in international law as non-international armed conflicts). While there is little disagreement over the authority of international law regarding the former, traditionally states have jealously asserted their sovereignty involving armed violence that occurs within their borders, particularly when it involves rebels, insurgents, and guerrilla forces. Thus, even though most legal analysts and political leaders agree that the four Geneva Conventions are part of customary international law binding on all states, this does not affect the use of state violence during internal armed conflicts.[7]

This chapter will examine how the regulation of domestic armed conflicts, and in particular the protection of civilians and civilian objects during such conflicts, evolved into a universal legal norm binding on all states even if they have not signed the Second Protocol to the Geneva Conventions.[8] While the term "non-international armed conflict" covers a number of different situations involving nonstate actors, I will limit my focus to those that involve insurgent forces and a sitting government within the borders of a state. Although the rules also address the treatment of those detained as prisoners of war, I will concentrate on those aspects of international law that prohibit attacks on civilians and civilian objects.

---

[6] See Theodor Meron, "The Humanization of Humanitarian Law," *The American Journal of International Law*, vol. 94, no. 2, April 2000; Amanda Alexander, "A Short History of International Humanitarian Law," *The European Journal of International Law*, vol. 26, no. 1, 2015; and Gasser, *International Humanitarian Law*.

[7] See, for example, International Committee of the Red Cross, *Customary International Humanitarian Law* (Cambridge University Press, 2005); Theodor Meron, "The Geneva Conventions as Customary Law," *The American Journal of International Law*, vol. 81, no. 2, April 1987; Jean-Marie Henckaerts, "The Grave Breaches Regime as Customary International Law," *Journal of International Criminal Justice*, vol. 7, no. 4, September 2009.

[8] An optional protocol to a treaty or convention is a legal instrument that establishes additional rights and obligations. While the original agreement remains binding on all parties, the protocol creates new legal obligations only for those who specifically ratify it. Thus, under the doctrine of consent, states who signed the 1949 Geneva Conventions but refused to endorse the two 1977 protocols are not bound by their additional obligations.

The Limitations of the LOAC during Internal Hostilities

Since the end of World War II, the overwhelming majority of armed conflicts in the world have been internal to states.[9] Yet the laws and customs of war, as they have developed over the past few centuries, have focused almost exclusively on conflicts between states.[10] Civil wars were considered to be purely domestic affairs in which the international law of armed conflict did not apply, unless the state recognized the insurgents as belligerents, a rare act of admission. Thus, while IHL has attained a relatively high level of codification and acceptance in customary law with respect to international armed conflicts, this did not traditionally extend to internal hostilities where the rules are less clear, particularly in distinguishing between military action and law enforcement.[11] This is because governments resist acknowledging that the LOAC could be applied to internal disputes.

The regulation of internal conflicts has always been difficult, for several reasons. First, the principle of sovereignty traditionally shielded states from international scrutiny over how they respond to armed challenges to their authority within their own borders. Such challenges have taken various forms: rebellions, insurrections, revolutions, coups, and guerrilla insurgencies. Generally, states have long sought to limit international legal oversight in these matters inasmuch as such scrutiny could affect them in the future. All states share an interest in suppressing challenges to their authority from rebels. In fact, it was their concern to protect the ability to respond to such challenges against comprehensive international regulation that led them to limit the substantive provisions of what has become known

---

[9] See Uppsala Conflict Data Program and Peace Research Institute Oslo, "Armed Conflict Data Set, Version 4-2009," at: https://www.prio.org/Data/Armed-Conflict/UCDP-PRIO/Armed-Conflicts-Version-X-2009 (accessed 10 April 2021). According to research conducted by David Laitin and James Fearon, between the end of World War II and 2002, there were 122 civil wars, compared with 25 conventional wars. See their "Ethnicity, Insurgency and Civil War," *American Political Science Review*, vol. 97, no. 1, February 2003, p. 75.

[10] For example, Article 2 of the 1899 Hague Convention states, "The provisions contained in the Regulations mentioned in Article I are only binding on the Contracting Powers, in case of war between two or more of them." Similarly, the 1907 Hague Convention declares that "the provisions contained in the Regulations referred to in Article 1, as well as in the present Convention, do not apply except between Contracting powers, and then only if all the belligerents are parties to the Convention." See Convention (II) with Respect to the Laws and Customs of War on Land, The Hague, 29 July 1899 and Convention (IV) Respecting the Laws and Customs of War on Land and Its Annex: Regulations Concerning the Laws and Customs of War on Land, The Hague, 18 October 1907.

[11] Watkin, "Controlling the Use of Force," p. 10.

as Common Article 3 when the 1949 Geneva Conventions were negotiated (see below).[12]

Second, the LOAC were traditionally based on the principle of reciprocity, the notion that states will accept certain obligations with the expectation that others will abide by them equally.[13] This expectation is not only principled but also practical. Governments often adhere to a particular rule in part because they fear that a violation by their own state would likely result in similar violations by others against them. Thus, states may refrain from attacking their adversary's populated areas to avoid their own populated areas being attacked in return.

However, internal conflicts tend to be highly asymmetric, allowing government forces to engage in horrendous violence without fear of significant retaliation. Asymmetry is a condition of substantial inequality in resources such as personnel, weapons, equipment, and finances, as well as their application in terms of power projection, range, precision, command and control, training, and intelligence.[14] Governments also enjoy legal authority and international recognition, two attributes denied to their opponents. Insurgents often employ guerrilla warfare tactics to overcome their vast asymmetrical disadvantage, relying on the organization of small groups of combatants who use stealth, mobile military tactics, and maneuver to combat a larger, less mobile, and more powerful government army.[15]

This wide disparity in resources and status gives governments far less incentive to abide by any rules. Moreover, nonstate actors do not sign treaties, do not interact with other states on a regular basis, and are not members of international organizations. Governments therefore often feel less constrained by norms of reciprocity and are often less willing to apply international law to their relations with nonstate actors.

---

[12] See *Final Record of the Diplomatic Conference of Geneva of 1949*, vol. 2-B, pp. 10–15, referred to in International Committee of the Red Cross, *Commentary on the First Geneva Convention* (Cambridge University Press, 2016), fn. 191.

[13] See Bryan Peeler, *The Persistence of Reciprocity in International Humanitarian Law* (Cambridge University Press, 2021).

[14] See Michael Schmitt, "Asymmetrical Warfare and International Humanitarian Law," in Wolff Heintschel et al. (eds.), *International Humanitarian Law Facing New Challenges* (Springer, 2010), p. 17. See also David L. Buffaloe, "Defining Asymmetric Warfare," Institute of Land Warfare Papers, No. 58, September 2006, pp. 3–6 and 9–13; Michael Gross, *Moral Dilemmas of Modern War: Torture, Assassination, and Blackmail in an Age of Asymmetric Conflict* (Cambridge University Press, 2009), pp. 3–4; Toni Pfanner, "Asymmetrical Warfare from the Perspective of Humanitarian Law and Humanitarian Action," *International Review of the Red Cross*, vol. 87, no 857, March 2005, p. 151.

[15] Anthony James Joes, *Guerrilla Warfare: A Historical, Biographical, and Bibliographical Sourcebook* (Greenwood, 1996).

Third, the line between an armed conflict and other forms of political violence within a state is often unclear and contested. Civil wars do not usually begin as armed conflicts, but rather as political protests that escalate into armed hostilities, usually after the government employs brutal methods to suppress them.[16] It is often unclear exactly when the transition from violent protest to warfare occurs. This makes it difficult to objectively establish when internal violence has reached the level of an armed conflict that can be distinguished from other forms of political violence.

For example, in early 2011 hundreds of thousands of Syrians began a widespread campaign of protest against the authoritarian government of Bashar al-Assad, actions that were part of the Arab Spring. The Syrian government responded by deploying police, military, and paramilitary forces to violently suppress the demonstrations. Yet it was not until 18 months later that the International Committee of the Red Cross (ICRC) declared that the conflict constituted a civil war under international law, a declaration that was shared by many governments. Even then, President al-Assad continued to reject this characterization.[17]

The distinction between civil unrest and armed conflict is further complicated in cases where insurgents simultaneously engage in both military operations (which are regulated by the LOAC) and terrorism (which is typically treated by governments as criminal activity). The Irish Republican Army (IRA) in Northern Ireland in the late 20th century is a good example.[18] This ambiguity enables governments to claim that the authorities are engaging in law enforcement and domestic security operations rather than military ones, and are therefore not bound by the LOAC. Indeed, governments themselves often blur the line between law enforcement and military action when they employ military tactics, weapons, and paramilitary forces against political protest and those engaged in civil unrest. Again, the brutal British response to the IRA uprising is instructive.[19]

---

[16] Brandon Ives and Jacob Lewis, "From Rallies to Riots: Why Some Protests Become Violent," *Journal of Conflict Resolution*, vol. 64, no. 5, 2020.

[17] Neil MacFarquhar, "Syria Denies Attack on Civilians, in Crisis Seen as Civil War," *New York Times*, 15 July 2012.

[18] See Richard English, *Armed Struggle: The History of the IRA* (Oxford University Press, 2003).

[19] Many view the Northern Ireland conflict as having occupied the gray area between some form of non-international armed conflict and the lower-intensity category of "situations of internal disturbances and tensions." The British government claimed that it represented the latter rather than the former. See Colm Campbell, "Wars on Terror and Vicarious Hegemons: The UK, International Law, and the Northern Ireland Conflict," *International and Comparative Law Quarterly*, vol. 54, no. 2, April 2005, p. 331.

Finally, the principle of state supremacy has traditionally held that waging war is an exercise of sovereign authority, a prerogative held solely by states, and that only these acts could be regulated by international law.[20] From this perspective, internal violence is not warfare, and actions taken against armed groups within a state's borders fall within the category of law enforcement and internal security. This has allowed governments to derogate from human rights commitments by declaring a public emergency which "threatens the life of the nation," an action permitted under the International Covenant for Civil and Political Rights, while simultaneously denying the authority of the LOAC.[21]

States therefore have an interest in denying their political opponents the status of combatants, thereby freeing themselves from the restrictions imposed on their actions under IHL. For this reason, the primary obstacle to states extending the LOAC to internal disputes has been the fear that doing so would result in the recognition of insurgents as belligerents with the same rights as sitting governments.[22]

As a result, states generally resist acknowledging that even intense fighting on their territory constitutes armed conflict, since to do so is to admit failure and a loss of control to opposition forces and could be seen as recognizing a status for insurgents.[23]

In fact, unless forced by circumstances, governments tend to regard rebels and their armies as common criminals, bandits, and terrorists to be dealt with as a law enforcement matter, often denying that a state of war exists even in the face of evidence to the contrary.

International Humanitarian Law in Internal Disputes

Over the past half-century several factors have challenged this paradigm. First, following World War II, diplomats and legal advisors began to recognize that internal conflicts were not only common but were more

---

[20] See the discussion in Roda Mushkat, "Who May Wage War? An Examination of an Old/New Question," *American University Law Review*, vol. 2, no. 1, 1987.

[21] See, for example, International Covenant on Civil and Political Rights, entered into force 23 March 1976, Article 4(1).

[22] For a discussion of the long debate on the issue during the Diplomatic Conference, see David A. Elder, "The Historical Background of Common Article 3 of the Geneva Convention of 1949," *Case Western Reserve Journal of International Law*, vol. 11, no. 1, 1979, pp. 42–48.

[23] International Law Association, "Final Report on the Meaning of Armed Conflict in International Law," presented at the Hague Conference, 2010, p. 4.

numerous and often more vicious than interstate wars. Thus, when the delegates gathered for the Diplomatic Conference for the Establishment of International Conventions for the Protection of War Victims in 1949 (where the four Geneva Conventions were drafted), the previous two world wars were not the only events that haunted their discussions. The brutality of the Spanish Civil War (1936–1939) had foreshadowed the brutality of the global war that would soon follow. An estimated 200,000 civilians died as a result of extrajudicial executions and bombing attacks by fascist forces on Spanish cities with Republican leanings. This does not include the thousands of other civilians who died as a result of disease and malnutrition in overcrowded and unhygienic prisons and concentration camps.[24]

This factor became even more important in the following decades. Decolonization and the rise of revolutionary challenges to corrupt autocratic states in the developing world led to a dramatic increase in civil wars, national liberation movements, and guerrilla insurgencies that were internal to states.[25] The formation of new states often sparks internal conflict over the type of governing regime, economic system, and political institutions. This is particularly the case in low-income societies that are rich in natural resources and characterized by high poverty rates and ethnic fragmentation and inequality, in which some groups are excluded from the fruits of growth.[26] Moreover, states with weak central governments and few resources to satisfy the needs of their populations make insurgencies not only more attractive but also more effective.[27] This political instability, as well as ideological fissures fueled by the rapid growth in social movements and the involvement of regional and global powers, has made internal conflicts more likely.

At the same time, internal conflicts have tended to be not only more likely but also more brutal, at least in terms of their effect on civilians. A primary feature of guerrilla warfare is the close relationship between the fighters

---

[24] Paul Preston, *The Spanish Holocaust: Inquisition and Extermination in Twentieth-Century Spain* (W. W. Norton & Company, 2013).

[25] Ann Hironaka, *Neverending Wars: The International Community, Weak States, and the Perpetuation of Civil War* (Harvard University Press, 2005).

[26] See "Civil Wars in Developing Countries," special issue of *Journal of Peace Research*, vol. 39, no. 4, July 2002. In particular, see in that issue S. Mansoob Murshed, "Conflict, Civil War and Underdevelopment: An Introduction." Also see the study conducted by Quy-Toan Do and Lakshmi Iyer, *Poverty, Social Divisions, and Conflict in Nepal,* Policy Research Working Paper, No. 4228 (World Bank, 2007).

[27] David Laitin and James Fearon, "Ethnicity, Insurgency and Civil War," *American Political Science Review*, vol. 97, no. 1, February 2003.

and the communities in which they operate and upon whom they depend for support, intelligence, and sanctuary. This leads to a close association of fighters with noncombatant members of their communities.[28] As a result, government forces are more likely to view civilians as potential adversaries and will engage in mass killing of civilians as a military strategy to eliminate those they view as sympathetic to the rebels. For that reason, mass killing of civilians is significantly more likely during domestic guerrilla conflicts than during other kinds of wars.[29]

Second, there has been a significant growth in both human rights and international criminal law since the conclusion of the four Geneva Conventions in 1949. Neither was a major factor at the time, but over the subsequent decades both have become firmly established in international law and diplomatic practice. The proliferation of human rights treaties, international organizations, humanitarian norms, and international criminal tribunals has significantly reduced the barrier that protected political leaders from legal scrutiny of internal state violence.

Finally, and perhaps most important, the development of IHL since the 1970s shifted the focus in the LOAC from regulating combat to protecting civilians and other noncombatants.[30] Under the current rules—which are now universally applicable for international armed conflicts—soldiers are required at all times to distinguish between civilians and combatants and between military objectives and civilian objects when planning and engaging in attacks. They may not launch indiscriminate attacks or treat separate targets as a single objective. This is known as the principle of distinction, a bedrock rule from which combatants may not derogate.[31] Under this principle, all attacks must be limited to military targets, which are defined as those that, by their nature, location, purpose, or use, make an effective contribution to military action *and* whose destruction or neutralization offers a definite military advantage in circumstances ruling at the time.[32]

Moreover, although combatants are permitted to employ a wide range of weapons and strategies to secure a military advantage, the use of force by

---

[28] Mao Tse-Tung, *On Guerrilla Warfare* (Dover Publications, 2005 [1937]).

[29] Benjamin Valentino, Paul Huth, and Dylan Balch-Lindsay, "Draining the Sea: Mass Killing and Guerrilla Warfare," *International Organization*, vol. 58, no. 2, 2004.

[30] See Ruti Teitel, *Humanity's Law* (Oxford University Press, 2013) and Meron, "The Humanization of Humanitarian Law."

[31] Jean-Marie Henckaerts and Louise Doswald-Beck, *Customary International Humanitarian Law, vol. 1: Rules* (Cambridge University Press, 2009), chapters 1 and 2; Article 52(2) of the First Protocol Additional to the Geneva Conventions.

[32] Henckaerts and Doswald-Beck, *Customary International Humanitarian Law*, Rule 8.

combatants must be strictly limited to goals that are consistent with *military necessity*. This is defined as the amount and kind of force necessary to compel the submission of the enemy with the least possible expenditure of time, life, and money, subject to the laws of war.[33]

The uneasy tension between military advantage and civilian immunity is mediated by the third principle of IHL, the principle of proportionality. Proportionality holds that in all circumstances, the anticipated military advantage of an attack or action must be balanced against the probable or expected civilian losses. The expected casualties or damage to civilian property from an attack cannot be "excessive" in relation to said advantage gained from the attack.[34] Thus, combatants may not attack even a legitimate military target if the collateral damage to civilians is likely to be disproportionate to the specific military gain from the attack.[35] Moreover, they are required to take *feasible precaution* in the choice of means and methods of attack to avoid, or at least minimize, incidental loss of civilian life, injury to civilians, and damage to civilian objects, which are practicable taking into account circumstances ruling at the time.[36]

None of this is controversial or seriously contested by political and military leaders, although there may be disagreements on how they are interpreted and applied to specific cases. The principle of civilian immunity has been a foundation of our moral and legal understanding of armed conflict since the 1970s. Indeed, it is rooted in codes that date back to medieval times. It is embedded in both treaty and customary international law and has been reaffirmed by multiple international and regional organizations, ever since the UN Security Council passed its first resolution explicitly addressing civilian protection as an international obligation in 1999.[37]

---

[33] United States Military Tribunal, Nuremberg, "The Hostages Trial: Trial of Wilhelm List and Others," Case No. 47, Part IV, United Nations War Crimes Commission, Law Reports of Trials of War Criminals, vol. 8, 1949, p. 66.

[34] Henckaerts and Doswald-Beck, *Customary International Humanitarian Law*, chapter 4; Articles 51(5b) and 57(2iii) of the First Protocol Additional to the Geneva Conventions.

[35] International Court of Justice, "Legality of the Threat or Use of Nuclear Weapons," Advisory Opinion of 8 July 1996, General List No. 95, Opinion of Judge Higgins, p. 587.

[36] The principle of feasible precaution is articulated in the Protocol Additional to the Geneva Conventions of 12 August 1949, and relating to the Protection of Victims of International Armed Conflicts (Protocol I), 8 June 1977, article 57.

[37] In 1999, the Security Council convened a two-day meeting to address the universal protection of civilians in armed conflict. They concluded the meeting by passing Resolution 1265, reiterating support for the legal protection of civilians. United Nations Security Council, "Security Council Concludes Two-Day Meeting on Protection of Civilians in Armed Conflict," press release, 17 September 1999, SC 6730, available at: https://www.un.org/press/en/1999/19990917.sc6730.doc.html (accessed 25 April 2021).

There is an ongoing debate over which of these principles apply to non-international armed conflicts in the same way as they do to interstate wars. However, according to the International Tribunal for the Former Yugoslavia, the nature of modern armed conflict and the universal adoption of basic principles of IHL have almost rendered irrelevant the legal distinction between types of armed conflict, at least in regard to the protection of noncombatants.[38]

From this perspective, neither the legality of the armed challenge to the government nor the status of the fighters is relevant in the obligation to adhere to the principle of civilian immunity; governments have a nonderogable obligation to shield civilians from military operations in all types of conflicts, to the degree possible. Most legal scholars would agree with Michael Schmidt that once the conditions that define an internal conflict are satisfied, IHL governs all conflict-related activities, including the rules on targeting, detention, and the protection of civilians and civilian objects.[39]

This raises three questions. First, at what point do internal hostilities between a government and its challengers reach the level of an armed conflict, such that IHL applies? Second, which rules applicable to international armed conflicts are also universally in force for internal hostilities? Third, are states that have specifically refused to sign the Second Protocol to the Geneva Conventions exempt from these rules?

Defining a Non-international Armed Conflict

The most important factor in determining the degree to which governments are required to adhere to the principles of IHL when confronting violent challenges to their authority is whether the challenge is characterized as an armed conflict. Although there is no single definition of armed conflict in international law, even for international disputes, a comprehensive and exhaustive study by the International Law Association found that there is a general consensus within the international community that all armed conflicts have two defining characteristics that, at a minimum, distinguish

---

[38] This was the conclusion of the International Tribunal for the Former Yugoslavia in its widely cited Tadic decision. See *Prosecutor v. Tadic Case*, No. IT-94-I-AR72, Decision on the Defence Motion for Interlocutory Appeal on Jurisdiction, 2 October 1995, paras. 97 and 98.

[39] Michael N. Schmitt, "Charting the Legal Geography of Non-International Armed Conflict," *International Law Studies*, vol. 90, 2014, p. 14.

it from situations of peace: (1) the existence of at least two organized armed groups that are (2) engaged in ongoing hostilities of some intensity.[40] This, of course, requires a bit more development.

For international armed conflicts, the condition is simple: any resort to armed force between national armies is sufficient to make IHL immediately applicable between them.[41] However the threshold for non-international armed conflicts is higher and requires the nonstate party to meet additional criteria. Meeting these criteria determines whether the principles of IHL will apply in circumstances involving a violent challenge to the authority of the state within its borders.

Over the past few decades, a general consensus has emerged among international institutions that define the conditions under which hostilities would rise to the level of an internal armed conflict. According to the International Criminal Court for the Former Yugoslavia in its *Tadic* decision:

> [A]n armed conflict exists whenever there is . . . protracted armed violence between governmental authorities and organized armed groups or between such groups within a State. International humanitarian law applies from the initiation of such armed conflicts and extends beyond the cessation of hostilities until . . . a peaceful settlement is achieved. Until that moment, international humanitarian law continues to apply in the whole territory . . . under the control of a party, whether or not actual combat takes place there.[42]

These criteria are very similar to those enumerated in the Rome Statute to the International Criminal Court.[43] The key concepts in these definitions are "protracted" and "organized." There is broad agreement among legal analysts that a protracted conflict is one that is ongoing and achieves a level of intensity that identifies it as more than civil unrest, intermittent violence, or

---

[40] International Law Association, "Final Report on the Meaning of Armed Conflict in International Law," p. 2. For a discussion of the process through which the International Law Association developed this key report, see Mary Ellen O'Connell, "Defining Armed Conflict," *Journal of Conflict and Security Law*, vol. 13, no. 3, 2008, pp. 396–398.

[41] International Committee of the Red Cross, *Commentary on the First Geneva Convention*, para. 416.

[42] International Criminal Tribunal for the Former Yugoslavia, *Prosecutor v. Dusko Tadic A/K/A Dule*, "Decision on the Defence Motion for Interlocutory Appeal on Jurisdiction," 2 October 1995, para. 70. I edited out the references to international armed conflicts, leaving only the definition relevant to non-international ones.

[43] United Nations General Assembly, Rome Statute of the International Criminal Court (last amended 2010), 17 July 1998, Article 8(2)f.

terrorism. The ICTY listed several indicators that would determine the intensity of the fighting: the seriousness of attacks, the spread of clashes over territory and over a period of time, the number of government forces employed, the distribution of weapons among both parties to the conflict, and whether the conflict is addressed by the United Nations Security Council.[44]

Others add that the hostilities must exhibit such intensity that the government is compelled to employ its armed forces against the insurgents rather than relying on regular police and internal security officers.[45] Internal conflicts having a lesser degree of intensity, even instances of minor rebellion, did not fall within the scope of hostilities covered by these rules.[46]

The other key concept, "organized armed violence," requires that the insurgents exhibit a minimum amount of organization with the capacity to engage in military operations and that they operate under a responsible central command, occupy a substantial part of the territory of the state, exercise some orderly administration within the area they control, and observe the LOAC.[47]

There is a spirited debate over the degree to which armed insurgents must meet all of these conditions in order to be considered belligerents under international law.[48] Unless the UN Security Council addresses a particular internal conflict, the determination of whether internal violence has risen to the level of an armed conflict is often made by the government itself, which usually has an interest in rejecting that characterization. However, for the purposes of applying the protection to civilians contained in IHL to an internal conflict, this is irrelevant. IHL focuses solely on shielding noncombatants from the effects of military operations, which makes it unnecessary to determine the legality of an insurgent rebellion against the state. Regardless of the status of the insurgents, once hostilities reach the level of intensity defined by the ICTY, ICTR, ICC, and others, the protections afforded to noncombatants guaranteed under IHL apply.

---

[44] International Committee of the Red Cross, *Commentary on the First Geneva Convention*, fn. 141.

[45] Dietrich Schindler, "The Different Types of Armed Conflicts according to the Geneva Conventions and Protocols," *Collected Courses of the Hague Academy of International Law*, vol. 163, 1979, p. 146.

[46] Antonio Cassese, "The Geneva Protocols of 1977 on the Humanitarian Law of Armed Conflict and Customary International Law," *Pacific Basin Law Journal*, vol. 3, nos. 1–2, 1984, p. 105.

[47] Valentina Azarov and Ido Blum, "Belligerency," in *Max Plank Encyclopedia of International Law*, Rudiger Wulfrum, ed. (Oxford University Press, 2011). The classic work on belligerency that outlines these criteria is Lassa Oppenheim, *International Law: A Treatise*, 7th edition, edited by Hersch Lauterpacht, vol. 1 (Longmans Green & Co., 1952), p. 249.

[48] See the discussion on this in Yair M. Lootsteen, "The Concept of Belligerency in International Law," *Military Law Review*, vol. 166, December 2000, p. 109.

The definitions established by these institutions reflect the requirements of international criminal law inasmuch as the tribunals must first establish the existence of an armed conflict in order to exercise jurisdiction in the cases that came before them. Moreover, to some extent the tribunals represent the will of the international community, since they were created by either the UN Security Council (which has the authority to speak for the UN membership) or a widely supported multilateral treaty, the Rome Statute.

Sources of Universal IHL in Internal Conflicts

Until 1977, the only provision under international law that applied to internal armed conflicts was Article 3, common to all four Geneva Conventions of 1949. This article, identically worded in all of the treaties, applies to conflicts "not of an international character." This phrase is a catch-all to describe any hostilities in which at least one of the belligerents is a nonstate actor. It primarily refers to internal conflicts and civil wars, but it also describes internal armed conflicts that spill over into other states or those in which third states or a multinational force intervenes alongside the government (such as the U.S. wars in Iraq and Afghanistan in the early 21st century).[49]

The purpose behind Common Article 3 was to extend some of the rules of international armed conflict that are enumerated in the four Geneva Conventions to those who take no active part in hostilities in internal wars. Like the four Conventions in general, the article applies primarily to the treatment of prisoners of war and other combatants who have become *hors de combat,* although it also stipulates some regulations concerning civilians living under a military occupation. Thus, the article begins by referring to "persons taking no active part in the hostilities, including members of armed forces who have laid down their arms and those placed 'hors de combat' by sickness, wounds, detention, or any other cause."

According to the language of the article, detainees "shall in all circumstances be treated humanely," and "outrages upon personal dignity, in particular humiliating and degrading treatment and torture," are prohibited.

---

[49] See Dapo Akande, "Classification of Armed Conflicts: Relevant Legal Concepts," in Elizabeth Wilmshurst (ed.), *International Law and the Classification of Conflicts* (Oxford University Press, 2012), p. 62. Many civil wars attract external state involvement, and these are known informally as internationalized armed conflicts. However, because there are only two types of conflicts under the LOAC, international and non-international, this term does not create any new obligations. See Kubo Macak, *Internationalized Armed Conflicts in International Law* (Oxford University Press, 2018).

Moreover, it prohibits murder, hostage-taking, and unfair trial for those in this protected class.

Although a number of delegates to the Diplomatic Conference made numerous attempts to apply *all* existing law to non-international armed conflicts, this position was ultimately rejected by the conference since states were not prepared to accept an obligation to apply the fullness of the detailed provisions of the Conventions in internal situations.[50] As a result, the final wording of Article 3 was purposely vague and severely limited; what it specifically mandates and what it forbids are still subject to debate. Moreover, it does not specifically limit the effects of military operations on civilians and civilian objects such as hospitals, schools, and residences. Indeed, it does not mention civilians at all, nor does it address the conduct of hostilities and their effect on noncombatants. This minimalist approach to extending the LOAC to internal hostilities represented a compromise between those who advocated extending the full protections of the Geneva Conventions—regardless of the type of conflict—and those who tended to view non-international conflict as strictly within the police jurisdiction of the territorial sovereign.[51]

Therefore, even if the four Geneva Conventions have become part of customary international law, Common Article 3 does not provide significant legal protection to civilian populations during internal conflicts.

At the same time, Common Article 3 established the principle that the LOAC could apply to militarized disputes that fall outside the traditional state-on-state model. It is clear from the *travaux préparatoires* of the Diplomatic Conference where the Conventions were drafted that the delegates were keenly aware of the implications of extending the laws of war to domestic conflicts. The documents show that the representatives developed a strong consensus during the long and often heated discussions of the various meetings that, at a minimum, fundamental humanitarian norms would be binding in armed conflicts "not of an international character" when such conflicts surpass in severity and organization mere rioting or terrorism.[52]

---

[50] J. Pictet (ed.), *Commentary on the First Geneva Convention for the Amelioration of the Condition of the Wounded and Sick in Armed Forces in the Field* (International Committee of the Red Cross, 1952), p. 38.

[51] Eugene D. Fryer, "Applicability of International Law to Internal Armed Conflicts: Old Problems, Current Endeavors," *International Lawyer*, vol. 11, no. 3, 1977, p. 569.

[52] Elder, "The Historical Background of Common Article 3 of the Geneva Convention of 1949," p. 38.

These obligations would not be based on reciprocity but on a legal commitment to provide some basic humanitarian protections to noncombatants regardless of the status of the belligerents. Thus, although the proposals by several states to provide stronger protections for civilians and civilian institutions such as hospitals were not included in the final draft of Article 3, the principle that humanitarian principles should be applied to internal conflicts was established. Moreover, since virtually all states have signed the four Conventions, it is safe to conclude that this principle is universally recognized. The International Court of Justice affirmed this point, observing that Common Article 3 provides a "minimum yardstick" that applies to both international and non-international conflicts.[53] A very minimum yardstick.

The most important legal instrument for protecting civilians in internal conflicts is the Second Protocol to the Geneva Conventions, which was concluded in 1977 and entered into force the following year. In the years following the drafting of the 1949 Geneva Conventions, the changing nature of armed conflict in terms of means, methods, and participants—as well as the increase in frequency and brutality of non-international armed conflicts—made it clear that Common Article 3 had proven to be woefully inadequate to deal with the widespread deprivations of human rights in civil wars.[54] The political environment in the world had changed significantly between 1949, when the Geneva Conventions were concluded, and adoption of the First and Second Protocols almost 30 years later. Decolonization, wars of national liberation, proxy wars supported by the superpowers, the U.S. wars in Korea and Vietnam, and violent conflicts over government and regime type had raged around the globe, mostly in the developing world. These events, rather than the last great world war, were on the minds of the delegates attending the meetings where the Second Protocols was drafted.[55]

---

[53] ICJ, *Military and Paramilitary Activities in and against Nicaragua case*, Merits, Judgment, 1986, para. 218.

[54] This was the general consensus among those who advocated for greater humanitarian protection. See Emily Crawford, "Unequal before the Law: The Case for the Elimination of the Distinction between International and Non-international Armed Conflicts." *Leiden Journal of International Law*, vol. 20, no. 2, June 2007, p. 448 and R. R. Baxter, "Humanitarian Law or Humanitarian Politics—The 1974 Diplomatic Conference on Humanitarian Law," *Harvard International Law Journal*, vol. 16, Winter 1975.

[55] See Official Records of the Diplomatic Conference on the Reaffirmation and Development of International Humanitarian Law Applicable in Armed Conflicts, Convened by the Swiss Federal Council for the Preparation of Two Protocols Additional to the Geneva Conventions of 12 August 1949, held at Geneva, 1974–1977, vol. 4.

Like other major multilateral agreements, the Protocol was developed at a broad-based conference consisting of numerous working groups, state delegations, and legal specialists meeting in dozens of sessions over a long period of time. Unlike the others, however, it was not the United Nations that called the conference, but an NGO that political leaders had accepted as a legitimate authority on the LOAC. The ICRC had been working for at least two decades to update the Geneva Conventions to reflect the growing belief that greater protection for noncombatants was needed. The group extended a general invitation to all parties to the Conventions to appear for the second Conference of Government Experts, which was held in Geneva in 1972. Seventy-seven states sent delegations.

The Diplomatic Conference met from 1974 to 1977 not only to increase legal protection of noncombatants but also to more stringently regulate the means and methods of combat. It consisted of four sessions, each ranging from one to three months. These sessions were the culmination of two decades of meetings by government representatives to address the protection of civilians in armed conflict, convened by the ICRC in New Delhi (1957), Vienna (1965), Istanbul (1969), the Hague (1971), Geneva (1971), Vienna (1972), Geneva again (1972), and Tehran (1973).[56]

Although the ICRC strongly advocated for a single protocol relating to the protection of the civilian population in all types of conflicts, the majority of delegates expressed a preference for maintaining the distinction between international and non-international armed conflict. As a result, the ICRC proposed separate protocols and introduced into the draft of Protocol II a part on the protection of the civilian population, following the example of draft Protocol I.[57] The protections in the Second Protocol are not as detailed or extensive as in Protocol I, which addresses international conflicts; however, the essential principle of civilian immunity in internal conflicts is unambiguously maintained. The Protocol applies to armed conflicts fought between a state and "dissident armed forces or other organized armed groups which, under responsible command, exercise such control over a part of its territory as to enable them to carry out sustained and concerted military

---

[56] International Committee of the Red Cross Library and Archives, "Drafting History of the 1977 Additional Protocols," 16 October 2019.

[57] International Committee of the Red Cross, Protocol Additional to the Geneva Conventions of 12 August 1949, and relating to the Protection of Victims of Non-International Armed Conflicts (Protocol II), adopted on 8 June 1977 by the Diplomatic Conference on the Reaffirmation and Development of International Humanitarian Law Applicable in Armed Conflicts, 8 June 1977, Commentary of 1987, para. 4386.

operations and to implement this Protocol."[58] Its focus was on the legal obligations of states; conflicts between nonstate actors only were not covered.

The key section of the Second Protocol is Article 13, which provides the fundamental principle of civilian immunity in internal armed conflicts: "The civilian population and individual civilians shall enjoy general protection against the dangers arising from military operations. . . . The civilian population as such, as well as individual civilians, shall not be the object of attack. Acts or threats of violence the primary purpose of which is to spread terror among the civilian population are prohibited."[59] This means that the obligation goes beyond abstaining from attacks against civilians to avoiding or minimizing incidental civilian casualties and taking proactive safety measures to protect them.[60]

In addition, Protocol II prohibits attacks on objects "indispensable to the survival of the civilian population" and "historic monuments, works of art or places of worship which constitute the cultural or spiritual heritage of peoples." It also bans "pillage" against civilian property, and the forced displacement or movement of the population.[61] The ban on attacks indispensable to survival is particularly important. It means that governments may not prevent food shipments or the delivery of fuel, electricity, or other necessities to towns and cities that are sympathetic to the rebels. It could also be reasonably interpreted to forbid attacks against commercial establishments that provide important resources to civilians. Indeed a literal interpretation would also proscribe attacks on the homes, infrastructure, or businesses of those who support or are sympathetic to the insurgents but are not participating in the conflict.

Finally, the treaty bans collective punishment (harassment, violence, or administrative action taken against a group in retaliation for an act committed by individuals who are considered to be part of the group).[62] This is particularly important in internal conflicts inasmuch as belligerents in these circumstances often represent an ethnic group, clan, or tribal association,

---

[58] International Committee of the Red Cross, Protocol Additional to the Geneva Conventions of 12 August 1949, Article 1(1).
[59] International Committee of the Red Cross, Protocol Additional to the Geneva Conventions of 12 August 1949, Article 12(2).
[60] International Committee of the Red Cross, Protocol Additional to the Geneva Conventions of 12 August 1949, Commentary of 1987, para. 4770.
[61] International Committee of the Red Cross, Protocol Additional to the Geneva Conventions of 12 August 1949, Articles 14, 16, and 17.
[62] International Committee of the Red Cross, Protocol Additional to the Geneva Conventions of 12 August 1949, Article 4(2).

political party, religious order, or other identifiable collectivity. The use of government military force against such groups to suppress support for insurgents, intimidate their members, or retaliate against insurgent actions has long been an issue in wartime.

Other Legal Instruments

Although Protocol II is the most focused and comprehensive instrument providing protection to civilians in internal conflicts, 25 states have refused to sign the agreement. These include countries that have been deeply involved in internal conflict, for example, Syria, Sri Lanka, Somalia, Eritrea, Pakistan, Myanmar, India, Israel, and Turkey.[63] Under the doctrine of consent, their explicit refusal to sign constitutes a persistent objection to its provisions, exempting them from any obligations that one may argue exist under customary law. Yet the international community, as represented by the United Nations (including the Security Council), the European Union, the African Union, the Organization of American States, and several international criminal tribunals, still hold them responsible for the principle of civilian immunity in internal conflicts. Therefore we need to look beyond one specific treaty and examine the wide range of agreements and judicial rulings that support the universality of civilian immunity.

The Rome Statute of the International Criminal Court includes within its jurisdiction war crimes committed during non-international armed conflict. Specifically, it considers as a violation any action that "intentionally direct(s) attacks against the civilian population as such or against individual civilians not taking direct part in hostilities" and "against buildings dedicated to religion, education, art, science or charitable purposes, historic monuments, hospitals" during both international and internal armed conflicts.[64]

The Convention on Certain Conventional Weapons and its three Protocols applies both to international conflicts and "in case of armed conflicts not

---

[63] For a complete list of parties to Protocol II, see International Committee of the Red Cross, "Treaties, State Parties and Commentaries," in Protocol Additional to the Geneva Conventions of 12 August 1949, at: https://ihl-databases.icrc.org/applic/ihl/ihl.nsf/States.xsp?xp_viewStates=XPages_NORMStatesParties&xp_treatySelected=475 (accessed 3 April 2021).

[64] UN General Assembly, Rome Statute of the International Criminal Court (last amended 2010), 17 July 1998, Article 8(2)e.

of an international character."[65] Its purpose is to provide new rules for the protection of civilians from types of weapons that are particularly injurious to them, including landmines, booby traps, blinding lasers, and explosive remnants of combat. Thus, for example, it is "prohibited in all circumstances to make any military objective located within a concentration of civilians the object of attack by air-delivered incendiary weapons; 125 states have signed the convention; the overwhelming majority of nonsignatories are African states.[66]

The principle of civilian immunity in internal armed conflicts has also been addressed in a number of soft law instruments. Both the UN General Assembly and Security Council, for example, have passed multiple resolutions to this effect. In 1968 and 1970, before the conclusion of the two Geneva Protocols, the General Assembly outlined the basic principles of distinction that would apply in all armed conflicts, without distinguishing between their forms.[67] Similarly, the Security Council reaffirmed this principle several times, as have regional organizations such as the African Union, the Organization of American States, and the European Union, which also passed strong resolutions recognizing the authority of IHL in internal conflicts.[68]

The Role of NGOs in Universalizing the Rules

Over the past three decades, humanitarian and human rights NGOs have played a major role in universalizing the legal protection of civilians in internal conflicts, regardless of the status of the parties or whether they have

---

[65] United Nations, Convention on Prohibitions or Restrictions on the Use of Certain Conventional Weapons Which May be Deemed to Be Excessively Injurious or to Have Indiscriminate Effects (and Protocols) (As Amended on 21 December 2001), 10 October 1980, Article 1(3).
[66] United Nations, Office for Disarmament Affairs, "The Convention on Certain Conventional Weapons," available at: https://www.un.org/disarmament/the-convention-on-certain-conventional-weapons.
[67] UN General Assembly, "Basic Principles for the Protection of Civilian Populations in Armed Conflicts," A/RES2675, 9 December 1970; UN General Assembly, "Respect for Human Rights in Armed Conflicts," A/RES/2444, 19 December 1968.
[68] See Security Council Resolution 1295 (UN Doc. S/RES/1295), 17 September 1999. See also Resolutions 1674 (UN Doc. S/RES/1674), 28 April 2006 and 1894 (S.RES/1894), 11 November 2009; African Union, "Progress Report of the Chairperson of the Commission on the Development of Guidelines for the Protection of Civilians in African Union Peace Support Operations" (PSC/PR/2—CCLXXIX), May 2011, para. 5; Organization of American States, "Promotion of and Respect for International Humanitarian Law," AG/RES. 2052 (XXXIV-O/04), 8 June 2004.

signed the Second Protocol. The most important organization is the ICRC.[69] The ICRC is an NGO based in Geneva with the mandate to monitor and oversee the protection of victims of armed conflict, principally civilians and other noncombatants, prisoners of war, the forcibly displaced, and the wounded. It was founded in 1863 by Swiss activist Henri Dunant to prevent and alleviate suffering during armed conflicts.[70]

For more than a century, the organization's primary activity was its field operations in aid of prisoners of war and victims of armed conflict and internal violence around the world. However, since the end of World War II the ICRC has been the major force in the progressive development of IHL and the institutionalization of its principles in all conflicts, international and internal.

The ICRC is widely regarded within the international community as a highly knowledgeable authority about IHL.[71] Its status and authority in this area are derived from two sources. First, the four Geneva Conventions make reference to the organization in more than a dozen articles and provide the ICRC with the mandate to inspect prisoner-of-war camps, organize relief operations, reunite separated families, and provide other humanitarian activities during armed conflicts.[72]

Second, the ICRC's Statutes encourage it to undertake similar work during internal conflicts where the Geneva Conventions do not directly apply. The Statutes are adopted and revised periodically at the International Conference of the Red Cross and Red Crescent (the organization's supreme deliberative body), which takes place every four years and at which states that are party to the Geneva Conventions participate. The breadth of participation, along

---

[69] The ICRC is one of three related NGOs that use the phrase "red cross": National Societies, which are accredited and located in more than 100 countries; the League of Red Cross Societies; and the International Committee of the Red Cross. This chapter is concerned only with the last one.

[70] The cross in this case is not a religious symbol. Rather, it represents the emblem on the Swiss flag, reflecting the national origin and headquarters of the organization.

[71] See, for example, David Forsythe and Barbara Ann Rieffer-Flanagan, *The International Committee of the Red Cross: A Neutral Humanitarian Actor* (Routledge 2016); Steven R. Ratner, "Law Promotion beyond Law Talk: The Red Cross, Persuasion, and the Laws of War," *The European Journal of International Law,* vol. 22 no. 2, 2011; R. Geiß, A. Zimmermann, and S. Haumer (eds.), *Humanizing the Laws of War: The Red Cross and the Development of International Humanitarian Law* (Cambridge University Press, 2017); Abdullahi Bala Ado, Ya'u Ibrahim Saleh, and Musa Garba Usman, "Contribution of the International Committee of the Red Cross (ICRC) to the Development and Implementation of International Humanitarian Law," *International Journal of Multidisciplinary Research and Development,* vol. 2, no. 4, April 2015.

[72] The ICRC is mentioned by name in 5 different articles in the First Convention, 4 in the Second Convention, 11 in the Third, and 18 in the Fourth.

with the deliberative process that sets policies and missions, confers a soft-law authority to the meetings.

According to the Statutes, the role of the organization is "to undertake the tasks incumbent upon it under the Geneva Conventions, to work for the faithful application of international humanitarian law applicable in armed conflicts and to take cognizance of any complaints based on alleged breaches of that law," and also "to work for the understanding and dissemination of knowledge of international humanitarian law applicable in armed conflicts and to prepare any development thereof."[73]

The ICRC has five primary functions: (1) reviewing humanitarian law to reflect changing conflict situations, and preparing for their adaptation and development when necessary; (2) stimulating ongoing discussion of problems with applying current rules; (3) advocating with states to adopt national measures necessary for its implementation; (4) defending IHL against legal developments that disregard its existence or might tend to weaken it; and (5) interpreting the treaties and customary practices, particularly in practical situations of armed conflict, and highlighting serious violations of the law as they occur.[74] Toward this end, the organization publishes regular commentaries, analyses, and manuals addressing the obligations of state and nonstate actors in both international and internal armed conflicts.

Throughout the first half of the 20th century, the ICRC continually tried to expand the rules of armed conflict to include internal hostilities, raising the issue at numerous international forums and pressuring governments to accept the authority of international law in these circumstances.[75] In the latter area, results have been mixed.[76]

As an NGO, the ICRC has no formal authority to interpret or implement IHL, but its prestige, experience, and expertise in this area provide a type of political and technocratic legitimacy and authority. Indeed, the organization

---

[73] Articles 5(2c) and 5(2g).

[74] Yves Sandoz, "The International Committee of the Red Cross as Guardian of International Humanitarian Law," 12/31/1998 at https://www.icrc.org/en/doc/resources/documents/misc/about-the-icrc-311298.htm. Accessed May 31, 2023.

[75] For a comprehensive history and analysis of the ICRC, see David Forsythe, *The Humanitarians: The International Committee of the Red Cross* (Cambridge University Press, 2009). For a discussion of ICRC activities in this area during the first half of the 20th century, see International Committee of the Red Cross, *Commentary on the First Geneva Convention*, chapter 1, article 3.

[76] For a discussion of specific cases where the ICRC has pressured states to accept the obligations articulated in IHL in internal conflicts, see Mary Ellen O'Connell, "Humanitarian Assistance in Non-International Armed Conflict: The Fourth Wave of Rights, Duties, and Remedies," *Israeli Yearbook on Human Rights*, vol. 31, 2001.

CIVILIAN IMMUNITY IN DOMESTIC ARMED CONFLICTS 179

itself can be viewed as constituting an international epistemic community in the area of armed conflicts.

The ICRC Commentaries on the Geneva Conventions and Protocols are a soft law instrument that has been periodically updated to reflect current consensus and political conditions in the world. The Commentaries are developed by teams of renowned legal specialists charged with documenting developments and providing up-to-date interpretations. They are reviewed by dozens of practitioners and academics from all regions of the world, providing comments and input into the final product. This elaborate process helps to ensure that all main views are taken into account, and therefore represents at least a representative consensus from the epistemic community of international law analysts. Since their publication in 1950s and 1980s, the Commentaries have become a major reference for the application and interpretation of IHL by legal advisors and international law scholars.[77]

The first editions from the 1950s were largely based on the preparatory work for the 1949 Conventions and on the experience of the Second World War; subsequent publications reflect the changing consensus of states regarding their obligations and the shift toward internal conflicts as the primary form of armed hostilities. Neither the drafters of the 1949 Geneva Conventions nor the authors of the initial Commentary in 1952 anticipated the dominant role that non-international armed conflicts would take in the decades following the adoption of the Convention. The updated Commentaries therefore focus on applying IHL to these developments in great detail.[78] This does not mean that all legal analysts and political leaders accept the ICRC views. Clearly there are disagreements.[79] However, the reports are well-respected and often cited as authorities in interpreting how IHL is applied, in this case, to the protection of civilians in internal conflicts.

Since the 1990s, traditional human rights organizations, such as Human Rights Watch and Amnesty International, have begun to monitor, investigate,

---

[77] See, for example, Bruno Demeyere, Jean-Marie Henckaerts, Heleen Hiemstra, and Ellen Nohle, "The Updated ICRC Commentary on the Second Geneva Convention: Demystifying the Law of Armed Conflict at Sea," *International Law Studies, U.S. Naval War College,* vol. 94, 2018.

[78] Jean-Marie Henckaerts, "Bringing the Commentaries on the Geneva Conventions and Their Additional Protocols into the Twenty-first Century," *International Review of the Red Cross,* vol. 94, no. 888, 2012, p. 1211.

[79] For some critiques of ICRC analyses, see Michael A. Newton, "Contorting Common Article 3: Reflections on the Revised ICRC Commentary" and Nicholas Mull, "A Critique of the ICRC's Updated Commentary to the First Geneva Convention: Arming Medical Personnel and the Loss of Protected Status (October 23, 2016)," both in *Georgia Journal of International and Comparative Law,* vol. 45, 2017; and Yorum Dinstein, "The ICRC Customary International Humanitarian Law Study," *International Law Studies,* vol. 82, 2006.

and issue reports on armed conflicts, both international and internal. These reports offer a neutral analysis of how the belligerents adhered to their obligations to shield civilians from the effects of combat.[80] While these reports have no legal standing under international law, they help to promote the universality of IHL in domestic conflicts. This does not mean that interested parties always or even usually accept their conclusions, but the reports become part of the public record.

Summary

Civilian immunity in armed conflict has become a universal legal norm in both international and internal conflicts. This was not always the case, and the levels of protections between the two are still different in some ways. The legal protection of civilians in international armed conflicts is built on centuries of codes and customs that crystallized in the 1977 First Protocol to the four Geneva Conventions. This agreement established the bedrock principles of distinction, proportionality, military necessity, and feasible precaution as the foundation of IHL. These principles are now part of customary international law.

However, traditionally governments were shielded from the obligation to adhere to the law of armed conflict when confronting challenges by armed groups within their own borders. Customary law did not apply in cases of internal armed conflicts and civil wars, and the continued persistent objections by a number of states suggest that it still has not. However this does not release any state from its obligation to adhere to the basic rules underlying civilian immunity even in domestic conflicts. The line that protected states from international scrutiny slowly dissolved over the 70 years since the conclusion of the four Geneva Conventions in 1949. There is now a firm corpus of universal legal norms embedded in multiple treaties, organizational resolutions, soft law instruments, and rulings by international tribunals that establish the basic legal protection of civilians in domestic armed conflicts.

---

[80] See, for example, Human Rights Watch, *World Report, 2016,* particularly the reports investigating violations during internal conflicts in Burma, Iraq, Libya, Yemen, Somalia, and South Sudan; Human Rights Watch, "Unacknowledged Deaths: Civilian Casualties in NATO's Air Campaign in Libya," 2012; Human Rights Watch, "Why They Died: Civilian Casualties in Lebanon during the 2006 War," vol. 19, no. 5(E), September 2007; Amnesty International, "NATO/Federal Republic of Yugoslavia: 'Collateral Damage' or Unlawful Killings? Violations of the Laws of War by NATO during Operation Allied Force," 5 June 2000.

These principles, rules, and institutions now comprise a robust civilian immunity regime at both the global and regional levels. States cannot avoid these regulations by refusing to sign particular agreements or making a persistent objection.

This does not mean that all of the LOAC apply to domestic conflicts. Even though governments are required to treat their opponents humanely, they do not have to recognize them as belligerents unless a number of strict conditions are met. Even then, they are permitted to put them on trial for insurrection and for killing members of security forces, something that they cannot do with foreign combatants.

Still, the protection of civilian populations has become universal in non-international armed conflicts, and states may not derogate from its core principles even if they believe that their hold on power is threatened.

7
International Consensus and the Future of International Law

Despite the institutionalization of global human rights norms, governments have considerable leeway under international law to address internal security and challenges to their authority from their own populations. This leeway is restricted by voluntarily accepted agreements that allow international regulation of certain types of state violence toward these populations. However, under the doctrine of consent, these agreements are binding only on those who ratify them, and even then, states can renounce their obligations by withdrawing from the treaties. Moreover, some practices are not specifically covered by treaty, and others are ambiguous in some key details, such as Common Article 3 of the 1949 Geneva Conventions. The frequency of various types of atrocities practiced in all regions of the world, as well as the failure of states and international institutions to consistently act against violators, makes it difficult to argue that customary international law can be substituted for explicit agreement in many of these cases.

Yet the empirical evidence suggests that political leaders and legal analysts do in fact consider that some acts of internal state violence constitute violations of international law under all circumstances, regardless of whether states have signed agreements prohibiting them or whether such bans reflect state practice. In popular discourse, these acts are referred to as "atrocities." They include the violent persecution of minorities; widespread, systemic, one-sided violence against a population; torture; and deliberate assaults on civilians during an internal armed conflict. What links them conceptually is that they all fall within the broad category of "excessive state violence," which I define in Chapter 1 as a level of coercive force that the international community considers to be disproportionate and illegitimate for pursuing state interests within a state's own borders.

This suggests that there are limits to the doctrine of consent. The previous pages discussed how a universal ban on excessive state violence evolved over the past several decades. I argued that this was the result of an expansion of international law that was facilitated by the proliferation of institutions of global governance and the adoption of multilateralism as the legitimate process for creating new rules. This has made a new source of international law possible. This source is based on an international consensus that states consciously develop over time through deliberation within these institutions. Political leaders, diplomats, and legal advisors derive consensus-based legal norms from an overlapping body of multilateral lawmaking treaties and conventions, soft law created by broad-based international and regional institutions, principles contained in organizational charters and institutions, and legal norms that have achieved the status of *jus cogens*. This consensus is reflected in multiple rulings and opinions by international courts and other legal bodies, such as the UN International Law Commission.

This final chapter will examine the degree to which the empirical chapters have successfully demonstrated that this is in fact the case and whether a new source of international law is required to explain it. In doing so, it will discuss the implications for the doctrine of consent, theories of consensus-based international law, the future of international law, and the regulation and enforcement of human rights norms.

Deliberation and Process

The previous chapters support the proposition that the increased globalization of world politics through the expansion of multilateral institutions is leading to a larger role for international consensus as the foundation for legal rules. Chapters 3 through 6 illustrate how the universalization of particular human rights norms—the prohibitions of crimes against humanity, violent persecution, torture, and attacks on civilians during civil wars—was facilitated by extensive deliberation among states within a wide variety of international and regional forums. This deliberation resulted in several groundbreaking lawmaking treaties, key rulings by international tribunals established by the United Nations, and resolutions by broad-based deliberative bodies such as the UN General Assembly, the African Union, the European Union, and the Organization of American States.

The major human rights lawmaking treaties generated legal norms that went beyond the list of state parties. In doing so, they established definitions and obligations that have become embedded in general international law. All of the major treaties were developed at broad-based conferences consisting of numerous working groups, government delegations, and legal specialists meeting in dozens of sessions over long periods of time. The Genocide Convention was the product of a two-year process at an international conference in which state representatives repeatedly revised multiple drafts. Both the definition and obligations associated with the practice emerged from discussion, debate, and compromise. Indeed, at the beginning of the process it was not even clear that there was the political will to develop a treaty on genocide. It was during months of deliberation that state representatives developed a consensus around the main principles that currently constitute the definition and legal prohibition of genocide. A similar dynamic was present during the development of the Convention Against Torture and the Second Protocol to the Geneva Conventions. The CAT took six years to complete, while the Second Protocol took five.

The conceptualization of crimes against humanity and ethnic cleansing is the product of several decades of discussion and development, culminating in Article 7 of the Rome Statute of the International Criminal Court, which entered into force in 1999. The final document was the result of several years of multilateral negotiations, culminating in a six-week session involving representatives from 161 states, whose intent was to outline universal offenses against the international community.

The United Nations played a main role in facilitating these processes. Ostensibly the UN is simply a collective security organization established by states to provide for mutual cooperation, resolution of conflicts, and the prevention of military aggression. Yet the organization's goals, practices, and institutional structure suggest a far broader and more ambitious social agenda, including the promotion of human rights and the progressive development of international law. In pursuing this agenda, the UN system includes a wide network of specialized agencies, legal and technical experts, and NGOs.[1]

Member states clearly resisted endowing the organization with either legislative powers or the authority to create new international law. However, through its extensive network of semi-autonomous organizations (such as the International Law Commission), General Assembly committees (such as the Sixth Committee, which addresses legal issues), and independent experts (such as the Special Procedures of the Human Rights Council), the

---

[1] Bruce Cronin, "The Two Faces of the United Nations: The Tension between Intergovernmentalism and Transnationalism," *Global Governance*, vol. 8, no. 1, January–March 2002.

organization constantly evaluates current international law and acts to expand, extend, and amend it by mobilizing states to develop new legal norms.

This is particularly true with the development of lawmaking treaties designed to address atrocities. The Genocide Convention, the Convention Against Torture, and the Rome Statute of the International Criminal Court were all initiated by the UN General Assembly. The development of each agreement involved several UN bodies and agencies, culminating in widely attended conferences of state representatives. As a universal global organization encompassing all recognized states, its deliberative forums represent both the will of the international community and the interests of its members (which often conflict). The decision to expand its focus to include the regulation of excessive internal state violence evolved over time as the General Assembly and Security Council—both deliberative bodies—attempted to address discrete security issues.

The previous four chapters demonstrated that the universalization of legal norms prohibiting excessive state violence was also facilitated by regional security bodies and human rights institutions in Europe, the Americas, and Africa. These deliberative bodies strengthened the global consensus in this area by drafting parallel regional agreements that closely mirrored those concluded by international organizations. The Organization of American States, the Council of Europe, and the African Union have all passed resolutions, drafted treaties, and created monitoring bodies and judicial institutions addressing these issues.

In addition to highlighting the role played by international political institutions in universalizing certain legal norms banning atrocities, the previous chapters demonstrated how the expansion of international judicial bodies has also helped to institutionalize these norms. Building from the precedent established decades earlier in Nuremberg, the UN Security Council criminalized acts of excessive internal state violence by creating a series of international and hybrid tribunals to prosecute atrocities committed in the former Yugoslavia, Rwanda, Sierra Leon, Cambodia, and East Timor. The resolutions and statutes that established these courts cited torture, genocide, ethnic cleansing, war crimes (including those committed during internal armed conflicts), and systemic attacks on civilians as universal violations. This process helped lead to the creation of a permanent tribunal to prosecute these violations, the International Criminal Court, an act that formalized the prohibition of excessive state violence.

As Chapters 3 through 6 illustrate, these various courts have played an important role in universalizing the legal norms against certain types of atrocities. While the tribunals did not create new law, their rulings formally reflected a broad consensus within the legal community that the prohibition of atrocities could be universally applied to individuals from all states, regardless of whether such states have signed human rights agreements. Their decisions were the result of deliberation among judges and legal analysts, who form a type of epistemic community, in addressing specific cases. As discussed in the previous chapters, legal advisors, political leaders, and domestic courts continue to cite these rulings extensively and apply them to situations that were not addressed by the judges or the cases before them.

The lack of a hierarchical legal system at the global level means that there is technically no concept of precedent in international law. Therefore, despite the inclusion of "judicial decisions and the teachings of highly qualified publicists" as secondary sources of international law in Article 38 of the ICJ Statue, these rulings are not legally binding beyond each particular case. Moreover, as sources of international law, they are inconsistent with the doctrine of consent inasmuch as the rulings reflect the consensus of the international legal community, not necessarily individual states. However, lawyers and legal analysts frequently evoked these decisions in subsequent cases. In particular, rulings by the International Criminal Tribunal for the Former Yugoslavia established precedents that have helped to universalize the prohibitions against excessive state violence.[2] We can consider these key rulings, discussed in the previous four chapters, as a form of soft law created by international judicial institutions.

In all of the areas of excessive state violence discussed in the previous chapters, rulings by the above-mentioned tribunals—as well as those issued by the International Criminal Court, regional human rights courts, and the International Court of Justice—have been accepted by political leaders as evidence that the prohibition of atrocities has achieved universal status. Thus, although the International Criminal Court is a treaty-based body, its rulings and opinions have an influence that goes well beyond the member states.

---

[2] For a discussion of the increasing use of precedent by international courts, see Harlan Grant Cohen, "Theorizing Precedent in International Law," in Andrea Bianchi, Daniel Peat, and Matthew Windsor (eds.), *Interpretation in International Law* (Oxford University Press, 2018).

Identifying the Tipping Point of a Universal Legal Norm

In Chapter 2 I suggested that one could determine the degree to which a consensus-based legal norm has become embedded in general international law by tracing the process through which it evolved from an idea held by a small group of legal entrepreneurs to one where a critical mass accepted it as a standard. Finnemore and Sikkink refer to this process as a norm's life cycle.[3] By tracing the process, we try to determine the tipping point after which agreement becomes widespread, a key event that Scharf refers to as a Grotian moment.[4] Chapters 3 through 6 confirm that this process was present in the development of general international law prohibiting excessive internal state violence.

Each of the legal norms banning atrocities began as an innovative idea that initially lacked widespread international support but over time became widely received within the international community. All were eventually accepted into general international law. Each legal norm had its own life cycle, but as a group the tipping point was the entry into force of the Rome Statue of the International Criminal Court. The Statute was the first legal document that tied together the individual atrocities—genocide, ethnic cleansing, torture, civilian victimization during armed conflicts, and one-sided systemic attacks on a population.

Not even countries that refused to join the ICC challenged the notion that the specified atrocities (called core crimes) are prohibited acts. Rather, as discussed in Chapter 3, opposition was focused on the Court's structure, operation and procedures for prosecuting suspects as well as the mandate of the prosecutor.[5] In fact, even the key states that failed to ratify the final treaty—such as the United States, China, Israel, and the Russian Federation—attended the Rome conference, participated in the deliberations and debates, and publicly expressed support for the legal prohibition of atrocities.[6]

---

[3] Martha Finnemore and Kathryn Sikkink, "International Norm Dynamics and Political Change," *International Organization*, vol. 52, no. 4, 1998.

[4] Michael Scharf, "Seizing the 'Grotian Moment': Accelerated Formation of Customary International Law in Times of Fundamental Change," *Cornell International Law Journal*, vol. 43, April 2010.

[5] See, for example, Teresa Young Reeves, "A Global Court? U.S. Objections to the International Criminal Court and Obstacles to Ratification," *Human Rights Brief*, vol. 8, no. 1, 2000.

[6] See the summary of statements made by individual state representatives in United Nations, "UN Diplomatic Conference Concludes in Rome with Decision to Establish Permanent International Criminal Court," 1998, press release, 20 July 1998, available at: https://www.un.org/press/en/1998/19980720.l2889.html.

Subsequently both the United States and China demonstrated their willingness to cooperate with the Court in 2005 when they refused to cast a veto in a Security Council resolution referring the situation in Darfur to ICC prosecutors, even though Sudan was not a party to the Rome Statue.[7] This allowed the resolution to pass.[8]

The Rome Statute may have been the tipping point for the universalization of a legal ban on committing atrocities within state borders. However, as previous chapters demonstrated, each of the legal norms went through its own particular life cycle through which an increasing number of organizations, resolutions, and agreements led to a cascade, resulting in a general consensus within the international community.

As discussed in Chapter 3, the concept of crimes against humanity was officially introduced to the world in the 1945 Charter of the International Military Tribunal at Nuremberg, but it took decades before its prohibition became widespread enough to be considered a universal legal norm. Moreover, the concept was originally an adjunct to war crimes inasmuch as they were limited to acts occurring during an armed conflict. Similarly, although Raphael Lemkin coined the term "genocide" in 1944, the Nuremberg Charter did not even mention the act as an offense, nor was anyone prosecuted by the Tribunal for committing it.

The ICTY and ICTR breathed new life into the development of these concepts by issuing broadly accepted and widely cited rulings that can be viewed as a key tipping point for expanding international law to include certain acts of state violence committed within their juridical borders (see Chapters 3 through 6). In particular, the ICTR forever removed the legal requirement that there be a nexus with an armed conflict for an act to constitute an atrocity under international law. The judgments issued by both tribunals confirmed that individual leaders could be prosecuted for committing specified acts, even though there was no treaty (prior to the creation of the ICC) that provided for that. These rulings could be viewed as the apex of the life cycle of legal norms prohibiting these atrocities, reflecting a legal consensus within the international community.

The universal prohibition of torture also evolved over the course of several decades. Although it has been mentioned in virtually every human rights

---

[7] The Rome Statue allows for the Security Council to refer any state for investigation and prosecution, even those that refuse to sign treaty.

[8] UN Security Council, Resolution 1593 (2005) [on Violations of International Humanitarian Law and Human Rights Law in Darfur, Sudan], 31 March 2005, S/RES/1593.

agreement since the Universal Declaration was approved by the UN General Assembly in 1948, it was not until the late 1990s that it became part of general international law binding even on those who were not party to these agreements. In fact it was not considered an international crime until the end of the decade. The 1984 Convention Against Torture entered into force in 1987; however, at the time, only 20 states had ratified it.[9] Yet each time its prohibition was stipulated in an international or regional agreement over the following decades, the legal norm was strengthened.

The tipping point occurred on 24 March 1999, when the British House of Lords ruled that General Augusto Pinochet was not entitled to immunity from prosecution for committing torture, and as such could be tried for this act under the principle of universal jurisdiction. The United Kingdom had joined the Convention Against Torture in 1988, which allowed its government to exercise universal jurisdiction under British law, but the House of Lords was not concerned with Chile's status regarding the treaty. The Pinochet case has been cited by numerous legal analysts and jurists, and no political leader has publicly acknowledged use of torture since that time.[10]

The laws of armed conflict date back hundreds of years, but the idea that they could apply to internal disputes is of recent vintage. Moreover, the protection of civilians was not considered to be a substantial part of the laws and customs of war until the conclusion of the First and Second Protocols to the Geneva Conventions in 1977. The recently coined term "international humanitarian law" to describe this set of protections did not emerge until the Protocols. While the ICTY solidified these principles as part of general international law binding on all states, the Second Protocol was almost certainly the tipping point for applying these principles to internal conflicts. Combined with the rulings from the ICTY, the drafting of the Rome Statute, and the subsequent prosecution of war criminals for actions during civil wars, the life cycle of civilian immunity in internal conflicts demonstrates the depth of these legal norms in the body of international law.

---

[9] See Han Danelius, "Convention Against Torture," United Nations Office of Legal Affairs, Audiovisual Library of International Law, at: https://legal.un.org/avl/ha/catcidtp/catcidtp.html#:~:text=The%20Convention%20against%20Torture%20and,been%20ratified%20by%2020%20States.

[10] See Andrea Bianchi, "Immunity versus Human Rights: The Pinochet Case," *European Journal of International Law*, vol. 10, no. 2, 1999.

Consensus and the Future of International Law

The empirical chapters support the proposition that legal norms based on international consensus can coexist with those grounded in state consent. Unless states establish a global authority with the power to legislate for the entire international community, the sources of international law will remain a mix of various instruments, primarily customary practice, multilateral treaty, Security Council directives, and international consensus. This makes it possible to expand international law without undermining its traditional foundation. While the principle of sovereignty has traditionally strongly favored consent-based sources, the globalization of world politics has opened up the possibility for universally binding legal norms derived from deliberation and broad agreement by the international community. This is essentially *opinio juris* without corresponding state practice.

Multilateral treaties will likely remain the primary source of international law in those areas where states prefer to stipulate their legal obligations with some precision, usually based on the principle of reciprocity, for example in the areas of security, arms control, environmental policy, governance of the high seas, trade, and the treatment of refugees. They will also continue to be a key method for codifying and expanding existing practice, particularly in the issue areas that were traditionally covered by customary law.

In cases where states have signed particular human rights treaties, these agreements will likely remain the primary source of obligation recognized by other states and international institutions. Thus, for example, the UN Security Council resolution establishing the ICTR cited Common Article 3 and the Second Protocol to the Geneva Conventions as the primary foundation for the charges. Rwanda was a party to these agreements. Similarly, the resolution creating the ICTY cited "grave breaches" of the Geneva Conventions, to which Yugoslavia was a party.[11] At the same time, the Council did not cite the Genocide Convention (which Rwanda had ratified) or any other treaty when enunciating the charges of genocide and crimes against humanity against the accused perpetrators.[12] They chose to rely on general international law prohibiting these practices.

---

[11] United Nations Security Council, Resolution 827, adopted by the Security Council at its 3217th meeting, on 25 May 1993, S/RES/827.

[12] United Nations Security Council, Resolution 955, adopted by the Security Council at its 3453rd meeting, on 8 November 1994, S/RES/955.

The approach taken by the Council in addressing violence in the former Yugoslavia is equally instructive. The resolution creating the ICTY limits its jurisdiction to actions that occurred beginning in January 1991, a time when Yugoslavia was still a unified state. Thus, under international law, any violations that occurred were technically during a non-international armed conflict. Yet Yugoslavia had not signed the Second Protocol, and therefore international humanitarian law in this area did not technically apply.[13] From the Security Council actions regarding Rwanda and the former Yugoslavia, one can deduce that the Council was using a mix of treaty law and general international law.

Customary law will continue to be important in areas where there is a relatively long history of consistent state practice—such as the use of the high seas, diplomatic relations, and the general laws of international armed conflict—that states recognize as regulating not only their own policies and behavior but those of all other states as well. All of these areas have been codified into treaties; however, customary law will be essential for ensuring that new states who have not signed these agreements accept the basic foundations for coexistence and international relations.

At the same time, as I argued in Chapter 1, there is a limit to trying to apply customary law to areas where there is a lack of uniform, consistent state practice. The frequent attempts to expand it to new areas of international law by some scholars have proven to be problematic, particularly in regard to regulating the internal behavior of states. This is especially the case in those areas in which the norms are of relatively recent vintage and where the practice is inconsistent.

The examination of atrocities in the previous chapters bears this out. While there is clear *opinio juris* regarding the prohibition of genocide, ethnic cleansing, torture, and one-sided violence against civilians and minority populations, this was not preceded by consistent state practice. Indeed, torture is still regularly practiced, albeit at a lower rate than in the past; civilians are still routinely victimized in internal armed conflicts; governments continue to persecute minorities, often violently; and ethnic cleansing and one-sided attacks on populations by states continue to be common in various parts of the world. Moreover, the reaction by the

---

[13] As mentioned in Chapter 6, although Common Article 3 is binding on all signatories to the four Geneva Conventions, it does not directly provide significant protection of civilians from indiscriminate or direct attacks by military forces. Clearly the charges stipulated in the Statute went well beyond this article.

international community to these offenses has been inconsistent; in many cases, the response to these atrocities has been muted, suggesting a lack of uniform practice.

Still, some legal scholars continue to cite customary law as the basis for arguing universal obligations in regard to these practices. The irony of this is that since the early part of the 20th century, states have demonstrated a clear preference for codifying customary law into written agreements. Attempts to invigorate the customary source of legal norms by expanding their application to cover internal state violence actually go against this trend.

Moreover, in the case of atrocities, most political leaders and legal analysts do not view the persistent objector rule—which is so crucial for customary law to be consistent with the doctrine of consent—as a legitimate means to circumvent the general prohibitions against excessive state violence. Thus, for example, states may not legally commit genocide or torture by explicitly refusing to ratify the respective conventions even as they were being drafted.

The previous four chapters demonstrate how consensus can be created through deliberation among a wide range of states and supported by overlapping treaties, resolutions by international and regional organizations, rulings by international tribunals, Security Council actions, and other soft law instruments. Consensus was not imposed by powerful states on the world; indeed, the most powerful country (the United States) rarely led or even supported many of the efforts to criminalize internal violence. Rather, the *travaux préparatoires* where multilateral lawmaking treaties prohibiting atrocities were drafted, negotiated, and approved demonstrate that the delegates from smaller countries led the efforts.

This book focused on internal state violence; however, a theory of consensus-based international law can also be applied to other types of state behavior where the international community has consciously tried to create universal legal norms. For example, one can make a *prima facie* case that states consider the use of chemical and biological weapons a violation of international law, even if those employing them have refused to sign the chemical weapons and biological weapons treaties. For example, when the Syrian government used chemical weapons against rebel positions in the city of Homs in December 2012 and August 2013, it led to an international outcry and demands for international action; the UN secretary-general referred to this as a war crime. However, at the time Syria was not a party to the

Chemical Weapons Convention. It did not accede to the agreement until 12 September 2013.[14]

Implications for Enforcement

The degree to which states and institutions enforce a legal norm both reflects and reinforces the strength of the particular norm. It also influences how states and international and regional organizations attempt to enforce international human rights law.

States have established at least four methods for enforcing the universal prohibition of atrocities: UN Security Council sanctions, international criminal tribunals, humanitarian intervention, and the exercise of universal jurisdiction by domestic courts. All of these are strongly influenced by the degree to which potential enforcers determine whether internal state violence is protected by the principle of sovereignty or whether such violence is a violation of general international law. The previous chapters strongly suggest that international institutions do in fact consider certain acts to constitute universal violations. One of the remaining questions, then, is what states can do—and have done—to enforce them and what this tells us about limits on the doctrine of consent.

As argued in Chapter 2, one of the most important institutional developments in world politics has been the gradual self-expansion of the UN Security Council's mandate to address internal state violence. This represents a growing consensus among the five major powers that sovereignty and state autonomy no longer automatically protect governments from international scrutiny when their actions breach the prohibition against committing certain types of atrocities. In all cases during the 1990s and early 2000s, the Council acted on the basis of the "breach of the peace" clause, which, as a matter of international law, subjects all states in the world to its authority. By reconceptualizing certain types of internal state violence as threats to

---

[14] See UN Secretary General, "Secretary-General's remarks to the Security Council on the Report of the United Nations Missions to Investigate Allegations of the Use of Chemical Weapons on the Incident That Occurred on 21 August 2013 in the Ghouta Area of Damascus," 16 September 2013, at: https://www.un.org/sg/en/content/sg/statement/2013-09-16/secretary-generals-remarks-security-council-report-united-nations. See also Arms Control Association, "Chemical Weapons Convention Signatories and States-Parties," June 2018, at: https://www.armscontrol.org/factsheets/cwcsig.

international peace and security, the Council has essentially universalized the legal prohibition of such violence.

Under Chapter VII of the UN Charter, the Council may employ virtually any type of enforcement action at its own discretion, including imposing mandatory sanctions, and if it deems it necessary, authorizing or initiating military force. However, according to Article 2(7) of the Charter, "Nothing contained in the present Charter shall authorize the United Nations to intervene in matters which are essentially within the domestic jurisdiction of any state." This clause reflected the overwhelming consensus at the time of the UN founding that the purpose of Chapter VII was to provide for international security, not the protection of populations from human rights violations.

Article 2(7) continues, "[B]ut this principle shall not prejudice the application of enforcement measures under Chapter VII," essentially giving the Council a blank check to act at its own discretion. Traditionally the Council avoided becoming involved in the internal affairs of the UN member states, and the political interests of the five permanent members often prevented direct action even in the most egregious cases of internal state violence.

Certainly the Council's actions have often been and will continue to be inconsistent and self-interested. The Council does not respond to many cases of internal state violence, and the permanent members usually avoid taking action against their allies. China, for example, initially refused to join with the other permanent members seeking to act to stop the genocide in Darfur, and Russia prevented any unified action against Syria during its government's widespread attacks on its civilian population during the Syrian Civil War.[15] The United States has never approved a resolution condemning Israel's attacks on Palestinian civilians.[16]

As a deliberative body, rather than a global police force, the Council is not required to act even if there is a violation of the Charter. As a political body, rather than legal one, it usually does not act when specific members believe that doing so would harm its national interests, even if all of its members believe that international law has been violated. Still, as demonstrated in the previous chapters, the Council has acted in enough cases to establish a firm

---

[15] See "Security Council—Veto List," Dag Hammarskjöld Library, at: https://research.un.org/en/docs/sc/quick (accessed 22 May 2021).

[16] See American-Israeli Cooperative Enterprise, "U.N. Security Council: U.S. Vetoes of Resolutions Critical to Israel (1972–Present)," at: https://www.jewishvirtuallibrary.org/u-s-vetoes-of-un-security-council-resolutions-critical-to-israel (accessed 23 May 2021).

position that certain types of atrocities do in fact violate international law and the UN Charter, even when initiated within a state's own borders.

Specifically, as discussed in the previous chapters, the Council demonstrated its deference to international law when it created international tribunals to try individuals for violations in the former Yugoslavia, Rwanda, and Sierra Leon. It did so on the basis of a well-defined legal standard regarding the prohibition of atrocities that applied to all sides in the conflicts. Nothing in either the Charter or international law gave the Council, or any other international body, the authority to establish such tribunals. Rather, the Security Council used its Chapter VII powers granted under the "breach of the peace" clause of the Charter to establish tribunals to try individuals accused of genocide, crimes against humanity, and grave breaches in the laws of armed conflict. The Security Council did this on the basis of general international law rather than specific treaties.[17] In fact, nowhere in the resolutions authorizing the creation of these tribunals did the Council cite specific treaty violations. This is in part because at the time no treaty existed that mentioned, defined, or criminalized crimes against humanity.

Moreover, although some argued that the core crimes referenced by the Council had become embedded in customary law, up to that point there was nothing in customary practice that allowed for the prosecution of individuals accused of violating the laws of internal armed conflict. (The Geneva Conventions apply only to states.)[18] Indeed, prior to the Council's actions in the early 1990s, there had not been any international action opposing crimes against humanity since 1945, despite the many atrocities that were committed regularly throughout the world during this period. So it is difficult to argue that this reflected state practice. Thus, customary law cannot provide a legal justification for attaching criminal responsibility to the types of atrocities discussed in the previous four chapters.

It is significant that the Council chose to cite international law as its basis for establishing the tribunals inasmuch as they had the authority to act by simply evoking their powers to maintain international peace and security under the Charter, without any regard for legal considerations. Although some political leaders at the time questioned whether the Council could in fact legally create the ICTY, the authority of the Council to do so was soon

---

[17] See Security Council Resolutions 955 (UN Documents S/RES/955, 1994); 827 (UN Documents, S/RES/827, 1993), and 1315 (UN Documents S/RES/1315, 2000).

[18] Guenael Mettraux, *International Crimes and the Ad Hoc Tribunals* (Oxford University Press, 2006), p. 8.

broadly accepted and ultimately reaffirmed in the *Tadić* case.[19] Thus, when the Council created a similar court to try extreme violations of human rights in Rwanda a year later, there was little opposition. In fact with Rwanda, the Council took the extraordinary step of expanding the scope of its authority to include domestic human rights violations that occurred outside of an armed conflict, something it did not attempt with the former Yugoslavia.

The choice of which offenses would fall within the jurisdiction of the newly created courts can tell us a lot about the role of the Council in the interpretation of international legal obligation. The Council decided to focus only on those areas in which there was a broad consensus concerning the universality of international law. They developed a list of core crimes that were considered universally recognized offenses against the international community under international law regardless of whether they violated a specific treaty.

In addition to actions taken by the Security Council, the universal prohibition of atrocities also provides the legal and political foundation for the practice of humanitarian intervention.[20] Humanitarian intervention is a direct challenge to the United Nations Charter, the only truly universally adopted multilateral treaty. There is nothing in the document that even implies a humanitarian exception to the prohibition on the use of force; the only exemptions are immediate self-defense and collective action authorized by the Security Council. Yet the adoption of the "responsibility to protect" by 170 heads of state at the 2005 World Summit—subsequently validated by consensus in the UN General Assembly—carved out such an exception in cases of internal atrocities.[21] Significantly, neither resolution refers to any treaty or customary law when asserting the right and responsibility to take forceful action in cases of internal state violence that rise to the level of atrocities.

Of course, humanitarian intervention is highly controversial as a legal, political, and diplomatic matter. This is not because there is disagreement over whether states have the legal right to commit atrocities within their own

---

[19] ICTY, "Opinion and Judgment," The Prosecutor v. Duško Tadic, Case No.: IT-94-1-T, Trial Chamber II, 7 May 1997.

[20] Humanitarian intervention is the use of armed force by a state against another state without the consent of its government, for the purpose of preventing or halting gross and massive violations of human rights or international humanitarian law. See Danish Institute of International Affairs, *Humanitarian Intervention: Legal and Political Aspects*, 1999, p. 11.

[21] United Nations, "2005 World Summit Outcome," Resolution adopted by the General Assembly on 16 September 2005 (A/60/1).

borders under the protection of sovereignty, but because many scholars and practitioners doubt whether such intervention is effective or wise. Indeed some consider it to be counterproductive and are concerned that it can easily be used as a cover for pursuing state interests unrelated to the protection of victim populations.[22] It is not the wisdom of the practice that is significant for our discussion, however, but the fact that the international community considers certain types of internal state violence to warrant international intervention regardless of whether the offending state has signed a particular treaty.

The current conceptualization of intervention in cases of excessive international state violence can be found in the 2001 report of the International Commission on Intervention and State Sovereignty, *The Responsibility to Protect*. This document formulated the principle based not on the legal right to intervene but on the *responsibility* of all states to do so in order to protect populations from atrocities. Specifically, the report asserted that it was every state's responsibility to protect its citizens from "genocide, war crimes, ethnic cleansing, and crimes against humanity." If a state fails to do so—or, more commonly, when the state itself is the perpetrator—it then becomes the responsibility of the international community to protect that state's population, regardless of whether the offending state was a party to a particular treaty or whether such offenses violated customary international law.[23]

In 2011 the UN Security Council invoked the responsibility to protect doctrine for the first time by adopting Resolution 1973 authorizing member states to "take all necessary measures" to protect civilians under attack from Libyan leader Muammar al-Qaddafi's government.[24] The subsequent exploitation of this authorization by NATO to engage in regime change undermined the possibility for future actions, but the principle of protecting populations under threat from atrocities itself was never rejected.[25]

---

[22] See, for example, Rajan Menon, "R2P: It's Fatally Flawed," *The American Interest*, vol. 8, no. 6, June 2013; Benjamin Valentino, "The True Costs of Humanitarian Intervention," *Foreign Affairs*, vol. 90, no. 6, November–December 2011; David N. Gibbs, *First Do No Harm: Humanitarian Intervention and the Destruction of Yugoslavia* (Vanderbilt University Press, 2009).

[23] International Commission on Intervention and State Sovereignty, "The Responsibility to Protect: Report of the International Committee on Intervention and State Sovereignty," International Development Research Centre, December 2001.

[24] UN Security Council Resolution 1973, adopted by the Security Council at its 6498th meeting, on 17 March 2011, S/RES/1973.

[25] See, for example, Hannah VanHoose, "Understanding the Russian Response to the Intervention in Libya: Moscow Delivered at the United Nations but Its Critical Statements Reflect Real Concerns," 12 April 2011.

The principle of universal jurisdiction is still highly controversial, particularly in determining the basis for overriding what has traditionally been bedrock standards in international relations, state sovereignty and the Act of State Doctrine.[26] Moreover, legal analysts from many states have expressed concern that an unwarranted expansion beyond the most heinous crimes would distort the purpose of the principle and provide opportunities for abuse, thereby putting its legitimacy into question. For this reason, states have been reluctant to apply it beyond the most egregious cases.[27]

In Chapter 4, I discussed how some states have claimed universal jurisdiction over cases involving torture by foreign officials. Over the past few decades, this has been extended by courts to include a wider set of offenses that legal experts consider to be universal crimes, which include crimes against humanity, war crimes, genocide, and terrorism.[28] Some of these acts are mentioned as universal offenses in multilateral treaties, such as the Geneva Conventions and Protocols, the Convention Against Torture, the Genocide Convention, and the International Convention on Enforced Disappearances. Others, such as crimes against humanity, are accepted on the basis of general international law. In all of the cases, however, the decision by domestic legal activists and courts to prosecute is strengthened by a broad consensus that the international legal prohibition against certain atrocities is a universal principle.

Implications for Human Rights

Political leaders have traditionally prioritized security and economic interests over the protection of foreign populations from egregious human rights abuses. This is not likely to change significantly over the coming years.

---

[26] See, for example, African Union and European Union, "Technical Ad Hoc Expert Group on the Principle of Universal Jurisdiction," report, 15 April 2009. I should note that most legal analysts find the Act of State Doctrine to be ambiguous, based on Anglo-Saxon common law more than on a principle of international law. See Joseph W. Dellapenna, "Deciphering the Act of State Doctrine," *Villanova Law Review*, vol. 35, no. 1, February 1990 and Gregory H. Fox, "Reexamining the Act of State Doctrine," *Harvard International Law Journal*, vol. 33, 1992.

[27] See, for example, United Nations, *Report of the International Law Commission Seventieth Session* (30 April–1 June and 2 July–10 August 2018), Annex A: Universal Criminal Jurisdiction, A/73/10 and United Nations General Assembly, Sixth Committee, 71st session, "The Scope and Application of the Principle of Universal Jurisdiction (Agenda Item 85)," 2016.

[28] See Howard Varney and Katarzyna Zduńczyk, "Advancing Global Accountability: The Role of Universal Jurisdiction in Prosecuting International Crimes," report, International Center for Transitional Justice, 2020.

Moreover, there appears to be a clear hierarchy of human rights within international law and diplomacy. Virtually all governments violate human rights, and routine abuses such as the denial of due process or freedom of expression tend to be treated by states as diplomatic or political rather than legal issues. To a large extent, they fall within the internal jurisdiction of states, even if they are prohibited by agreements such as the Covenant on Civil and Political Rights.

At the same time, states and international organizations have demonstrated that the principle of sovereignty is limited when it comes to certain types of abuses. The trend since the end of the Cold War has been steadily moving toward greater legal liability for governments that engaged in specified practices deemed by the international community to constitute universal offenses.

This book focused on the most egregious forms of human rights abuses, atrocities, because this is the area where there appears to be a general consensus that they constitute universal violations of international law. Human rights are as much a political question as they are a legal one. For this reason, the list of abuses that rise to the level of atrocities may grow over the coming period, although we obviously do not know which ones will be included. One thing is certain: the days when governments could avoid legal liability (although not necessarily punishment) for engaging in excessive violence against their populations by refusing to consent to the norms prohibiting appear to be over.

Index

For the benefit of digital users, indexed terms that span two pages (e.g., 52–53) may, on occasion, appear on only one of those pages.

Abbott, Kenneth, 71
Act of State Doctrine, 78–79, 86, 198
Afghanistan War (2001-21), 170
African Charter on Human and Peoples' Rights (Bangui Charter), 42, 138
African Court on Human and Peoples' Rights, 62–63, 98–99
African Union, 57–58, 175, 176, 183, 185
Albania, 110
Alvarez, Jose, 66
American Convention on Human Rights, 42, 138
American Declaration on the Rights and Duties of Man, 42
Amin, Idi, 79–80
Amnesty International, 155, 179–80
Apartheid Convention (1974), 101, 125–29, 137–38, 150
apartheid policies
    armed conflict contexts and, 127
    civil and political rights denied through, 124, 128
    consensus-based international law and, 4–5, 36, 126, 128
    crimes against humanity and, 125, 126, 127
    Israel and, 129
    persecution law and, 123–29
    race as underlying basis for, 123–24
    soft law and, 127
    in South Africa before 1990, 123–25, 128–29
    territorial separation and, 123–24, 128
    torture and, 127
    United Nations Charter and, 125
    United Nations Security Council and, 125

Arab Charter of Human Rights, 138
Arab Spring (2011), 162
Arend, Anthony, 54
Armenian genocide (1915-22), 86–87, 97, 112–13
al-Assad, Bashar, 162
Association for the Prevention of Torture, 155–56
Austria, 110

Bangui Charter (African Charter on Human and Peoples' Rights), 42, 138
Bassiouni, Mahmoud Cherif, 50, 82
Baylis, Elena, 62–63
Berlin Treaty (1876), 110
Bosnia, 80–81, 107, 120–21, 122
Bothe, Michael, 45–46
Bulgaria, 110
Bybee, Jay, 145–46
Byers, Michael, 35

Cairo Declaration of Human Rights in Islam, 138
Cambodia, 79–80, 81, 98–99, 113, 185
Campaign for the Abolition of Torture, 155
Catholic Church, 20–21, 22, 97, 133–34
Champetier de Ribes, Auguste, 111–12
Charney, Jonathan, 29, 58, 64
Chemical Weapons Convention, 192–93
Cheng, Bin, 11–12
Cherokees, 121
Chile, 82, 86, 141, 189
China
    Buddhists as subject to persecution during Tang Era in, 97
    Falun Gong movement in, 107

China (*cont.*)
  Sudan's war in Darfur and, 187–88, 194
  tributary system before 1900 in, 24
  Uyghur population in, 112–13
  World War II and, 74
Christenson, Gordon, 49–50
Churchill, Winston, 111
civilians' immunity in domestic armed conflicts
  consensus-based international law and, 4–5, 33–34, 36, 64–65, 180–81
  Convention on Certain Conventional Weapons and, 175–76
  international criminal tribunals and, 167, 169, 180–81
  international humanitarian law and, 158–59, 165–67, 169
  laws of armed conflict and, 122, 165, 180
  proportionality principle and, 166
  Second Protocol to the Geneva Conventions (1977) and, 1, 159, 173–74, 189
  United Nations General Assembly's recognition of, 176
  United Nations Security Council's recognition of, 166, 175, 176
civil wars. See non-international armed conflicts
Coalition for the International Criminal Court (CICC), 90
Cold War, 79
Common Article 3. See *under* Geneva Conventions (1949)
Community of Latin American and Caribbean States, 93
Concert of Europe, 22
Congress of Vienna (1815), 21–22
consensus-based international law
  apartheid policies and, 4–5, 36, 126, 128
  civilians' immunity in domestic armed conflicts and, 4–5, 33–34, 36, 64–65, 180–81
  common consent and, 34
  customary international law compared to, 32–35, 38
  deliberation through international institutions and, 32–34, 38
  domestic and international judicial decisions as sources for, 38–39, 71
  ethnic cleansing and, 4–5, 36
  excessive internal state violence and, 4–5, 36, 37, 64–65
  genocide and, 4–5, 36, 64–65, 118–19
  global governance and, 26–27
  human rights and, 3, 18–19, 38, 71
  jus cogens norms and, 38–39, 47–58, 118, 182–83
  methods for determining norms in, 52–56
  multilateral treaties and conventions as a basis for, 6–7, 39–42, 51, 63–65, 69–71, 182–83
  opinio juris and, 7, 34, 35, 52–53
  positive law and, 6–7
  regional agreements and, 42
  soft law as a basis for, 38–39, 42–47, 51
  state practice and, 33–34
  tipping points in establishing, 187–89
  torture and, 33–34, 36, 131–33, 134–35, 188–89
  United Nations Security Council and, 65–68
Convention Against Torture (CAT, 1984)
  absolute nature of prohibition against torture under, 140, 141, 147–48
  Committee Against Torture's role in monitoring, 71, 153
  definition of torture in, 41, 135–36
  doctrine of consent and, 131
  drafting of, 136–37, 139, 184, 185
  nongovernmental organizations' role in establishing, 30–31
  non-refoulement principle and, 140, 146–47
  nonsignatories of, 1, 132, 150, 152–53, 188–89
  number of signatories to, 139, 156
  Optional Protocol for the Convention Against Torture and, 154
  states' criminal jurisdiction for acts of torture under, 136, 139–40
  states' right to withdraw from, 2
  universal jurisdiction principle and, 150–51
  wartime conditions and, 140

Convention Governing the Specific
  Aspects of Refugee Problems in
  Africa, 105
Convention on Certain Conventional
  Weapons, 175–76
Convention on the Elimination of
  Discrimination against Women, 101
Convention on the Prevention and
  Punishment of the Crime
  of Genocide. *See* Genocide
  Convention (1948)
Convention on the Rights of Persons with
  Disabilities, 137–38
Convention on the Rights of the Child,
  30–31, 137–38
corporal punishment, 145
Council of Europe, 93, 185
Council of the League of Nations, 110
Covenant on Civil and Political
  Rights (1966)
  consensus-based international law and,
    71, 82–84
  genocide and, 84
  public emergency exceptions in, 83, 163
  torture prohibition in, 84, 131–
    32, 137–39
  Universal Declaration of Human Rights
    codified in, 14, 82–83
Criddle, Evan, 49–50
crimes against humanity
  apartheid policies and, 125, 126, 127
  Armenian genocide and origins of the
    term, 86–87
  erga omnes obligations and, 76–77
  ethnic cleansing and, 121, 123
  excessive internal state violence and, 82,
    87–88, 89, 94–95
  genocide distinguished from, 112
  humanitarian intervention and, 84–85
  individuals' criminal responsibilities
    for, 85–86, 87–88
  international criminal tribunals and, 84,
    89, 93, 112
  International Law Commission and, 63,
    85–86, 89–90, 91, 93, 98–99
  International Military Tribunal and, 89
  jus cogens norms and, 50–51
  natural law and, 87

Nuremberg Charter (1945) and, 188
peacetime applications of, 93
rape and, 144
Responsibility to Protect principle
  and, 197
Rome Statute and, 1, 89–90, 91–92, 94,
  112, 123, 184
state sovereignty doctrine and, 88
threshold test for, 94
United Nations Charter and, 92–93
universality of, 87, 92, 198
as war crimes, 76–77, 188
customary international law (CIL)
  collective knowledge and, 35
  consensus-based international law
    compared to, 32–35, 38
  diplomatic law and, 18
  European origins (1648-1945) of, 18, 23
  Geneva Conventions (1949) and,
    159, 171
  human rights and, 11, 14–15, 16–17,
    18–19, 35
  implied consent and, 7, 15, 34–35
  multilateralism and, 29
  non-international armed conflicts, 195
  North Continental Shelf case and, 15
  opinio juris as a basis for, 11–12, 15–
    16, 34–35
  persecution prohibition and, 130
  persistent objector exception and, 16–
    17, 25–26, 46, 132, 192
  slavery and, 36
  state practice as a basis for, 11, 13, 15–
    16, 18, 24, 29, 182
  states' prosecution of enemy
    combatants prior to World War II
    and, 75
  states' refusal to ratify international
    treaties and, 2
  torture and, 132
  United Nations and, 29
  Universal Declaration of Human Rights
    and, 14
  universal legal norms and, 11–19
  verbal conduct and, 11–13
Czechoslovakia, 110

D'Amato, Anthony, 48–49

Darfur conflict (Sudan), 187–88, 194
decolonization
    dramatic increase in number of
        international states and, 15–16
    jus cogens norms and, 50
    non-international armed conflicts
        and, 164
    UN Declaration on the Granting of
        Independence to Colonial Countries
        and Peoples and, 39
    wars of national liberation and, 172
    weak central governments and political
        instability following, 164
Denmark, 141
Deudney, Daniel, 27–28
Diplomatic Conference for the
    Establishment of International
    Conventions for the Protection of
    War Victims (1949), 163–64
diplomatic law, 18, 64
doctrine of consent
    Convention of Torture's nonsignatories
        and, 131
    Genocide Convention (1948) and,
        1, 115–16
    human rights and limits to, 4–5, 182–
        83, 193
    international criminal tribunals and,
        92–93, 186
    persistent objector exception and, 16–
        17, 25–26
    Second Protocol's nonsignatories
        and, 1, 175
Dunant, Henri, 176–77

East Pakistan genocide (1971), 79–80
East Timor, 46–47, 65–66, 80–81, 185
Economic Community of West African
    States, 30–31
The Enlightenment, 21
Estonia, 110
ethnic cleansing
    armed conflict contexts and, 120, 122
    in Bosnia, 120–21, 122
    consensus-based international law and,
        4–5, 36
    crimes against humanity and, 121, 123
    critics of the concept of, 121
    definition of, 119–20
    genocide compared to, 119–21
    humanitarian intervention and, 84–85,
        123, 130
    international humanitarian law
        and, 122
    lack of international law regarding, 1,
        121, 123
    laws of armed conflict and, 121–22, 123
    mass displacements of civilians
        and, 122–23
    mass rapes and, 120–21, 122
    in medieval and early modern
        Europe, 120
    military attacks on civilian areas
        and, 122
    in Myanmar, 1
    persecution law and, 119–23
    Responsibility to Protect principle
        and, 197
    Rome Statute and, 184, 187
    Second Protocol to the Geneva
        Conventions and, 122–23
    torture and, 122
    US interactions with Native American
        populations before 1900 and, 121
    Yugoslavia Wars (1990s) and, 120–
        21, 122
European Convention for the Prevention
    of Torture, 42, 155–56
European Convention for the Protection
    of Human Rights and Fundamental
    Freedoms, 42, 138
European Court of Human Rights, 62–
    63, 143–44
European Union, 57–58, 104, 175,
    176, 183
excessive internal state violence. *See also*
    non-international armed conflicts
    consensus-based international law, 4–5,
        36, 37, 64–65
    crimes against humanity and, 82, 87–88,
        89, 94–95
    Genocide Convention and, 77–78
    human rights and, 81–82, 157
    international criminal tribunal rulings
        and, 186, 188, 195–96
    international stability and, 80–81, 82

mass killings of civilians in non-
international conflicts and, 164–
65, 182–83
persecution of minorities and, 96, 98–
99, 182–83
refugees and, 80–81
regional security organizations and, 185
"shocking the conscience of humanity"
threshold and, 82
torture and, 134, 182–83
Universal Declaration of Human Rights
and, 77
extraordinary rendition, 147

Falk, Richard, 52
Falun Gong movement, 107
Feierstein, Daniel, 111–12
Finnemore, Martha, 53–54, 187
First Protocol to the Geneva Conventions
(1977), 127, 180, 189
Fox-Decent, Evan, 49–50
France, 48–49, 109, 115–16, 126. *See also*
French Revolution
Franck, Thomas, 16
Free Imperial Cities, 20–21
French Revolution, 22, 108

Garcia Castellon, Manuel, 86
Garzon, Baltasar, 86
Geneva Conventions (1949)
apartheid policies and, 127
civilian immunity in domestic armed
conflicts and, 1, 158, 159, 173–74, 189
Common Article 3 and, 170–72,
182, 190
consensus-based international law
and, 71
customary international law and,
159, 171
ethnic cleansing and, 122–23
First Protocol and, 127, 180, 189
nondiscrimination provisions of, 101
nonsignatories of, 17
prisoners of war and, 101, 158, 170, 177
Second Protocol and, 1, 122–23, 159,
167, 172–75, 176–77, 183–84,
189, 190–91
torture prohibition in, 135n.16, 170–71

genocide. *See also* Genocide
Convention (1948)
in Cambodia during 1970s, 79–80, 81
consensus-based international law and,
4–5, 36, 64–65, 118–19
Covenant on Civil and Political Rights
and, 84
crimes of humanity distinguished
from, 112
in East Pakistan (1971), 79–80
ethnic cleansing compared to, 119–21
The Holocaust and, 77, 97, 111
humanitarian intervention and, 84–85
international criminal tribunals and, 84,
112, 130, 190
internationally accepted
definition of, 41
jus cogens norms, 50, 118–19
persecution law and, 111–19
Responsibility to Protect principle and,
119, 197
in Rwanda (1994), 80–81, 113
target and intent questions in
defining, 113–14
United Nations Charter and, 92–93
universal jurisdiction principle and, 198
Genocide Convention (1948)
consensus-based international law and, 71
definition of genocide in, 41, 183–84
doctrine of consent and, 1, 115–16
individuals' criminal liability under,
78–79, 85–86
nonsignatories as subject to jurisdiction
of, 1, 79, 113, 115–17, 119
on "odious scourge" of states
committing atrocities against their
own populations, 3
process of drafting, 183–84, 185
states' criminal liability under, 78
state sovereignty doctrine and, 115–16
states' right to withdraw from, 2
United Nations General Assembly
involvement in establishing,
78, 114–15
United Nations Security Council
and, 115–17
universal jurisdiction confirmed (2006)
for, 116–17

Ghana, 141
Gonzales, Alberto, 145–46
Gowlland-Debbas, Vera, 42
Greece, 110
Grotius, Hugo, 17, 21
Guzman, Andrew, 25

Haas, Ernst, 31
Hague Conventions (1899-1907), 24, 73–74, 135n.16, 158n.3, 160n.10
Haiti, 65–66
Harkavy, Robert, 8n.21
Helfer, Laurence, 25–26, 71
Henkin, Louis, 18, 38
Hoffman, Tamas, 117
The Holocaust, 77, 97, 111. *See also* Nazi Germany
Holy Roman Empire, 20–21, 22
Holy SeeM (The Vatican), 20–21
Homs chemical weapons attacks (Syria, 2012-13), 192–93
House of Lords (United Kingdom), 86, 189
humanitarian intervention
  crimes against humanity and, 84–85
  ethnic cleansing and, 84–85, 123, 130
  genocide and, 84–85
  in Libya (2011), 197
  opinio juris and, 13, 35
  Responsibility to Protect principle and, 80, 84–85, 119, 130, 196–97
  United Nations Charter and, 196
  United Nations Security Council and, 65–66
human rights
  consensus-based international law and, 3, 18–19, 38, 71
  customary international law and, 11, 14–15, 16–17, 18–19, 35
  doctrine of consent and, 4–5, 182–83, 193
  domestic courts' assertion of universal jurisdiction regarding, 82, 86
  as *erga omnes*, 4
  excessive internal state violence and, 81–82, 157
  jus cogens norms and, 50, 51
  "naming and shaming" and, 9
  opinio juris and, 13, 35, 191–92
  regional agreements and, 42
  soft law and, 43–44
  state consent doctrine and, 25
  state sovereignty doctrine and, 81, 198–99
  Universal Declaration of Human Rights, 14, 50, 77, 82–83, 98, 100–1, 131–32, 137–39, 188–89
Human Rights Watch, 179–80
Humphrey, John, 14
Hungary, 110

ICC Statute. *See* Rome Statute (1998)
Ikenberry, John, 63–64
India, 70, 79–80, 175
Indonesia, 46–47, 141
Inter-American Court of Human Rights, 62–63
International Atomic Energy Agency (IAEA), 70
International Committee of the Red Cross and Red Crescent (ICRC), 173–74, 176–79
International Convention on Enforced Disappearances, 198
International Convention on the Elimination of All Forms of Racial Discrimination (ICEARD), 101, 126, 137–38
International Convention on the Suppression and Punishment of the Crime of Apartheid. *See* Apartheid Convention (1974)
International Court of Justice (ICJ)
  Article 38 and, 45–46, 60, 186
  on Geneva Conventions' Common Article 3 as baseline for international and non-international conflicts, 172
  North Continental Shelf case and, 15
  selection process for judges at, 59–60
  South Africa's colonization of Namibia and, 128
  on state behavior violating customary international law, 14
  on torture's *jus cogens* status, 133
International Covenant for Civil and Political Rights. *See* Covenant on Civil and Political Rights (1966)

INDEX 207

International Criminal Court (ICC). *See also* Rome Statute (1998)
  doctrine of consent and, 92–93
  establishment of, 116–17, 185
  ethnic cleansing and, 121
  influence beyond member states of, 186
  jurisdiction of, 84, 92–93
  nonsignatories to, 113, 187–88
  Sudan and, 92–93
  United Nations Security Council referrals to, 92–93
International Criminal Tribunal for Rwanda (ICTR)
  crimes against humanity and, 89, 93, 112
  criminal responsibility for individuals who plan mass violence established in, 85
  establishment of, 65–66, 71, 81, 89, 93, 116–17, 185, 190, 195–96
  ethnic cleansing and, 121
  genocide and, 112, 130, 190
  jurisdiction of, 84, 93–94
  persecution law and the statute of, 98–99, 105, 129
  precedents regarding excessive internal state violence established by, 188, 195–96
  torture and, 144
International Criminal Tribunal for the Former Yugoslavia (ICTY)
  civilians' immunity in domestic armed conflicts and, 167
  crimes against humanity and, 89, 112
  criminal responsibility for individuals who plan mass violence established in, 85
  definitional questions regarding non-international armed conflicts and, 168–70
  establishment of, 65–66, 71, 81, 89, 93–94, 116–17, 185, 190–91, 195–96
  genocide and, 112, 130
  jurisdiction of, 84
  persecution law and the statute for, 98–99, 104, 105, 129
  precedents established by decisions at, 186, 189
  torture and, 137, 143, 148–49, 151
international humanitarian law (IHL)
  civilians' immunity in domestic armed conflicts and, 158–59, 165–67, 169
  ethnic cleansing as a violation of, 122
  international agreements serving as sources of, 170–75
  International Red Cross and Red Crescent and, 177–79
  nongovernmental organizations' role in promoting the norms of, 176–80
  non-international armed conflicts and, 160, 163, 165, 167–75
  proportionality principle and, 166, 180
  soft law and, 179
  wounded or detained combatants and, 158
International Labor Organization, 24
International Law Commission (ILC)
  circulation of draft articles as standard practice at, 61
  consensus-driven deliberation process at, 61
  on definition of non-international armed conflicts, 167–68
  Draft Articles on Prevention and Punishment of Crimes Against Humanity, 63, 85–86, 89–90, 91, 93, 98–99
  establishment (1947) of, 58–59
  jus cogens norms and, 49, 54–55, 56–57, 58–63, 182–83
  Nuremberg Principles (1950) and, 77–78
  progressive development of international law and, 62, 184–85
  Rome Statute and, 89–90, 91
  selection process for, 59–60
  soft law and, 62
  Statute of, 59–60
  on threshold for customary international law, 15–16
  on torture's *jus cogens* status, 148–49
  on verbal conduct and international customary law, 11–13
  Vienna Convention on the Law of Treaties and, 64

International Military Tribunal, 75-76, 77-78, 89, 188. *See also* Nuremberg Tribunal (1945-46)
International Tribunal for the Law of the Sea, 62-63
Iraq, 110, 170
Ireland v. United Kingdom, 143-44
Irish Republican Army (IRA), 143, 162
Israel, 70, 129, 175, 187-88, 194

Jackson, Andrew, 121
Jennings, Robert, 15
Jews, 77, 97, 111, 120
Johnstone, Ian, 29, 45, 68
Joyner, Christopher, 12
jus cogens norms
  consensus-based international law and, 38-39, 47-58, 118, 182-83
  crimes against humanity, 50-51
  decolonization and, 50
  definition of, 47
  genocide and, 50, 118-19
  human rights and, 50, 51
  international institutions with legitimacy to interpret, 56-58
  legal positivism and, 52-53
  methods for determining, 52-56
  multilateral treaty regimes and, 56-57, 69-71
  natural law and, 48, 52-53
  self-determination rights and, 46-47, 50
  slavery and, 50, 51
  state consent doctrine and, 48
  terrorism and, 50
  torture and, 50-51, 137-38, 148-51
  universal applicability of, 47, 49-50, 54
  Vienna Convention on the Law of Treaties and, 48-49
just war doctrine *(jus ad bellum)*, 20

Kelly, J. Patrick, 16
Kirgis, Frederic, 13, 40
Korean War, 172
Kosovo Law on Specialist Chambers and Specialist Prosecutor's Office, 98-99
Krisch, Nico, 25

Latvia, 110

Law of Nations, 14, 21, 22
Law of the Seas Convention, 17, 24
Law on the Extraordinary Chambers in the Courts of Cambodia, 98-99
laws of armed conflict (LOAC). *See also* Geneva Conventions (1949); war crimes
  civilian immunity under principle of distinction in, 122, 165, 180
  ethnic cleansing and, 121-22, 123
  international criminal tribunals and, 84
  interstate war and, 157, 160
  military necessity principle and, 157-58, 165-66, 180
  non-international armed conflicts and, 160-63, 169, 181, 189
  reciprocity principle and, 161
  terrorism and, 162
  torture and, 138
  United Nations Charter and, 92-93
  war crimes and, 88
League of Nations, 24, 110
Lee, Roy, 29, 91
legal positivism, 7-8, 37, 52-53, 64-65
Lemkin, Raphael, 111, 113-14, 188
Liberia, 80-81
Libya, 65-66, 197
Li Hongzhi, 107
Lingaas, Carola, 102-3
Lippman, Matthew, 111-12
Lithuania, 110
London Agreement of 1945, 75-76

maritime law, 17, 62-63
McBride, Sean, 155
Meron, Theodor, 13, 42
Millett, Lord, 82
Montenegro, 110
Montevideo Convention on the Rights and Duties of States (1933), 24
Morocco, 141
multilateralism
  attenuated consent and, 27-28
  Cold War's end and increased opportunities for, 80
  consensus-based international law and, 6-7, 39-42, 51, 63-65, 69-71, 182-83

customary international law and, 29
expansion since 1945 of, 27–28, 57, 63–64, 182–83
global governance and, 26–27, 182–83
international organizations and, 27–29
opinio juris and, 12, 28–29
Myanmar, 1, 112–13, 175

Namibia, 46–47, 128
Napoleonic Wars, 21–22
natural law
crimes against humanity and, 87
early modern European monarchies and, 19–22
The Enlightenment and, 21
jus cogens norms and, 48, 52–53
jus naturae et gentium and, 20
just war doctrine and, 20
opinio juris and, 34, 35
state consent doctrine's rejection of, 22–23, 26
Stoicism and, 19–20
Nazi Germany, 74–75, 77, 79, 111, 119, 125
nongovernmental organizations (NGOs)
consensual knowledge and, 31
international agreements influenced by, 30–31
international humanitarian law norms promoted by, 176–80
international law as a basis for mobilization among, 5, 30–31
regional organizations' subcontracting of tasks to, 30–31
Rome Statute and, 30–31, 90–91
torture prohibition promoted by, 155–56
non-international armed conflicts. *See also* excessive internal state violence
asymmetrical nature of, 161
customary international law and, 195
decolonization and, 164
Geneva Conventions and, 159
guerrilla warfare and, 159, 161, 164–65
increase since 1945 in number of, 160, 163–64
international criminal tribunals' decisions regarding, 168–70

international humanitarian law and, 160, 163, 165, 167–75
laws of armed conflict and, 160–63, 169, 181, 189
mass killings of civilians in, 164–65
soft law and, 177–78
Spanish Civil War and, 163–64
state sovereignty doctrine and, 159, 160–61, 163
Tadic decision and, 168, 195–96
threshold questions regarding existence of, 167–70
United Nations Security Council and, 168–69
North Atlantic Treaty Organization (NATO), 30–31, 197
North Continental Shelf case, 15
Northern Ireland, 162
North Korea, 70–71
Nowak, Manfred, 144
Nuclear Non-Proliferation Treaty (NPT), 70–71
nullum crimen nulla poena sine lege principle (there can be no crime or punishment without law), 75–76
Nuremberg Charter (1945), 75, 77–78, 85–86, 105, 112, 125, 137–38, 188
Nuremberg Principles (1950), 77–78, 98–99, 114
Nuremberg Tribunal (1945-46), 75–77

Operation Condor, 86
opinio juris (legal obligation)
consensus-based international law and, 7, 34, 35, 52–53
customary international law and, 11–12, 15–16, 34–35
humanitarian intervention and, 13, 35
human rights and, 13, 35, 191–92
international institutions and, 25
multilateralism and, 12, 28–29
natural law and, 34, 35
political leaders' collective perceptions and, 43
soft law and, 45
torture and, 132–33
United Nations General Assembly resolutions and, 11–12

Oppenheim, Lassa, 34
Optional Protocol for the Convention Against Torture (OPCAT), 154
Organization for Security and Cooperation in Europe, 80
Organization of American States, 24, 30–31, 175, 176, 183, 185
Osbourne v. Jamaica, 145
Ottawa Convention, 30–31
Ottoman Empire, 24, 108–9, 110, 112–13

Pakistan, 70, 175
pariah states, 8n.21
persecution of minorities
  apartheid policies and, 123–29
  armed conflict contexts and, 107, 120
  consensus-based international law and, 4–5
  Covenant on Civil and Political Rights and, 84
  customary international law and, 130
  discrimination element of, 100–3
  ethnic cleansing and, 119–23
  excessive internal state violence and, 96, 98–99, 182–83
  fundamental identity standard and, 105
  gender persecution and, 105, 117
  genocide and, 111–19
  historical permanence of former status standard and, 105
  human rights and, 94–95, 100
  immutable characteristic standard and, 105
  international criminal tribunals and, 98–99, 104, 105, 129
  nationalism and, 109
  political persecution and, 105–7, 117
  protective measures to prevent, 108–11
  racial or ethnic persecution and, 96, 97, 105, 106, 109, 114, 118, 123–29, 130
  refugee law and, 97–98, 104–5
  religious persecution and, 96, 97, 105, 106, 109, 114, 118, 130
  sexual orientation and, 105, 117
  soft law and, 98–99, 130
  state-approved violence as element of, 99–100
  state sovereignty doctrine and, 108
  systemic oppression element of, 99–100, 103–7
  threshold tests in establishing, 104
  Universal Declaration of Human Rights and, 98
Pinochet, Augusto, 82, 86, 189
piracy, 50
Poland, 110
prisoners of war
  Geneva Conventions and, 101, 158, 170, 177
  Hague Conventions and, 73
  International Committee of the Red Cross and Red Crescent and, 176–77
  non-international armed conflict and, 170
  torturing of, 134–35

Qaddafi, Muammar, 197
Qānūn legal code, 24

rape, 120–21, 122–23, 144
Refugee Convention (1951), 97, 105
Responsibility to Protect principle, 80, 84–85, 119, 130, 196–97
Rhodesia, 65–66
Roberts, Anthea Elizabeth, 12
Rohingya population (Myanmar), 1, 112–13
Roma, 111
Romania, 110
Roman law, 4, 23
Rome Statute (1998). *See also* International Criminal Court (ICC)
  apartheid policies and, 127, 129
  Article 7 of, 89–90, 145, 184
  civilians' immunity in armed domestic conflicts and, 187
  crimes against humanity and, 1, 89–90, 91–92, 94, 112, 123, 184
  criminal responsibility for individuals who plan mass violence established in, 85
  domestic and international judicial decisions as subsidiary sources for, 32
  ethnic cleansing and, 184, 187
  genocide and, 112, 130, 187
  multilateral negotiations on, 89–91

nongovernmental organizations' role in
  establishing, 30–31, 90–91
non-international armed conflicts and,
  168–69, 175
nonsignatories of, 92–93
persecution law and, 98–99, 103, 105
process of drafting, 184, 185
Rome Conference and negotiation of,
  90–92, 187–88
as tipping point in establishing
  international law against excessive
  internal state violence, 187–88
torture and, 136–37, 187
universal values enshrined in, 92
Ruggie, John, 19, 28, 63–64
Ruhashyankiko, Nicodeme, 116
Russia, 108–9, 110, 187–88, 194
Rwanda genocide (1994), 80–81, 113. See
  also International Criminal Tribunal
  for Rwanda (ICTR)

Sadat, Leila, 92
Schachter, Oscar, 40
Scharf, Michael, 19, 187
Schmidt, Michael, 167
Scott, Shirley, 69
Second Protocol to the Geneva
  Conventions (1977)
  civilian institutions and property
    protected in, 174
  civilians immunity in domestic armed
    conflicts and, 1, 159, 173–74, 189
  collective punishment banned
    in, 174–75
  doctrine of consent and, 1, 175
  ethnic cleansing and, 122–23
  International Committee of the Red
    Cross and Red Crescent's role in
    establishing, 173–74
  nonsignatories to, 1, 159, 175
  process of drafting, 183–84
  as response to shortcomings of Geneva
    Conventions' Common Article 3, 172
  states' right to withdraw from, 2
September 11 terrorist attacks (2001), 131,
  145, 147–48
Serbia, 107, 110. See also Yugoslavia
Sharia legal code, 24

Shaw, Malcolm, 39–40
Sierra Leone, 81, 98–99, 185, 195
Sikkink, Kathryn, 53–54, 187
slavery, 36, 50, 51, 84
soft law
  apartheid policies and, 127
  attenuated consent and, 45–46
  commonly held principles in a
    community and, 29–30
  consensus-based international law and,
    38–39, 42–47, 51
  decolonization and, 46–47
  human rights and, 43–44, 179
  International Law Commission and, 62
  non-international armed conflicts
    and, 177–78
  opinio juris and, 45
  persecution of minorities and, 98–
    99, 130
  political leaders' collective perceptions
    regarding, 43–44
  torture and, 141
  United Nations General Assembly
    resolutions and, 44–47
Somalia, 65–66, 175
South Africa
  Afrikaner population in, 108
  Apartheid policies before 1990 in, 123–
    25, 128–29
  Namibia and, 46–47, 128
  United Nations Security Council
    and, 65–66
Soviet Union, 115–16
Spain, 86, 120
Spanish Civil War, 74, 163–64
Stahl, Titus, 105–6
state consent doctrine
  Congress of Vienna (1815) and, 22–23
  critics of, 25–26
  definition of, 2
  Hague Conventions and, 74
  human rights and, 25
  international institutions established on
    the basis of, 6
  jus cogens norms and, 48
  natural law rejected under, 22–23, 26
  realism and, 7–8
  state sovereignty doctrine and, 22–23

state sovereignty doctrine
  crimes against humanity and, 88
  Genocide Convention and, 115–16
  human rights and, 81, 198–99
  non-international armed conflicts and, 159, 160–61, 163
  persecution of minorities and, 108
  state consent doctrine and, 22–23
Statute of the African Court of Justice and Human Rights, 98–99
Statute of the International Court of Justice, 32
Statute of the Special Court for Sierra Leone, 98–99
Stoicism, 19–20
Sudan, 65–66, 92–93, 112–13, 187–88, 194
Syria, 65–66, 162, 175, 192–93, 194
Szasz, Paul, 42

Tadic decision (1995), 168, 195–96
Tang dynasty, 97
Tanzania, 79–80
terrorism
  criminal law and, 162
  jus cogens norms and, 50
  laws of armed conflict and, 162
  September 11 terrorist attacks (2001) and, 131, 145, 147–48
  state consent doctrine and, 25
  United Nations Security Council and, 66
  universal jurisdiction principle and, 198
torture. *See also* Convention Against Torture (CAT, 1984)
  apartheid policies and, 127
  Catholic Church and, 133–34
  in Chile during Pinochet regime, 82
  consensus-based international law and, 33–34, 36, 131–33, 134–35, 188–89
  corporal punishment and, 145
  Covenant on Civil and Political Rights and, 84, 131–32, 137–39
  cruel and inhuman treatment compared to, 141–44
  customary international law and, 132
  definition in Convention Against Torture of, 41, 135–36
  efforts to circumvent universal prohibition of, 141–48
  erga omnes obligations and, 148
  ethnic cleansing and, 122
  excessive internal state violence and, 134, 182–83
  extraordinary rendition and, 147
  human rights and, 94–95, 131–32
  international agreements regarding prohibition of, 131–32, 133, 137–41
  international criminal tribunals and, 133, 137, 143, 144, 148–49, 151
  internationally accepted definition of, 41
  international organizations' role in promoting universal prohibition against, 151–54
  jus cogens norms and, 50–51, 137–38, 148–51
  laws of armed conflict and, 138
  nongovernmental organizations' role in promoting universal prohibition against, 155–56
  non-refoulement principle and, 140, 146–47
  nonstate agents' engagement in, 136
  opinio juris and, 132–33
  Pinochet case in United Kingdom (1999) and, 189
  police engagement in, 131, 134–35
  political prisoners and, 131, 134–35
  prisoners of war and, 134–35
  rape and, 144
  regional agreements and, 42, 138, 142
  security and intelligence services' engagement in, 134
  soft law and, 141
  ticking bomb scenario and, 147–48
  Torture Declaration (1975) and, 138–39
  universal jurisdiction principle and, 149–51
  US "enhanced interrogation" policies (2001-4) and, 145–46
Trail of Tears, 121
Treaty of Peace between Russia and Turkey (1829), 110
Tunki, Grigory, 39–40

INDEX 213

Turkey, 110, 112–13, 175

Uganda, 79–80
United Kingdom, 86, 126, 143, 162, 189
United Nations. *See also* United Nations General Assembly; United Nations Security Council
   Chapter VII and, 65–66, 194, 195
   Charter of, 45–46, 58–59, 66–67, 68, 92–93, 125, 128, 194–95
   Commission of Experts, 122
   Committee Against Torture and, 71, 153
   Committee on the Progressive Development of International Law and Its Codification and, 114–15
   Conference on Diplomatic Intercourse and Immunities and, 64
   customary international law and, 29
   Economic and Social Council (ECOSOC) of, 114–15
   establishment (1945) of, 24, 39
   Human Rights Commission of, 126, 139, 145, 151–52
   Human Rights Council of, 151–52, 184–85
   lawmaking conferences sponsored by, 63
   powerful nations' influence at, 57–58
   Responsibility to Protect doctrine and, 80, 196–97
   Special Rapporteur on Torture and Other Cruel, Inhuman and Degrading Treatment or Punishment and, 151–53
   universal jurisdiction principle and, 26
   World Summit (2005) and, 80, 84–85, 119, 196
United Nations General Assembly
   Apartheid Convention (1974) and, 126
   Convention Against Torture and, 141
   crimes against humanity and, 88, 90
   Declaration on Principles of International Law Concerning Friendly Relations and, 47
   Declaration on the Granting of Independence to Colonial Countries and Peoples and, 46–47
   ethnic cleansing and, 121

   Genocide Convention (1948) and, 78, 114–15
   opinio juris and, 11–12
   progressive development of international law and, 39, 58–59, 184–85
   Resolution 95 and, 47, 77–78, 114
   Sixth Committee of, 26, 61, 63, 90, 114–15, 184–85
   soft law and, 44–47
   Torture Declaration (1975), 138–39
United Nations Security Council
   apartheid policies and, 125
   breach of peace clause and, 193–94, 195
   Chapter VII authority of, 65–66, 194, 195
   civilians' immunity in domestic armed conflicts and, 166, 175, 176
   consensus-based international law and, 65–68
   crimes against humanity and, 88
   Darfur conflict in Sudan and, 187–88
   deliberation at, 67
   East Timor independence (1975) and, 46–47
   ethnic cleansing and, 121, 122
   Genocide Convention and, 115–17
   humanitarian intervention and, 65–66
   International Criminal Court referrals from, 92–93
   international criminal tribunals established by, 65–66, 71, 81, 89, 93–94, 170, 185, 190, 195–96
   jus cogens norms and, 53, 54–55, 56–57
   non-international armed conflicts and, 168–69
   nuclear nonproliferation and, 70–71
   permanent *versus* rotating members of, 67
   Resolution 1373 and, 66
   Resolution 1540 and, 66
   Responsibility to Protect doctrine and, 197
   South Africa's possession of Namibia and, 46–47
   United Nations Charter and, 66–67, 68
   veto power and, 53

United States
   Apartheid Convention and, 126
   Convention Against Torture and "enhanced interrogation policies" (2001-2004) in, 145–46
   Darfur conflict in Sudan, 187–88
   ethnic cleansing against Native Americans before 1900 in, 121
   Genocide Convention and, 115–16
   International Criminal Court nonsignatory status of, 187–88
   Israel and, 194
Universal Declaration of Human Rights (1948)
   Covenant on Civil and Political Rights as codification of, 14, 82–83
   customary international law and, 14
   excessive internal state violence and, 77
   jus cogens norms and, 50
   nondiscrimination provisions of, 100–1
   persecution of minorities and, 98
   torture prohibition in, 131–32, 137–39, 188–89
   violations of, 14
universal jurisdiction principle, 26, 149–51, 198
Uyghur Muslims, 112–13

Vattel, Emer de, 21–23

Vienna Convention on Diplomatic Relations (1961), 18, 24, 64
Vienna Convention on the Law of Treaties (1969), 2, 48–49, 64, 70–71, 118
Vietnam, 79–80, 172

war crimes. *See also* laws of armed conflict (LOAC)
   crimes against humanity as, 76–77, 188
   Nuremberg Tribunal (1945-46) and, 75–77
   Responsibility to Protect principle and, 197
   universal jurisdiction principle and, 198
Washburn, John, 91
Weisburd, A. Mark, 15–16
West Bank, 129
Westphalia Treaty (1648), 21–22
Whitaker, Benjamin, 116
World Organization Against Torture (Organisation Mondiale Contre la Torture), 155–56
World Trade Organization, 29, 55, 62–63
World War II, 74–75

Yoo, John, 145–46
Yugoslavia, 80–81, 110, 120–21, 122, 191. *See also* International Criminal Tribunal for the Former Yugoslavia (ICTY)